GUIDE TO
REAL ESTATE
LICENSE EXAMINATIONS

REVISED EDITION

A detailed up-to-date guide to state licensing examinations for real estate salesmen and broker license applicants. Designed as a text-workbook for classroom use or home study, it provides non-technical coverage of examination subjects and hundreds of examination-type questions.

GUIDE TO
REAL ESTATE
LICENSE EXAMINATIONS

REVISED EDITION

John T. Ellis

Prentice-Hall, Inc., Englewood Cliffs, New Jersey

Library of Congress Cataloging in Publication Data

Ellis, John T
   Guide to real estate license examinations, revised edition

   (Prentice-Hall series in real estate)
    1. Real estate business—United States. 2. Real
estate business—Examinations, questions, etc.
I. Title.
HD1375.E35   333.3'3   73-22125
ISBN 0-13-371005-X

PRENTICE-HALL SERIES IN REAL ESTATE

© 1974 Prentice-Hall, Inc., Englewood Cliffs, New Jersey

Printed in the United States of America

14   13   12   11   10   9

PRENTICE-HALL INTERNATIONAL, INC., *London*
PRENTICE-HALL OF AUSTRALIA, PTY. LTD., *Sydney*
PRENTICE-HALL OF CANADA, LTD., *Toronto*
PRENTICE-HALL OF INDIA PRIVATE LIMITED, *New Delhi*
PRENTICE-HALL OF JAPAN, INC., *Tokyo*

Contents

Solution of Percentage Problems and Tax and Insurance Prorations.
How to Solve Problems Involving Measurements, Area, and Volume.   Practice Problems.

Introduction

This book is written with a single purpose—to provide an applicant for licensure as a real estate broker or salesman with a sufficient amount of text material to study in preparation for his state license examination. In addition, a substantial, but not overwhelming, number of examination-type questions are provided at appropriate intervals in order to expose the applicant to the type of questions to be expected on the exam. These questions are furnished in order to test his understanding of the subject and for pre-examination drill.

Of course, not all state examinations are the same in scope or content. Throughout the United States, the most widely used examinations are those prepared and administered by the Educational Testing Service, or so-called "Princeton" exams. Since they are the closest thing to a uniform examination, the form of questioning used on these examinations is used in this book.

The principles, laws, and practices of real estate brokerage are not the same in all states. In order to provide for differences, at the end of many chapters a list of "points to be checked locally" is provided in order to compensate for any local deviations from the general text. In the chapter on Real Estate License Law, a work-study chart that categorizes the principal features of most state license laws is included in order to provide the applicant with an orderly approach to study his state's laws. This work-study chart has proven to be an effective learning device.

Definitions of words and phrases are the basis of many examination questions. At the end of each chapter a list of "words to watch" is provided. These words are selected from the glossary at the end of the book, and the words given in each list pertain to the chapter just studied. Over the years, I have found that this association with the immediate subject aids an applicant's retention, as opposed to simple memorization of the terms without any particular association.

All of the material in this book has been classroom tested by instructors in four states since the E. T. S. examinations were introduced in January 1971. Combined with a good program of instruction, it has proven to be an effective tool in preparing the applicant for license examination.

I would like to thank John E. Easter II, President of Virginia Farm Agency Realty, Inc., and Professor Carroll Gentry, Chairman, Division of Business, Virginia Western Community College, for reviewing the text and for their suggestions.

GUIDE TO
REAL ESTATE
LICENSE EXAMINATIONS

PART I

REAL ESTATE FUNDAMENTALS

Chapter 1

Introduction to
Real Estate Brokerage

Many persons who are interested in real estate, either as a career or for their own personal enlightenment, do not fully understand the operations of the real estate brokerage business. Those seeking licensure often do not understand the meaning of the terms *real estate broker* or *real estate salesman.*

The purposes of this introduction are to define the meaning of these terms and to give some insight into the broker-salesman relationship. The laws governing the licensure and regulation of brokers and salesmen will be discussed in detail later in this book.

Real Estate Broker Defined: License laws generally define a real estate broker as a person or business firm who, for compensation, engages to buy, sell, rent, lease, or exchange real estate for others.

A real estate broker is an entrepreneur, a businessman (or firm) who engages to act to bring together those who have real estate to be marketed in some manner and those who have a need for such real estate. He is a third party in the transaction, and receives his compensation in the form of a commission which is paid to him when he brings about a successful transaction. He may represent either the seller or the purchaser, but may not ordinarily represent both parties in the transaction. Most often, he will represent the seller, as an agent for the seller.

The laws permit a licensed real estate broker to hire others to work for him, in order to expand the perimeters of his operations by dealing with more than one person or property at the same time. For this purpose he hires real estate salesmen. These can only be actual persons (never a corporation or other form of business entity) who are licensed by the state as real estate salesmen. The basic relationship of a broker and salesman is that of an employer and an employee.

Real Estate Salesman Defined: Within the meaning of the license laws, a real estate salesman is a person who is employed by a licensed real estate broker to sell, buy, rent, lease, or exchange real estate, for others and for compensation, under the direction and guidance of the employing broker.

The salesman becomes, by licensure, an extension of the broker's physical facilities. Through the salesman the broker is able to deal concurrently with more than one person or property. A real estate broker who employed ten salesmen would, in theory, be able to produce eleven times as much business as if he operated alone. The relationship of the broker to the salesman is always that of an employer to an employee. Although many brokers, for tax purposes, contract with their salesmen as independent contractors, under the laws governing licensure as real estate brokers or real estate salesmen there exists an employer-employee relationship. Under this relationship, the broker is held responsible for the acts of his salesman, as any employer is with regard to his employees.

The salesman always acts in his dealings with the public as an agent for his employing broker, and not in an individual capacity. Contracts or agreements negotiated by the salesman are drawn in the name of the broker and generally must be signed by the broker in order to be valid. For example, if salesman "S," employed by broker "B," secures a listing on a property which belongs to owner "O," the listing will take the form of an agreement between broker "B" and owner "O," with the salesman identified merely as the person responsible for bringing in the listing. In the event of any litigation resulting from this agreement, the parties to the litigation would be the broker and the owner, with the salesman playing only an incidental role as an employee of the broker.

Most salesmen receive their compensation in the form of a percentage of the total commissions paid to the broker as a result of the transaction. The exact percentage is determined by prior agreement between the broker and the salesman, and is subject to many variables. A salesman who listed, but did not sell, a property would usually receive a portion of any commissions received from the sale of the property during the term of his listing, regardless of who made the sale. Another salesman who sold a property which was listed by someone else would receive a portion of the commission for having brought about the sale.

The salesman who listed and sold a property would usually receive one portion of the commission for bringing in the listing and another portion for making the sale. Other factors, usually determined in advance of any transactions, are governed by the particular agreement between the broker and salesman. As a general rule, the more a salesman receives from his broker in the form of office facilities, supplies, support, or assistance, the smaller will be his percentage of any commissions which accrue to his account. Because these percentages vary so much, no attempt will be made to discuss them here.

Since all agreements are drawn between the real estate broker and the principal, with the salesman acting as an employee or independent contractor for the broker, the salesman never enters into direct contractual relationships with the principle. He is, nevertheless, bound by the same strict rules as the broker, requiring him to exercise utmost good faith and fidelity toward the principal. The fiduciary relationship extends to the salesman as well as the broker. However, certain restrictions limit the activities of the salesman and distinguish him from the broker. License laws fix the responsibility for policy making with the broker, and regard one who is subject to these decisions of another as a salesman rather than as a broker. Other such responsibilities are those of collecting commissions, receipt of deposit monies, and advertising. A salesman who undertook to do any of these things without permission or approval of the broker would be in violation of the license law.

The Real Estate Brokerage Cycle

The operation of the real estate brokerage cycle from beginning to end requires four principle steps, with incidental steps being involved in each of the major categories.

The first step involves the *listing* of the property for sale by the real estate brokerage firm. This is accomplished by means of an agency contract, called a listing in the vernacular of the trade.

Once the listing is secured, the broker seeks a purchaser for the property. When one is found, an *agreement of sale* is drawn up between the purchaser and seller. This agreement, in some jurisdictions, takes the form of a deposit receipt, with the actual sales contract drawn at a later time.

The next step is to arrange for the financing of the sale. This requires a credit application and an *appraisal* of the property. Incidental to the financing it will often be necessary to arrange for a *survey* and/or *termite inspection.*

When all arrangements are completed for the financing, the transaction moves to the final phase, *title closing* or *escrow.* This final phase requires the preparation of a *deed* to the property, *mortgages* or *trust deeds* (sometimes called deeds of trust), notes or bonds for the repayment of the loan, title insurance, hazard insurance, and instrument recordation.

This book is arranged to follow the cycle described above. Text material on each subject is condensed to provide sufficient information for preparation for state license examinations, without encumbering an applicant with more study requirements than necessary to achieve this goal.

Of course, not all real estate transactions involve a sale of the property. Real estate brokers also participate in the leasing, and exchange of real property.

A chart showing the various steps in the brokerage cycle follows.

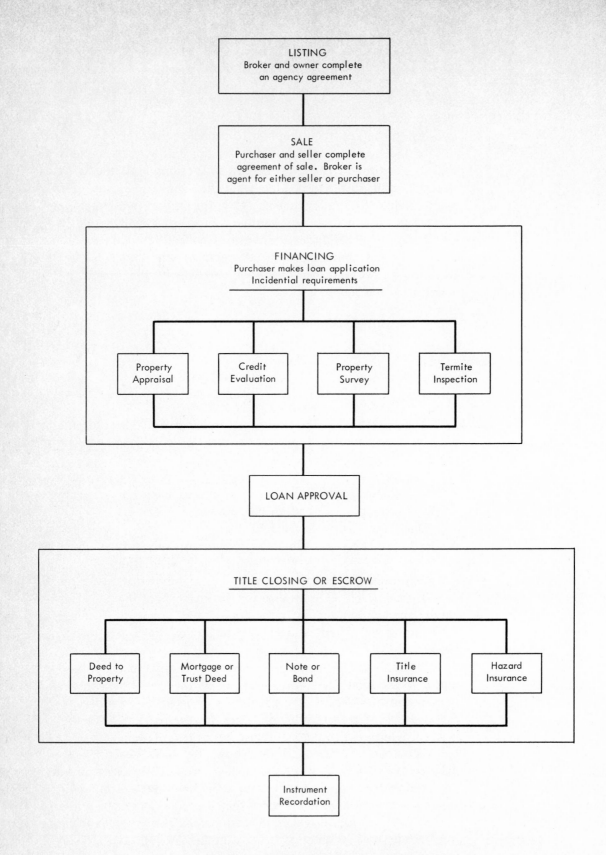

THE REAL ESTATE BROKERAGE CYCLE

Chapter 2

Contracts

Every business relationship entered into by a real estate broker involves the use of a contract in some form. His authority to sell or rent real estate is derived from his agency agreement, which is a contract. The subsequent sale or lease of the property is accomplished by the use of an agreement of sale or lease, another form of contract. At closing, the title to the property is passed by a deed, another form of contract. Various other instruments used in real estate, such as mortgages, deeds of trust, etc., are forms of contracts. It is imperative that a person licensed to do business as a real estate broker or salesman have at least a fundamental understanding of the legal principles governing contracts in order to avoid severe legal entanglements.

The Statute of Frauds

In most states, the law which governs all contracts is derived from the Statute of Frauds, a law enacted in the sixteenth century by Parliament in England and brought down through the ages in essentially its original form. Although this law governs contracts for many purposes, certain sections of it deal with contracts for specific purposes. This statute, or its provisions, has been adopted by most states. That section which deals with contracts for the sale or lease of real estate provides essentially as follows:

1. No contract for the sale of real estate *shall be enforceable* unless it is in writing and signed by the parties to be charged thereby.
2. No contract for the lease of real estate, for more than a specified

time *shall be enforceable* unless it is in writing and signed by the parties to be charged thereby.

It should be noted that the law does not require all contracts for the sale of real estate to be in writing before a conveyance can be made. If the parties agree orally to buy and sell real estate, and do subsequently transfer ownership by deed, the conveyance could be perfectly valid. However, after entering into an oral agreement to buy and sell real estate, if either party should desire not to consummate the agreement, the other party could not enforce the agreement through legal action. The same would be true of a lease for more than the statutory minimum period. To be governed by the Statute of Frauds, the lease must be for a period in excess of the minimum statutory period in that jurisdiction, usually one year.

Legal Status of Contracts

Contracts may be classified under the law as either *valid, void, voidable,* or *unenforceable.* Following is a brief explanation of each of these terms:

Valid. A valid contract is one that is legally binding and enforceable; one which contains all legal elements.

Void. Without legal force and effect; not really a contract.

Voidable. A contract which is valid and enforceable on its face, but which may be rejected by one or more of the parties at his option.

Unenforceable. A contract which was valid when drawn, but which cannot be proved or judgment obtained upon it by one or both parties, for some reason.

Essentials of a Contract

In order to be valid and enforceable, a contract must contain certain elements. The absence of any one of these elements would make the contract void or voidable. Generally, these elements are defined as follows:

1. There must be an offer and an acceptance.
2. There must be a seal or a consideration.
3. The parties must possess the legal capacity to contract.
4. There must be a reality of consent.
5. The object of the contract must be legal.

Following is a brief explanation of these elements:

1. Offer and Acceptance.

   The offer may originate with the seller, in the form of an offer to sell the property at a stipulated price. This offer may later be accepted by the buyer. The offer could originate with the buyer, in the form of an offer to purchase the property from the seller at a certain price. This price may or may not be accepted by the seller. In either case, the offeree must accept the conditions of the offeror's offer, or this requirement is not considered to be met.

   > Example: "A" offers his property for sale for $20,000, with the offer to include certain chattels, among them a washing machine and clothes dryer. "B" makes an offer to purchase the property at a price of $19,500, with the washer and dryer to be excluded from the sale.

   In this case there has not been an offer and an acceptance, and no contract exists unless "A" accepts the counteroffer made by "B." This form of negotiation often takes place in actual real estate transactions, with final agreement sometimes being reached only after several such offers and counteroffers.

2. There must be a seal or consideration.

   The seal is any mark intended by the party to be his seal. Historically, it consisted of an impression made in wax, affixed to the document next to the person's mark, and served to authenticate his signature. In modern usage, the addition of the word "seal," or the letters "L. S." next to the signator's signature is sufficient. The principal function of the seal today is to lessen the problem of proving a consideration, as the courts will not ordinarily look into the matter of consideration if the contract was made under seal. In some states, the statute of limitations is extended when the document is under seal.

   A consideration is something of value, exchanged for something of value. It is an essential part of any contract. Consideration may take the form of "valuable" consideration, such as a sum of money or its equivalent, or it may take the form of a "good" consideration, such as love and affection.

   Some contracts are based on promises of acts to be performed, and take the form of "unilateral" or "bilateral" contracts. A unilateral contract is one which places an obligation on one party without a corresponding obligation on the part of the other. It consists of a promise made in exchange for an act, as in a real estate listing.

   > Example: A poster which offers a reward for the apprehension of a criminal. The offeror of the reward agrees to pay a consideration

to anyone who causes the criminal's apprehension. This does not place a person who reads the poster under an obligation to search for the criminal.

A bilateral contract is one which is based on a promise exchanged for another promise.

Example: Marriage—a contract in which the consideration is one person's promise given in exchange for the promise of the other.

The consideration, whatever it may be, must not be trifling or inconsequential in nature, and should bear some relation to the value of the goods to be exchanged or the services to be performed.

3. The parties must have the capacity to contract.

Not all persons possess the legal capacity to enter into a contract. Generally, minors do not possess this capacity, and a contract entered into by a minor is voidable; that is, the minor can disaffirm the contract during his infancy or for a reasonable time thereafter. However, an infant is generally held liable for the reasonable value of necessaries which were furnished to him. Necessaries are those things which are essential to his existence in the society in which he lives, generally, food, shelter, and clothing.

Insane persons do not possess the capacity to contract. If a person entered into a contract while insane, his contract would be voidable, either by himself upon regaining his sanity, or by a guardian appointed by the court during his insanity.

4. Reality of consent.

In order to be recognized as valid, a contract must be free from mistake, misrepresentation, fraud, undue influence, and duress. The consent of the parties must be real, and the contract must reflect the true intent of the parties. Where the contract does not reflect such a condition, the result is that it would be either void or voidable. Following is a brief description of each of these conditions and the effect that its absence would have on a contract.

Misrepresentation. Misrepresentation is an innocent misstatement of fact without intent to deceive. If the misrepresentation proves to be of a material nature, the contract would be *voidable* by the party to whom the misrepresentation was made.

Example: "A" sells to "B" a tract of land which he honestly believed to contain 125 acres. A survey reveals only 120 acres in the tract. This was an innocent mistake on the part of "A"—misrepresentation.

Fraud. Fraud is the deliberate misrepresentation of the material fact, made with the intent that the other party act upon it in such a fashion as to cause himself some harm or injury. A contract based upon fraud is *voidable* by the party to whom the fraud is committed.

> Example: "A" deliberately tries to deceive "B" in selling property to him, by representing that the land had been approved for septic tanks, when he was aware that it would not pass percolation tests.

Undue Influence.   This is a mixture of fraud and force. It is the taking of an advantage of someone because of a particular and peculiar relationship that exists between the parties, or because of the distress of one of the parties. Such a contract is *voidable* by the person upon whom it is committed.

> Example: An agent who induces an owner to sell out of fear of changing racial character of the neighborhood—"blockbusting."

Duress. The actual or the threatening of personal injury or restraint in order to force someone to enter into a contract, against his own free will. Such a contract is *voidable* by the person upon whom it is committed.

> Example: From "The Perils of Pauline"—the villain who tied Pauline to the railroad track in order to force her to sign the deed to her home—duress.

5. Legal object.

Any contract based upon an agreement which would have as its object the violation of any federal or state law is on its face void. A contract which tends to interfere with the functions of government is also void.

> Example: Mrs. "X" hires an assassin to murder her husband, and pays him $500 in advance. The assassin fails to murder the husband. Mrs. "X" could not sue to recover her money, as her contract was based upon an illegal object.

Contract Form

There is no absolute form for any real estate contract. Any form which reflects all the conditions of the sale in such a manner as to meet the above requirements would probably be sufficient to make the contract enforceable. However, any contract should contain the following provisions:

1. Date
2. Names of the parties
3. Legal description of the property
4. Consideration

5. Terms of payment, including terms of any mortgages or deeds of trust
6. Any special agreements or contingencies
7. Date and place of closing

The above facts, if stated on any contract form, in a clear fashion, would probably make that contract legally sufficient. In practice, most brokers provide a standard form which meets these requirements and often will provide additional stipulations, based on prior experience of the broker.

One word of caution—as an agent, never draw up a contract of sale in its entirety. The courts have in the past held that a real estate agent may fill in the blank spaces on a contract form which had been prepared with competent legal advice, but that for him to write a contract in its entirety would constitute the practice of law without a license.

The Contract as an Executory Agreement

A contract for the sale of real estate is an *executory* agreement; that is, it is an agreement entered into at some point in time for the fulfillment of some act in the future. At the closing of the transaction, the seller transfers ownership to the buyer by means of a deed. This *deed,* which is an *executed* contract (one which has been fulfilled) then supersedes and replaces the contract of sale. Any provision of the contract of sale which was not included in the deed is no longer enforceable after the grantee has accepted the deed. Thus, the aggrieved party could not recover any damages for breach of contract because the terms of the contract have been merged in the deed. In order to insure the survival of a contract provision after the delivery of the deed, many brokers will insert in their contract form a provision similar to the following: "The terms of this contract will survive the settlement of the sale and not be merged in the deed."

Risk of Loss to Property during the Life of a Contract of Sale

When a contract of sale has been executed by all parties, the buyer acquires an *equitable title* to the property, although the legal title has yet to be delivered by deed. Effectively, the equitable title indicates a right, on the part of the buyer, to receive the legal title by deed according to the terms of the contract. This right can be enforced through court action. The passing of this equitable title to the buyer also places upon him the burden of the risk of loss to the property from any form of casualty during the life of the contract. Thus, if any such loss occurs, the buyer will assume the burden of such loss. This risk can usually be returned to the seller by contractual agreement, however, and it is not unusual to include in contracts of sale language which states that the seller will assume such risk of loss until the time of settlement. Often, the contract will require the seller to transfer to the buyer the seller's interest in any insurance policies currently in effect on the property. A few states have adopted the Uniform Vendor and Purchaser Risk Act. In these states, the risk of loss is placed on the seller, when title and/or possession of the property remains with the seller.

Assignment of Contracts

Unless the contract of sale contains a provision to the contrary, the buyer has the right to assign his interests (transfer of his equitable title) to another person. The assignee assumes all the rights of the buyer (assignor) and, of course, assumes all his responsibilities. However, the assignor continues to be liable to the seller for performance under the contract and does not relieve himself of such obligations by the assignment. The assignee is not liable unless he agrees to assume liability as a part of the assignment. Ordinarily, the assignee will perform in the same manner as the buyer would have performed, and difficulties do not often arise in this connection.

Breach of Contract; Rights of the Parties

If either party to a contract fails to perform according to the agreement, the other party has certain rights under the law. Briefly, listed below are the principal rights of the parties in this instance:

Buyer's Rights: (When seller fails to perform)
1. Rescission of the contract. This entitles the buyer to the return of all funds paid or other considerations given.
2. Damages. The buyer can sue for any damages incurred by him as a result of having acted in good faith under the terms of the contract. He must be able to prove actual damages.
3. Specific performance. The buyer may sue in court to require the seller to perform under the terms of the contract. Should he be successful in his suit, the court will order the seller to perform, and he may be jailed if he refuses to do so.

Seller's Rights: (When buyer fails to perform)
1. Rescission of the contract. As with the buyer, the seller may rescind. He must return to the buyer any consideration paid and recover possession of the real estate, unless provision is made for forfeiture of deposits.
2. Forfeiture of deposits. The seller may declare a forfeiture and

retain all considerations paid, provided the contract had stated this right as a part of its terms.

3. Damages. The seller may sue for any damages incurred, and recover through court action. As with the buyer, he must prove that damages had actually been incurred.

4. Specific performance. As with the buyer, the seller may sue for specific performance.

Termination of Contracts

There are two broad categories under which contracts may be terminated prior to the completion of performance. These are defined as

1. Acts of the parties
2. Operation of law

Examples of how these may apply will be found in the chapter on agency.

Questions on Contracts will be found in the Question Section, beginning on Page 175.

WORDS TO WATCH

Acceptance	Instrument
Agreement of Sale	Land Contract
Assignment	Lease
Assignor	Meeting of Minds
Assignee	Minor
Binder	Mutual Assent
Bona Fide	Offer
Breach	Offeree
Caveat Emptor	Offeror
Collusion	Option
Competent	Optionee
Conditional Sale Contract	Optionor
Consideration	Oral Contract
Contract	Parol
Contract of Sale	Rescission of Contracts
Duress	Sales Contract
Earnest Money	Seal
Et al	Specific Performance
Et ux	Statute of Frauds
Fraud	Time is of the Essence
Installment Contract	Undue Influence
Installment Land Contract	Uniform Commercial Code

Valid   Void
Vendee   Voidable
Vendor

POINTS TO CHECK LOCALLY

1. Does the Statute of Frauds in your state require
   a. All real estate sales contracts to be in writing, in order to be enforceable?
   b. All leases for more than a specified time to be in writing, in order to be enforceable?
      If so, what is the time required in your state?
2. Must contracts be under seal in your state?
3. Does placing a contract under seal extend the Statute of Limitations?
4. Does the Uniform Vendor and Purchaser Risk Act apply in your state?

Suggested Sources of Information

1. Attorneys
2. Title companies
3. Real estate manual (if published by the Real Estate Commission)

Chapter 3

Agency and Listings

The basis for a real estate broker's operation is his inventory of properties for sale or rent. However, unlike many other businesses involving the sale of a commodity, the broker does not ordinarily own his inventory. He secures his inventory by obtaining from the owner of the property the right to represent him in negotiations for the sale or lease of the property. He is paid a commission for his services, usually, but not necessarily by the owner. This creates an *agent-principal* relationship and is subject to the laws of agency. A real estate salesman is subject to the same laws, but, as an employee of the broker rather than as a principal party as in an agency agreement.

The Agent-Principal Relationship; Who May Be an Agent or Principal

An agency agreement is a contract. The most fundamental requirement for becoming a principal is that the party who is to be a principal possess the legal capacity to contract; that is, he be of sound mind and have reached majority. Since the principal, by means of the agency contract, conveys some authority upon the agent, the principal must possess such authority. One cannot convey to another any right or thing which he does not himself possess.

In order to become an agent, one must also possess the capacity to contract. This is the most fundamental requirement for becoming an agent. In addition, all states now require that real estate agents be licensed in order to collect a commission for services rendered to a principal as an agent for the sale or lease of real estate.

The relationship of a real estate broker to the owner of property usually follows this pattern, and a "listing" of real estate is therefore an agency contract. In this agreement, the owner of the property is the employer of the broker, and the relationship so created is a fiduciary relationship. It is not necessary for the broker to be employed by the owner of the property. Occasionally, a would-be buyer of real estate will employ a broker for the purpose of finding real estate which meets certain requirements. In this instance, the broker would be an agent for the buyer, rather than the seller, and would in effect be an employee of the buyer. This relationship is not common in the field of residential brokerage, though it is not uncommon in the areas of commercial or industrial real estate. Neither is the agency concept peculiar to the real estate business. Many other businesses are operated under this concept; securities brokers, insurance brokers, and many others operate under the agency concept.

Appointment of an Agent

An agent may in general be appointed by any of three methods.

Implication
Oral contract
Written contract

Under the statutes of many states, the appointment of a real estate broker by implication or by means of an oral contract has been made illegal, while in others it may still come about in this way. A few other states have not made an appointment by means of an oral contract illegal under the general statutes, but have made it a violation of the state's licensing laws for a licensee to accept an appointment by any means other than a written contract. Over the years, however, most brokers and principals have learned that an appointment by any means other than by a written contract often leads to misunderstandings and frequently to legal problems; and today most brokers make all possible effort to secure their appointment by means of a written listing, signed by the owner. This method has proven to be to the advantage of all concerned.

Other Contractual Principles Governing Agency Agreements

Since the agent's authority is derived from a contract with the owner, his employment is also subject to the basic legal principles governing contracts as well. Two such principles should always be remembered by the agent in accepting such appointment.

1. In case of a dispute arising out of an oral agreement, courts traditionally will place the burden of proof upon the broker to prove that an agency relationship existed.
2. In litigation arising out of the interpretation of a written agreement, courts will often interpret the document in the favor of the person who did not prepare the agreement.

These principles would seem to place the broker at a disadvantage in any litigation with a principal. In any relationship such as this, however, the court will look first to determine which party acted in good faith, and this examination will usually protect the broker if he has acted properly. This doctrine of good faith is perhaps the most important principle involved in an agent-principal relationship.

Types of Listings

The contracts that may exist between broker and principal are divided into two broad categories as follows:

General Listing: Often called an "open" listing. This is a listing wherein the owner lists the property for sale with one broker but reserves the right to list the property concurrently with as many other brokers as he may desire. This listing need not contain a definite termination date and may generally be terminated by either party's giving notice to the other of his desire to terminate prior to an actual sale of the property. It may also be terminated by the expiration of a reasonable time. In the event of a sale, only the broker who produced the buyer will receive any commission. Because of the strong possibility of another broker's receiving the commission by producing a sale first, most brokers will not obligate themselves for any considerable advertising or other expense with this type of listing.

Exclusive Listing: Exclusive listings are listings wherein for a stipulated time only one broker may be employed for the purpose of selling the property. They are divided into two types as follows:

Exclusive agency: This listing employs one broker as the agent for the property for a definite period of time but leaves the owner the right to sell of his own efforts without the obligation to pay a commission to the broker.

Exclusive authorization to sell: Also frequently called "Exclusive Right to Sell." This listing appoints one broker as sole agent for a stipulated period of time and entitles him to a commission if the property is sold within this time, no matter by whom. The owner must pay a commission even if he sells the property himself.

Multiple Listing: A multiple listing is an arrangement between a group of brokers, wherein all broker-members of the multiple listing service "pool" their listings in order to give maximum exposure to possible prospects. Any broker-member or salesman employed by a broker-member may show any current listing, and if a sale results, the commission is divided according to a predetermined arrangement between the listing and selling brokers. These listings are usually drawn on exclusive authorization to sell listing contracts, with the agreement to place the listing in the multiple listing service being a part of the consideration tendered by the listing broker.

All exclusive listings must contain a definite termination date and must be based upon a consideration, such as the broker's promise to use reasonable efforts to advertise and promote the sale of the property.

Obligations of the Agent to His Principal

In accepting appointment as an agent, a broker undertakes certain duties and obligations to his principal. Among these are:

1. *Loyalty:* The agent's first obligation is to his principal. An agency is a position of trust, and the agent must prove himself trustworthy. To fail to do so is illegal under the law.
2. *Notice:* An agent must always notify his principal of any information coming into his possession concerning the principal's property. This information must be communicated to the principal in a reasonable time.
3. *Obedience:* The agent must be obedient to his principal's instructions, even if he thinks them unwise. He may not substitute his judgment for that of the principal.
4. *Due Care:* He must exercise that degree of due care which a prudent businessman would employ in a similar situation. His failure to do so has been interpreted as negligence.
5. *Accounting:* The agent must always account to the principal for all of the principal's funds which come into his possession. Principal's funds must be maintained in a separate, insured bank account clearly labeled as an escrow account.

Termination of Agency

There are several ways by which an agency agreement may be terminated. Since the agency is a contract, it is terminable by the accepted means applicable to contracts, as follows:

Acts of the Parties: Terminated as the result of some action initiated by the parties themselves.

1. Mutual consent. By agreement of both parties.
2. Completion of the objective, such as the sale of the property.
3. Expiration. If the agreement carried a time limitation, the agency is terminated when the time is past. If there was no time limitation, it would be terminated by the expiration of a reasonable time.
4. Revocation by principal. This action could result in damage to the agent if done arbitrarily; and, if so, he might be able to recover through litigation.
5. Renunciation by agent. As above, if this action caused harm to the principal, the agent may be liable for damages.

Operation of Law: The law will act to terminate any agency when any of the following conditions exist.

1. Insanity. The insane party would lose his capacity to contract.
2. Death. The agency may survive the death of either party if the contract contains a provision making the agreement binding upon the estate of the deceased. This is not usual in an agency agreement.
3. Destruction of the property, or disposition for other reasons.

   Example: Property destroyed by tornado or sold for unpaid taxes.

4. Bankruptcy of either party. The bankrupt party loses his financial responsibility, and contracts made by him may be terminated.

Agent's Entitlement to a Commission

There will frequently arise a dispute between the agent and the principal as to whether a commission has been earned, and occasionally, as to the amount of commission earned. Generally, the law regards an agent's commission as earned when he has produced a buyer who is ready, willing, and able to buy on the principal's terms. If an agent finds a buyer who meets these qualifications, his commission is earned, even though the principal should refuse to sell, provided that the agency contract did not provide that the commission would be earned only if there were an actual transfer of title. However, the terms of the principal's offer must be substantially met by the buyer's acceptance, and it must be clear that he was ready, willing, and able to buy before an agent can collect when the principal does refuse to sell. An offer which is not in close substance with the principal's terms will not ordinarily qualify the agent for a commission unless the seller accepts the offer.

After an agreement of sale is reached, the fact that the sale does not reach consummation at closing will not bar an agent from collection of a commission, if the reason for failure to consummate was not the fault of the agent, and provided that there was no provision for title transfer as a condition of the commission's having been earned. In most cases the agent would have to prove that he did not and could not reasonably have been expected to know of the reason for the failure to consummate. In the case of a disputed commission when a sale does result, the agent can usually collect his commission if he can establish that he was the "procuring cause" of the sale; that is, if he can establish that the sale came about as a result of his efforts. In cases of a dispute over the amount of the commission due an agent, courts will generally award a commission equal to that usually paid under similar circumstances in the locality at the time of sale.

It is well to remember that many disputes over commissions arise out of oral or improperly prepared listings, and failure to have a clear understanding prior to the sale as to the amount of commission to be paid. A properly drawn listing contract will eliminate most disputes.

Questions on Agency and Listings will be found in the Question Section, beginning on Page 177.

WORDS TO WATCH

Agency
Agent
Broker
Exclusive Agency
Exclusive Authorization to Sell Listing
Fiduciary
Listing
Litigation
Multiple Listing
Net Listing
Open Listing
Principal
Procuring Cause
Revocation

POINTS TO CHECK LOCALLY

      1. Are oral listings legal in your state?

      2. Are net listings legal in your state?

Sources of Information

      1. Real Estate Manual, if published by the Commission in your state.

      2. Real estate brokers.

      3. Real estate board.

      4. Attorneys.

Chapter 4

Real Property Interests

Systems of Property Ownership

Historically, there have been two systems of real property ownership; the feudal system and the alodial system. The feudal system held that all land in the domain was owned by the sovereign, with the subject possessing merely a feud, or right to use the land in return for services to the sovereign. The alodial system held that land could be owned by an individual without any patent interest on the part of the sovereign. Although both these systems existed in England prior to the development of this country, from the beginning of our independence this country had adhered to the alodial system, although certain rights remain in the state, even in this country, on the theory that it is for the public good for the state to exercise these limitations. When a person owns land, he is said to hold it in "fee." Originally, this word was used to denote the rights of a serf who held land by virtue of services to the sovereign. In modern usage, it is used to denote ownership, as distinguished from rights of possession as under a lease.

Classifications of Property

Property is divided into two general classifications: real property and personal property. *Real property* is defined as the land itself and all that goes with it of an incidental nature. It includes not only the land itself, but all improvements to the land, the rights to all things under the surface and in the air above the land. *Personal property* is a right for less than a lifetime in real property, and any right or interest which a person possesses in things which are movable and not considered by law to be realty.

Property is generally classified according to usage into three broad categories: public, quasi-public, and private. Public property is property owned by the government, such as schools, roads, parks, etc. Quasi-public property is property which is privately owned, but its use dedicated to the public, such as property owned by utility companies. Private property is that held by individuals for their own pleasure or profit.

Within the realm of private ownership, there is no such thing as absolute ownership. No matter how strong an interest an individual may have in property, his rights to use and enjoy it are always subject to limitations imposed for the good of the general public. Certain limitations are, therefore, always present in private ownership, as follows:

> *Eminent Domain.* The right of the sovereign state to seize private property for public use. This right exists in any level of government and may be extended to private corporations such as utility companies, when it is for the public good to do so.
>
> *Police Power.* The right of the state to make reasonable rules for the use and enjoyment of the property in the public interest, such as zoning ordinances, etc.
>
> *Taxation.* The right of the state to tax the property and to deprive the owner of it for nonpayment of taxes.
>
> *Escheat.* The reverting of property to the state by reason of failure of persons legally entitled to hold, or when no heirs can be found.

Subject to these limitations, man can enjoy varying degrees of interest in real property. The measure of man's interest in any particular piece of property is known as his estate in land. An *estate in land* is the degree, quantity, nature, and extent of interest which one has in real property. It is not a measure of the amount of land owned, but rather the quality of ownership which one has in any certain piece of land. It is the measure of man's *degree of interest* in the land; i.e., how much interest, for how long a time, and what type of interest. These interests are defined as estates. Following is an explanation of the fundamentals of the various kinds of estates that exist in real property.

Estates in Land

Freehold Estates.   Any interest in land which lasts for at least a lifetime is classified as a freehold estate. These estates are further classified as estates of inheritance and life estates. The estate of inheritance continues beyond the life of the holder and descends to his heirs upon his death, while the life estate extends only for the term of a life.

When a person is the owner of a freehold interest in real property, he is said to hold the property in seisin. Seisin is defined as the possession of real estate with the intention of claiming at least a lifetime interest; seisin can be said to be the possession of a freehold.

Following is a brief description of the freehold estates:

FEE SIMPLE

This is the largest and best estate in real property. It is the least limited interest that one can possess in private property. This estate is, however, subject to the limitations of eminent domain, police power, taxation, and escheat and may be subject to the claims of a creditor or a surviving spouse's right of curtesy or dower. The fee simple owner, during his lifetime, may do anything he wishes with the land, as long as he does not violate the rights of others. He may sell it, build upon it, let it lie idle, or do with it as he pleases, subject to the limitations mentioned above.

Fee simple estates may be absolute or conditional. The *fee simple absolute* is the largest and most common form of interest in real property. It represents the most complete property interest without any limitation imposed by the grant which created it. The *fee simple conditional* estate is an estate in fee that is qualified to the extent that it is conditioned upon the happening of some future event.

> Example: "X" conveys property to his son, provided he marries before his twenty-fifth birthday. Should he fail to do so, on his twenty-fifth birthday, title would revert to "X" or his heirs.

When a person holds fee simple title to himself alone, he is said to hold the property in *severalty*. Severalty ownership is ownership by one person. Often, however, the title to property is shared by two or more persons who become *concurrent owners*. There are three basic types of concurrent estates.

Tenancy by the Entireties. This is a peculiar form of estate, which exists only in married couples. It is based on the common-law concept that a husband and wife are one person. In order for this estate to exist, the deed must be made out to both husband and wife, while they are married. If made out to them prior to marriage, no such tenancy can exist. In the event of the death of either husband or wife, the survivor receives a fee simple title to the property. Neither the husband nor the wife can sell or otherwise dispose of the property without the signature of the other spouse on the deed. Neither can they force a partition of the property. Should they be divorced, the tenancy by the entireties can no longer exist, and they become tenants in common. Property which is so held cannot be attached by a creditor unless he is the creditor of both husband and wife.

Only a limited number of states recognize this concept. It does not exist in community property states. In some states a tenancy by the entireties may exist between husband and wife only if it manifestly appears from the face of the granting instrument that such a tenancy was intended at the time of the grant. In certain other states, it exists automatically among husband and wife unless they specifically take title in some other form.

Joint Tenancy. Joint tenancy is the holding of simultaneous interest in one piece of real estate by two or more persons. For this estate to exist, the tenants must hold identical interests, simultaneously acquired, from the same source, in the same instrument, with the interests of all tenants commencing at the same time. For this reason, it is said that joint tenancy requires four unities.

1. Time
2. Interest
3. Title
4. Possession

Under joint tenancy, the parties are considered to have but one estate in the land with each considered to be owner of the whole. Under the so-called "grand incident" of common law, there existed among all joint tenants an automatic right of survivorship, which means that when a joint tenancy exists, title passes to the survivor upon the death of one of the tenants. This right has been modified by statute in certain states and no longer automatically exists in these states, although it may exist if the intention to create survivorship is expressed on the face of the granting instrument. When it does not exist, upon the death of one tenant, his interest will pass to his heirs rather than to the surviving tenants.

Tenancy in Common. Tenancy in common exists when two or more persons hold an estate in land by separate and distinct titles, but with a unity of possession. The owners may acquire their interests from different persons or from the same person, and the owners need not have identical interests at the same time. Each tenant in common holds an undivided interest in the entire property. Each tenant in common is responsible to the property in proportion to his interest in it; that is, each tenant will pay his share of the expenses of the property and receive his proportionate share of profits, if any. A tenant in common may dispose of all or part of his share in the property without disturbing the tenancies of the other tenants. There cannot be any right of survivorship among tenants in common. When a tenant in common dies, his estate in the property passes to his heirs rather than to the surviving tenants.

Survivorship. Under the so-called "grand incident" of the common law, whenever property is held as tenants by the entireties or as joint tenants, there automatically exists the right of survivorship; that is, in the event of the death of one tenant, his share passes to the surviving tenants, and the final surviving tenant becomes an owner in severalty.

Certain states have modified this concept by statute and allow survivorship only if it is clear from the face of the granting instrument that survivorship was intended at the time of the grant. When this rule applies, the usual language used to express this intent is "with survivorship as at common law."

LIFE ESTATE

A life estate is an interest in real property, which interest is to last for the term of someone's life. Its principal characteristic is that it will terminate upon the death of some person. It may be an estate in *reversion* or an estate in *remainder.* An estate in reversion will revert to the grantor upon the death of the person upon whose life it was founded, while an estate in remainder will pass to a third person.

> Example: If "X" grants a life estate to "Y" upon condition that upon "Y's" death the title will revert to "X," this is an estate in reversion. Should "X" grant to "Y" and stipulate that upon "Y's" death the title would pass to "Z," this is an estate in remainder.

Life estates are most commonly granted for the life of the grantee but may be founded upon the life of another person. A life tenant may, during his tenure, do almost as much with the property as he could with a fee simple title but is subject to certain restrictions:

A. He may sell, but he may sell only the interest which he possesses which is an interest for someone's lifetime. The grantee's estate would terminate upon the death of the person upon whose life the estate was predicated.
B. He has the right to rent from the property during his lifetime but must not commit waste upon the land.
C. He may use reasonable amounts of wood from the land for fuel or for repairs to buildings but may not sell timber off the land.
D. He is bound to make reasonable repairs to the land.
E. He must pay taxes and interest on encumbrances.
F. He may mortgage the property but, upon his death, the mortgage would terminate and no longer constitute a lien upon the property. For this reason, a mortgagee would usually require life insurance upon the life of the life tenant as a condition of the mortgage.

Non-Freehold Estates: Often a person has an estate in real estate in the form of the right to use and enjoy the property according to the terms of a contract called a *lease.* The estate which is created by the lease is known as a *leasehold.* A leasehold is the interest created and vested in the tenant by virtue of his lease. This interest in real property is regarded by law as *personal property,* since the title remains vested in the landlord. Since this estate is created for a period of less than a lifetime, it is an estate less than a *freehold.*

There are four principal types of estates that may be created by a lease. Each of these is an estate less than a freehold and is a personal interest in the real property under lease.

1. *Estate for Years.* Briefly, any tenancy for a definite period of time. This period may be for a year or for more or less than a year. If the lease stipulates a definite terminal date, it is a tenancy for years.

2. *Estate from Period to Period.* This type of tenancy exists when the tenancy is of an indefinite duration. It can continue for a day, week, month, year, or for years, as long as there is no stipulated terminal date in the agreement. The tenancy may be created by the contractual agreement at the outset, or by the tenant's hold over at the end of a tenancy for years. A tenant who holds over after the expiration of a tenancy for years is considered bound to the landlord for new lease of a like period as the original lease, or for one year, whichever is less, unless the lease contained a provision for a shorter holding period, such as an agreement for a month to month holding period. Many leases which are written as an estate for years contain a provision that if the tenant elects to remain after the expiration of the initial leasing period, he will be bound on a month to month basis.

3. *Estate at Will.* This is a tenancy of indefinite duration that exists whenever either party has the right to terminate at will and may be the result of implication of law or by agreement of the parties. The term of the estate so created is indefinite and may be terminated by either party giving proper notice.

4. *Estate by Sufferance.* A tenant by sufferance is a tenant who was initially in control of the premises with the consent of the landlord, but who holds over the termination of his rights, and without the consent of the landlord. This tenant is actually a trespasser and is subject to ejectment by the landlord.

See Page 31 for diagram "Estates in Land"

Miscellaneous Interests in Real Property

Some other general interests in real property exist in certain situations. The more important of these are as follows:

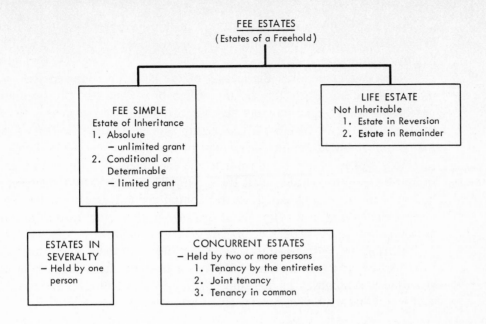

FEE ESTATES
(Estates of a Freehold)

FEE SIMPLE
Estate of Inheritance
1. Absolute
   – unlimited grant
2. Conditional or
   Determinable
   – limited grant

LIFE ESTATE
Not Inheritable
1. Estate in Reversion
2. Estate in Remainder

ESTATES IN
SEVERALTY
– Held by one
  person

CONCURRENT ESTATES
– Held by two or more persons
1. Tenancy by the entireties
2. Joint tenancy
3. Tenancy in common

All Fee Simple Estates Are Held in Seisin

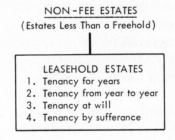

NON-FEE ESTATES
(Estates Less Than a Freehold)

LEASEHOLD ESTATES
1. Tenancy for years
2. Tenancy from year to year
3. Tenancy at will
4. Tenancy by sufferance

ESTATES IN LAND

Ground Rents.   In a few states a system of ground leasing is common in transfers of both improved property and unimproved property which is to be improved.

This system involves the leasing of the land for a long period, usually ninety-nine years, with the tenant either providing the improvements or purchasing them separately in the case of unimproved property. In effect, the lessee has all the benefits of ownership, subject to the payment of rent to the owner of the land. Such leases are redeemable at specific periods except for those which were created prior to the enactment of redemption statutes. In Maryland, for example, such leases may be redeemed by the lessee, at his option, for an amount equal to the annual ground rent capitalized at not more than 6 percent. The lessor cannot compel the lessee to redeem, however.

During the period of the lease, taxes and other assessments are assessed to the lessee, who has the responsibility for their payment. Ground leases are executed and recorded in the same manner as deeds and are purchased and sold by investors much as mortgages or other securities.

Dower.   When a woman marries, she automatically acquires the right to inherit, upon the death of her husband, at least a one-third life estate in all the real estate owned by the husband during the term of the marriage. The widow has dower in lands held by the husband as tenants in common, but not in lands held in joint tenancy. The dower is *not* the most that the husband may leave his wife but is the least that he may leave her under the law. If the couple has no children and the husband dies intestate, the wife will inherit a life estate in all real property owned by the husband during the marriage. Upon the death of the wife, the estate would then pass to the heirs of the husband. If there were children born of the marriage, and if the husband dies intestate, the wife will inherit dower interest (one-third life estate) in all real estate and the children will share equally in the remainder. Should the husband die testate, he may devise his wife not less than a one-third life estate in all his real property. The wife can surrender her dower interest in any or all of the real estate by joining with the husband in a deed of conveyance during his lifetime. However, should a husband convey any real estate during his lifetime without his wife's signature on the deed, upon his death, the wife may claim her dower interest.

The wife's dower will be terminated by:

1. Desertion or abandonment
2. Divorce
3. Murder of the husband to obtain the dower interest

In some states dower rights exist in the husband as well as in the wife. Certain states have abolished the dower by statute. It does not exist in community property states.

Community Property.   Certain states, mostly in the west, principally those whose laws are of Spanish origin, have community property laws. These laws are not uniform in all states, but the general concept is that all property held by husband and wife is owned equally by either. Certain exceptions are noted in every state which has community property laws. Because the laws are not consistent, as a real estate license applicant, it is recommended that you seek local advice on the applicability of these laws should you live in a community property state.

Fruits of the Soil.   This term refers to plant life on the land and to its disposition in the event of transfer of ownership of the land. Generally, the division follows the life expectancy of the plant, as follows:

Perennial plantings are plants that do not require annual planting and cultivation, though an original planting may have been necessary. This form of plant life is treated by law as real property, and the sale of land transfers ownership of such plants unless excluded in the deed of conveyance. An exception is timber that has been sold prior to the sale of the land but not yet severed from the land. If the contract for the sale of the timber predates the contract for the sale of the land, the timber is treated as personal property. Otherwise, a living, growing tree is real property while a tree cut down is personal property. Any perennial plant is included in this category.

Annual plantings, also called emblements, are any plants which must be planted annually and cultivated. All crops such as cotton, potatoes, corn, etc., are within this category. These plants are treated as personal property and the sale of the land does not include the crops unless specifically included in the deed of conveyance.

The seller of land on which emblements are growing has the right to continue to cultivate and harvest his crops after the sale of the land unless the crops are included in this deed of conveyance.

Easements.   An easement is any right which one person possesses in the lands of another. Its most common form is the right of way. Easements can be created by grant, reservation, implied grant, prescription, necessity, or condemnation. Following is a brief description of each method:

Grant. The easement is specifically created by agreement between the parties.

Reservation. At the time of a grant, the grantor reserves the rights in the easement for himself.

Implied Grant. Granted by law as having been implied in some prior agreement between the parties.

Prescription. Use of the land for a period of time, as under adverse possession.

Necessity. Held by law to be necessary for the benefit of the owner of the land, usually in the case of a "landlocked" parcel.

Condemnation. Acquired by the state under its powers of eminent domain.

Appurtenances.   An appurtenance is a right, privilege, or improvement which belongs with and passes with a principal property. Since it belongs to the property, rather than the tenant, it is considered to be real property. Some examples would be:

1. A right, such as the rights to subsurface minerals.
2. A privilege, such as the privilege of crossing another's land.
3. An improvement, such as a building.

These are considered to be appurtenances if their ownership would pass with change of ownership of the property.

Fixtures.   A fixture is an article of personal property that has become a part of the real estate by virtue of its attachment to the property. In determining whether an article has become a fixture, four principal tests are applied.

1. What was the purpose of its annexation to the property?
2. What was the form or nature of its annexation?
3. What was the intent of the parties who caused the annexation?
4. Would its removal damage the property?

If these tests are met affirmatively, the article would usually be held to be a fixture.

Adverse Possession.   A person may gain title to real estate by taking physical possession of the property and maintaining possession for the statutory period required in the jurisdiction. The period of time varies from state to state. Generally, public property (property owned by the government) may not be so acquired, but all private property is subject to the laws of adverse possession. The general requirements for title to be gained by adverse possession are:

1. *Actual Possession of the Property by the Occupant.* He must exercise some physical act of dominion over the land.
2. *Open and Notorious Possession.* The public in general, and the neighbors in particular, must know of the possession by the claimant. He must exercise such acts as would ordinarily be performed by the owner.

3. *Exclusive Possession.* The claimant's possession must be for himself alone and for no other person.

4. *Continuous Possession.* The claimant's possession must be continuous and uninterrupted for the statutory period of years. He does not have to be upon the land every day but must use the land for the purpose for which it is reasonably adapted without interruption for the necessary period.

5. *Tacking.* If an adverse claimant, before he has been in possession of the land for the necessary years, passes his interest to another person who takes immediate possession, he will be required to retain possession only for the balance of the statutory period. This is known as tacking.

6. *Claim of Ownership.* The adverse claimant must make an actual claim of ownership of the property. Possession without such a claim will not give the claimant title by adverse possession.

Extent of Title Acquired. Ordinarily, when the adverse claimant acquires title by adverse possession, the title given him will be a title in fee simple relating back to the date when he took possession of the land.

Questions on Real Property Interests will be found in the Question Section, beginning on Page 179.

NUMBER OF YEARS OF OCCUPANCY REQUIRED FOR A CLAIM OF TITLE BY ADVERSE POSSESSION

Alabama	20	Kentucky	7	North Dakota	20
Alaska	7	Louisiana	30	Ohio	21
Arizona	10	Maine	20	Oklahoma	15
Arkansas	7	Maryland	20	Oregon	10
California	5	Massachusetts	20	Pennsylvania	21
Colorado	18	Michigan	15	Rhode Island	10
Connecticut	15	Minnesota	15	South Carolina	10
Delaware	20	Mississippi	10	South Dakota	20
D. C.	15	Missouri	10	Tennessee	20
Florida	7	Montana	5	Texas	25
Georgia	20	Nebraska	10	Utah	7
Hawaii	20	Nevada	5	Vermont	15
Idaho	5	New Hampshire	20	Virginia	15
Illinois	20	New Jersey	20	Washington	10
Indiana	10	New Mexico	10	West Virginia	10
Iowa	10	New York	10	Wisconsin	20
Kansas	15	North Carolina	20	Wyoming	10

In certain states these periods may be modified under some conditions.

WORDS TO WATCH

Accretion	Joint Tenancy
Adverse Possession	Land
Air Rights	Landlord
Alluvium	Lease
Appurtenance	Leasehold
Avulsion	Lessee
Bundle of Rights	Lessor
Chattel Real	Life Estate
Chattels	Net Lease
Common Law	Notice to Quit
Community Property	Partition
Condemnation	Personal Property
Condominium	Personalty
Constructive Eviction	Police Power
Conveyance	Prescription
Curtesy	Property
Defeasible Fee	Quiet Enjoyment
Demise	Real Estate
Dispossess	Realty
Domicile	Remainder
Dower	Remainder Estate
Easement	Rent
Ejectment	Reservation
Emblements	Residuary Estate
Eminent Domain	Restriction
Encroachment	Reversion
Escheat	Reversionary Interest
Estate	Right of Survivorship
Estate at Sufferance	Right of Way
Estate for Life	Riparian Owner
Estate for Years	Riparian Rights
Estate from Period to Period	Seisin
Estate in Reversion	Separate Property
Estoppel	Severalty Ownership
Estovers	Squatters Rights
Eviction	Subletting
Fee	Surrender
Fee Simple	Tenant
Fee Simple Absolute	Tenant at Sufferance
Fee Tail	Tenancy at Will
Fixture	Tenancy for Years
Freehold	Tenancy in Common
Graduated Lease	Tenure in Land
Gross Lease	Trade Fixtures
Ground Lease	Warranty Deed
Hereditaments	Waste
Holdover Tenant	Zoning
Homestead	Zoning Ordinance
Homestead Exemption	

POINTS TO CHECK LOCALLY

1. Tenancy by the entireties:
   a. Does this tenancy exist in your state?
   b. Is it automatic between husband and wife or must the granting instrument specify?
2. Joint tenancy:
   a. Must joint tenancy be specified in the granting instrument?
   b. Is survivorship automatic or must it be specified?
3. Dower:
   a. Is dower recognized in your state?
   b. What share of the estate is the dower?
   c. Does dower or curtesy exist in the husband in your state?
4. Does your state have community property laws?
5. Are ground leases used in your state?
   If so, learn local regulations governing them.

Sources of Information

1. Real Estate Manual for your state.
2. Title companies or escrow companies.
3. Attorneys.
4. Real estate brokers.

Chapter 5

Appraising

Introduction

The appraisal of real estate is one of the more highly skilled fields of endeavor in this complex industry. A competent appraiser must have to his credit many years of study plus considerable experience in several areas. To attempt to appraise property without these qualifications would be, at the very least, unwise. This chapter will not attempt to prepare anyone for a career as a real estate appraiser. Its purpose is to acquaint the license preparation student with the terminology and techniques of the appraiser.

Appraisal Defined. An appraisal is defined as an estimate or opinion of value. This definition applies not only to an appraisal of real estate but also to any appraisal of anything of value—furs, jewelry, antiques, automobiles, or anything else. It can never be an exact statement of value for value is an intangible thing, subject sometimes to human emotions and all sorts of human frailties. It follows, therefore, that the accuracy of any appraisal depends upon the competence and integrity of the appraiser and on the skill which he employs in evaluation of the data concerning the property.

Although an appraisal may be in either written or oral form, most real estate appraisals are transmitted in the form of a written report, which will usually include a complete description of the property, relevant data concerning the property, and an analysis of that data. The real estate appraisal has been said to be the result of the application of an orderly program by which the problem of determination of value is solved.

Value Defined. Value is defined as the power of a property or commodities to command other properties or commodities in exchange in a free market. It is changeable and can be influenced by many things such as sentiment, necessity, utility, and the law of supply and demand. Nothing has value without use, and the ability of an owner to use or enjoy the property will, of course, influence his opinion of its value. Human factors must always be considered, since people make value. Most appraisals are based on the market value of the property, considering not only the present worth but also the future benefits that may be derived from its use.

Market value is defined as the price at which a willing seller would sell and which a willing buyer would pay, neither of them being under any compulsion to buy or sell. This definition assumes that both buyer and seller are fully informed as to the property and the state of the market for that property, and that reasonable time allowances are made for market exposure.

Market value should not be confused with *market price*, which is the amount, expressed in dollars, which was actually paid for a property. It is possible, under certain market conditions, for the market price of a property to be either higher or lower than its market value. It has been said that price is what you pay and value is what you get.

Many factors can influence the value of a property. Economic, political, or social factors within a community will often have a considerable influence upon the value of a property. Within the neighborhood itself, the same conditions will be reflected in the value of certain property. Finally, the characteristics of the particular site or location of a property will contribute to its value or lack of value.

Purpose of the Appraisal.   An appraiser makes an appraisal not for himself but for a client, and the opinion that he gives as to the value must not be his own opinion, but that of the average person reacting in the current market. It is extremely important for an appraiser to know for what purpose the appraisal is being made.

Generally, there are six reasons for having property appraised, as follows:

1. To determine its market value.
2. For purposes of condemnation.
3. To establish a basis for taxes (assessed value).
4. For insurance purposes.
5. For the settlement of an estate.
6. For an owner, who wishes to sell his property.

To some extent, the purpose of the appraisal will determine the approach to value determination which is to be used by the appraiser. There are three generally accepted methods or techniques which may be employed in the appraisal process. These methods are called "approaches" by the appraisers.

Approaches to Value

In arriving at his estimate of the value of a property through an orderly process, the appraiser has at his disposal three well-established techniques.

Cost approach. The current cost of reproducing a property, less depreciation from all sources.

Market data approach. The value of the property in relation to other properties of the same type and class. Often called the comparison approach.

Income approach. The value as indicated by the net earnings of the property.

Following is a brief description of the techniques employed in these approaches.

Cost Approach. This approach assumes that the reproduction cost of the property is its upper limit of value, and that a newly constructed building has an advantage over an older building. The appraiser must therefore evaluate the disadvantages of the existing building in comparison with the new building and make an allowance for these disadvantages. This allowance is called depreciation, and it may take either of three forms: physical deterioration, economic obsolescence, or functional obsolescence. Physical deterioration results from the physical wearing out of the property, is readily seen, and generally simple to identify. Economic obsolescence is the loss of value resulting from factors outside the property. It is the result of social changes which make the building less desirable because of the conditions within the community. Functional obsolescence is the result of outmoded function within the building itself. This includes such factors as layout, style, and design as compared with a new property serving the same function.

With the above factors as considerations, the cost approach consists of four steps.

1. The estimate of the value of the land as if it were vacant.
2. The estimate of the current cost of reproducing the improvements.
3. Estimation and deduction of depreciation from all causes.
4. The addition of the estimated value of the land and depreciated value of the improvements.

Market Data Approach. This approach is essential in almost every appraisal of real estate. Its application produces an estimation of the value of the subject property by comparing it with similar properties of the same type and class, which have been recently sold or are currently offered for sale in the same or competing areas. This comparative process requires considerable judgment as to similarity of the properties and must consider many factors such as location, construction, age, condition, layout, equipment, etc. Four categories of data are essential to this type of appraisal.

1. Sales or asking prices of comparable properties.
2. Conditions influencing each sale.
3. Location of each property.
4. Description of the land and improvements on each property.

This approach is usually given great reliance in appraising single family residential properties if adequate sales data on truly comparable properties is available.

Income Approach. This approach considers the present worth of the future potential benefits of a property. It estimates the current value of a property by the basis of its present and future income-producing capabilities. This is measured by the net income which a fully informed person is warranted in assuming the property will produce during its remaining economic life. Although income alone is not the sole factor used by the appraiser in arriving at his estimate or value, it is a major factor in this approach. Consideration must be given, however, to remaining economic life, not only of the building, but of other items within the property in estimating the value. The capitalization technique is employed in this method as follows.

Capitalization. This technique employs the division of the net income from the property by a predetermined capitalization rate according to the following formula:

$$\frac{\text{Net Income}}{\text{Capitalization Rate}} = \text{Value}$$

Selection of the proper capitalization rate is most important. A variation of less than 1 percent in capitalization rate can make a difference of thousands of dollars in the capitalized value of the property. Therefore, considerable care must be taken in selection of the proper capitalization rate.

The proper capitalization rate for a property consists of two factors: a return *on* the investor's capital, and the return *of* his original capital investment. Since the improvements will depreciate, while the land will not ordinarily depreciate in value, the residual technique is employed to determine the total capitalization rate.

For example: Assume that a property was producing a new income of $12,000 per year, on land which was valued at $30,000 by the comparison, or market data technique. Let us also assume a rate of earnings *on* capital of 6 percent. Thus, the portion of total income attributable to the improvements would be $10,200 [$12,000 − (.06 × $30,000)]. Assume also a remaining life of 40 years in the building, or $2\frac{1}{2}$ percent per year depreciation rate. This $2\frac{1}{2}$ percent depreciation rate on the building is added to the 6 percent return on capital, for a total capitalization rate of $8\frac{1}{2}$ percent. Using our basic capitalization formula, the value of the building is determined as follows:

$$\frac{\$10,200 \text{ net income from building}}{.085 \text{ capitalization rate}} = \$120,000 \text{ value of bldg.}$$

$$\begin{array}{l} \$\ 120,000 \text{ value of building} \\ +\ \ 30,000 \text{ value of land} \\ \hline \$\ 150,000 \text{ value of land and building} \end{array}$$

Gross Rent Multiplier. A method employed to assist in appraising properties on the basis of capitalization. This technique employs the relationship of the value of the property to its monthly rental income. A Monthly Gross Rent Multiplier (MGRM) for the property is determined, and the value of the property is estimated by multiplying the monthly income from the property by this factor as follows:

Monthly Gross Rent Multiplier × Monthly Rent = Value

From the above it can be seen that the MGRM is a factor reflecting a relationship between a sale price and rent. Use of this technique is generally restricted by the appraiser to rule of thumb estimates of general indications of value, and it is not used as a substitute for actual appraisals.

Correlation of Appraisal Estimates

In arriving at his final conclusion as to the value of a property, the appraiser takes into account the purpose of his appraisal, the type of property, and the adequacy of the data employed in each approach. He does not average the values indicated by each of the approaches, but weighs each in the light of the above considerations. He places the most emphasis on the approach which appears to be the most reliable in the light of the specific appraisal problem, but will temper this judgment with the conclusions of the other two techniques.

Employment of Appraisers

Generally, the employment of appraisers is divided into two groups, as follows:

Fee appraisers. These are self-employed businessmen who perform their services on an individual fee basis for each appraisal completed.

Staff appraisers. These are usually persons employed by institutions such as banks, savings and loan associations, or insurance companies to make appraisals for the employer.

Appraisal Societies

There are in this country two appraisal societies.

1. The American Institute of Real Estate Appraisers. Membership in this organization is designated by the letters M.A.I. following the member's name.
2. The Society of Real Estate Appraisers. Membership in this group is designated by the letters S.R.E.A. following the member's name.

These are professional societies similar in nature to national trade associations. Membership in either of these societies is earned only after considerable education, experience, and demonstrated capabilities in the field of real estate appraisal. A member of either of these societies can be considered a professional in this field.

Note: The discussion of real estate appraisal in this chapter is limited to the capability normally expected of real estate salesmen. Applicants for real estate broker licensure would do well to study additional subject matter on appraising prior to taking the E.T.S. examination. A good suggested text would be *The Valuation of Real Estate* by Alfred A. Ring and published by Prentice-Hall, Inc.

Questions on Appraising will be found in the Question Section, beginning on Page 183.

WORDS TO WATCH

Accrued Depreciation
Ad Valorem
Amenities
Appraisal
Appraiser
Appreciation
Assessed Valuation
Building Code
Building Line
Capitalization
Capitalization Rate
Cost of Reproduction
Curtilage
Deferred Maintenance
Deterioration
Economic Life
Economic Obsolescence

Front Foot
Functional Obsolescence
Gross Income
Highest and Best Use
Increment
M. A. I.
Market Price
Market Value
Net Income
Obsolescence
Setback
Setback Ordinance
Sinking Fund
Straight Line Depreciation
Unearned Increment
Valuation
Value

Chapter 6

Real Estate Finance

Introduction

Nearly all sales of real estate involve some sort of financing of part of the purchase price. It is essential that a real estate salesman have a fundamental knowledge of the principles which govern real estate finance. Seldom will a salesman encounter a buyer who is prepared to pay cash for the purchase price of real estate which he wants to buy. Usually, he must seek a loan from outside investment sources in order to make his purchase, and it often falls upon the agent to assist him in locating the necessary investment capital.

Mortgages and Trust Deeds

When a loan is made on real estate, the property itself becomes the security for the loan, through the process of hypothecation—the giving of property as security without giving up possession of the property. Hypothecation of real property is accomplished by means of a mortgage or trust deed (deed of trust). Although each of these instruments accomplish the same purpose, there is some difference in their standing under the law. A real estate agent should understand these differences.

In those states which employ the lien theory of mortgages, the mortgage creates a legal claim in favor of the mortgagee, against the mortgaged property. This lien becomes void when the debt is satisfied. In the event of default, the mortgagee must foreclose in order to collect the debt.

Foreclosure is a legal process which requires court action. In this action, the mortgagor is in default and asks for a judgment in favor of the mortgagee. The action further asks that the property be sold at auction in order to satisfy the indebtedness.

When a trust deed, or deed of trust, is used as security, a third party is brought into the picture. A trust deed conveys legal title to a third party, to hold as security until the debt is satisfied, at which time he will reconvey the title to the trustor (borrower). The principal difference in the operation of a trust deed, as distinguished from a mortgage, is in the event of default. Under the terms of the trust deed, the trustee is empowered to sell the property at auction and to use the proceeds to satisfy the indebtedness. This can often be accomplished more quickly and at less expense than foreclosure proceedings in court.

In some states which operate under the title theory of mortgages, a mortgage conveys legal title to the mortgagee, much as is done with a trust deed.

The Mortgagee's Role in Real Estate Finance

No understanding of real estate finance can be accomplished without a basic understanding of the position of the mortgagee in the transaction. Persons and firms which are engaged in this business are investors of funds, whose principal reason for lending is to make a profit on their investment. Usually, the lender is investing funds which he does not personally own, but over which he is serving as custodian. For example, banks and savings and loan associations invest funds belonging to their depositors. Insurance companies invest funds belonging to their policyholders. Eventually, these funds must be returned to their owners, and while in the custody of the bank, savings and loan association, or insurance company must earn a profit for the owner. The lender must invest the funds at a profit greater than the profit which it will have to repay to the owner of the funds. For this reason, the interest which they charge for the loan of the funds must be in excess of the interest which they will have to pay for the use of the funds.

A real estate agent must realize that money is a commodity, and it commands a price in the marketplace which is largely determined by the law of supply and demand. The greater the supply of available investment capital, the lower its price, and vice versa.

The lender must constantly seek the best possible combination of yield (profit) versus security, commensurate always with sound business practices and regulations imposed upon him by government regulations and the limitations of his charter. He must consider such factors as administrative costs, collection expenses, and myriad other factors which will influence his eventual profit picture. He must always be prepared to pay his sources (depositors, shareholders, policyholders) a profit on their investment which will attract them to continue to invest with him. In the light of these considerations, he must relate loans on real estate to other avenues of investment, such as loans to the government, loans to corporations, and investments in such fields as municipal bonds. All these fields of investment just mentioned are considered to be "prime" investment sources; that is, sources which are very secure and which require very little administrative cost or effort to collect. On the other hand, loans secured by real estate require extensive administrative machinery plus expensive collection procedures. In order to produce a net profit equal to that of a prime investment source, a real estate loan to an individual must return a higher yield to the investor.

One other principle of investment which must be recognized is that gain must always be commensurate with risk. The greater the risk undertaken by the lender, the greater his gain must be from the investment. For example, a bank may lend money on a personal loan to an established businessman with good security at a comparatively low rate of interest, while a small loan company must require a considerably higher rate of interest on a loan made without security to a high risk borrower.

There is a proven relationship also in the ratio of probability of default to the borrower's equity in the security. A person who has very little of his personal funds invested in the property is much less reluctant to relinquish it to foreclosure than one with a high ratio of equity to value.

The above is intended as background information for the understanding of the investment pattern of the various sources of real estate loans, and of the principles employed by these sources in deciding what loans they are interested in making. Following is a discussion of the various sources of funds and of their general policies and limitations. It should be recognized that the policies described here are general, and that occasionally a lender will establish policies not in full agreement with those detailed here.

Mortgages and Deeds of Trust as Negotiable Instruments

Mortgages and deeds of trust are negotiable instruments and are purchased and sold by investors much as shares of stock or other securities.

Some lenders originate loans directly to the consumer, while other lenders specialize in purchasing existing mortgages from other investors. When an existing mortgage is sold by one investor to another, this is known as trading in the secondary mortgage market (do not confuse this term with a "second" or junior mortgage).

When an existing mortgage or deed of trust is sold or traded, the borrower may receive notice to commence making his payments to the new owner, or in some instances, the original owner may continue to "service" the mortgage. In the latter circumstance, the borrower may not be made aware of the sale. In neither instance will the terms of the mortgage be changed in any way.

The Mortgage Loan Correspondent

A major factor in the real estate investment field is the mortgage loan correspondent. These firms act as representatives for many sources of investment capital and operate on a brokerage basis. The correspondent may represent a few or a great number of investment sources, such as insurance companies, mutal savings banks, pension funds, savings and loan associations, and commercial banks. Their role is to bring together the lender and the borrower, acting as agent or broker. They are paid a commission for their services in originating and processing the loan, and frequently also serve as a servicing agent after the origination of the loan.

In a sense the mortgage loan correspondent is to the finance industry what the real estate agent is to the real estate industry. He brings together the lender, who has the capital available for investment, and the borrower, who has a need for investment capital. He is paid a fee for his services, as the real estate agent is paid a fee for bringing together the buyer and seller of real estate.

A major role of the correspondent is the "servicing" of loans which he has originated. Servicing consists of handling the administration of the loan after its origination. He maintains a servicing department, charged with the responsibility of collecting payments, maintaining escrow accounts for taxes, insurance, F.H.A. mortgage insurance premiums, etc., and the disbursement of these funds to the proper parties at the proper time. Often, officers of the firm will serve as trustees on deeds of trust securing the loans, and will act in this capacity as necessary. The correspondent is paid a "servicing fee" for this endeavor.

Most correspondents are equipped to make direct loans from their own funds in many cases in order to provide the industry with faster service. By making loans based on his own evaluation of the risk, rather than waiting for the ultimate investor to do so, he can often provide the public with a needed service. The correspondent will assemble these loans into a "package" of loans, ranging from a few to twenty-five, fifty, or more loans which he will then sell in the secondary market, to an investor such as a mutual savings bank or insurance company, thus freeing his capital for investment in more loans to be sold by the same process when he assembles another package. This process is known as "warehousing." This ability to turn over his investment capital several times a year gives the correspondent a desirable flexibility and provides the industry with a much needed service. The information given above is, of course, an oversimplification of the role of the mortgage loan correspondent. Any new salesman or broker should thoroughly acquaint himself with the correspondents in his community and avail himself of their services whenever needed. They are often the best available source of financing of the sales made by the agent.

Sources of Funds

The sources of funds for real estate finance described here are those which are most generally available. In special situations or certain areas, sources other than these may be available. Any of these sources may originate loans or deal in the secondary market.

Savings and Loan Associations. Savings and loan associations are thrift institutions, chartered for the purpose of encouraging thrift, and for the purpose of making available investment capital for real estate finance. They are perhaps the largest single category of investor in real estate loans for financing the sale and purchase of single family dwellings. Their charters generally require that the institution make only loans on government securities or mortgages or deeds of trust on real estate or mobile homes.

Savings and loan associations derive their charters either from the federal government or from the state in which they operate. Federally chartered associations may always be identified by the use of the word "Federal" in their names (Example: First Federal Savings and Loan; Security Federal Savings and Loan, etc.). Insofar as the general public is concerned, there is little difference in the charter requirements of the state or federal charter.

A savings and loan association may be chartered as either a stock association or a mutual association. Stock associations are founded by a group of investors who put up the initial capital and own stock in the corporation, as with any other corporate business. A mutual association is owned by the shareholders (depositors) with each shareholder owning a share of the firm in proportion to the amount of his deposits. Most federally chartered associations are mutual associations, but state chartered institutions may be either stock or mutual associations. A mutual association is prohibited by law and regulation from making loans to anyone who is not a member of the association. However, regulations stipulate that anyone automatically and simultaneously becomes a member of the association when his loan application is accepted and a legal contract exists. It is not always necessary for a borrower to open a savings account in order to qualify as a member.

Both state and federal savings and loans are permitted at this time to make loans on real estate up to 95 percent of the appraised value of the property, or of the selling price, whichever is lesser. Both state and federally chartered institutions may make loans based on amortization periods of up to thirty years. Generally, the institution is prohibited from making loans on property more than one-hundred miles from its home office, but in some cases it is possible for them to exceed these limits.

All savings and loans have their deposits insured, usually with the Federal Savings and Loan Insurance Corporation. This is an agency of the federal government, originated in the early 1930s for the purpose of encouraging thrift and making investment capital available for real estate loans by insuring the deposits of shareholders in savings and loan institutions. At present, all accounts on deposit with member institutions are insured up to $20,000. Savings and loan institutions make loans for three major purposes, as follows:

1. New home construction
2. Loans on existing homes
3. Home improvement loans

Construction loans are usually non-amortized, or "straight" mortgages, while loans on existing properties and home improvement loans are usually repaid by means of an amortized mortgage.

Savings and loan associations make either conventional loans, F.H.A. insured loans, or V.A. guaranteed loans. Although the ratio of loan to value on loans made under F.H.A. insured and V.A. guaranteed loans may exceed the limitations of the institution's charter, because of the government insurance against loss by default, they are permitted to invest in loans of this type.

Commercial Banks. The role of the commercial bank in the financing of real estate purchases has been one of ever increasing participation for the past several decades. Until fairly recent times, mostly in the period since World War II, the commercial bank was not a major factor in this area, largely because of its broader investment portfolio. Commercial banks are designed to, and must, meet the financial needs of the total business community. Demand for short-term business loans, automobile loans, appliance and furniture loans, etc., has prevented the commercial bank from participating heavily in real estate loans. Also, the requirements of its charter place some limitations on the total percentage of investment portfolios that may be placed in long-term real estate loans. However, the tremendous growth of the banking industry over the past several decades has made considerably more funds available for investment, and this has led inevitably to a greater participation in real estate loans by these institutions.

Commercial banks are divided into two groups: federally chartered and state chartered. Federally chartered banks are called National banks and can be identified by the word "national" in their name. State banks can be identified by the absence of this word from their name. At present, both state and federally chartered banks may make real estate loans of up to 80 percent of the appraised value of the property or of the actual selling price, whichever is lower, for periods of up to twenty-five years. In practice, however, most banks limit their loans to somewhat lesser amounts and generally to shorter amortization periods.

Mutual Savings Banks. The mutual savings banks are specialized banking institutions, most of which are located in the north-east section of the United States. These banks operate in a fashion somewhat similar to savings and loans institutions. Historically, these banks have been heavy investors in F.H.A. and V.A. insured loans, in the secondary market, partly because they have difficulty in investing all their investment funds in their home communities. In recent years they have become somewhat heavier investors of funds in conventional loans, since their ratio of loan to value may sometimes exceed that of the commercial bank or savings and loan association. Since these institutions are often domiciled in another state, in investing in other areas they generally operate through mortgage loan correspondents, although in some cases they do make direct loans.

Insurance Companies. Traditionally, insurance companies have been heavy investors in real estate loans in the area of homes, apartments, commercial, and industrial properties. Their investment funds are derived from insurance premiums and from reinvestment of principal on present loans. These companies have been active in both conventional and government insured loans, and have over the past several decades been one of the prime sources of investment capital for the real estate industry. Depending on their size, they sometimes operate directly with the borrower and sometimes operate through mortgage loan correspondents.

Other Factors in Real Estate Investment Field. Several other sources of real estate loans are available, but usually on a limited scale. Some of these are:

1. Pension funds
2. Individual investors
3. College endowment funds

These sources generally operate through the trust department of commercial banks or mortgage loan correspondents and are not a major factor in the real estate investment field when considered in the light of other sources. They should not be discounted, however, and may provide a source of financing when other sources are not available.

As a real estate salesman, the placement of loans on sales made by you will usually be directed by your broker. However, you should be generally familiar with the sources as indicated in this chapter.

Types of Financing

In your capacity as a real estate salesman, you will have available to you three basic types of new financing for your sales of real estate. These are defined as conventional financing, F.H.A. insured financing, and Veterans Administration guaranteed financing. In addition to these methods, your purchaser's acquisition of the property can often be financed by the assumption of existing financing or by taking title subject to existing financing. Loans which are insured by F.H.A. or guaranteed by the Veterans Administration are commonly referred to as *government insured loans*. This description identifies the loan as one in which the lender is protected by an agency of the federal government against any financial loss he might suffer by reason of the borrower's default in the repayment of the loan. The procedures as to how this protection is applied will be explained in later discussion of the regulations which govern these loans. Because of this protection, the lender is persuaded to make the loans on terms which would not be agreeable to him without this protection.

A loan which is not insured or guaranteed by the government is known as a *conventional loan*. Without the government guarantee, the lender assumes a greater risk, and his terms for such loans will usually reflect this additional risk.

F.H.A. Insured Financing.   The Federal Housing Administration came into being as a result of the Federal Housing Act of 1934. It was originated as a means of attracting investment capital into real estate loans by insuring the lenders against loss caused by the borrower's default in the repayment of the loan. The F.H.A. is a government agency, and the assurance of this agency gave lenders the needed impetus to invest capital in real estate loans which they would not otherwise have been interested in making.

How F.H.A. Operates. F.H.A. is an insuring agency, which serves to insure lenders against loss by reason of a borrower's default on the repayment of a loan. It does not insure the property and does not make payments on the loan if the borrower misses a payment. Its function is to make up to the lender any loss that he suffers, after the loan has been foreclosed upon and the property sold at auction.

Example: Borrower secures a loan of $20,000, which he reduces through amortization to a balance of $18,000, when he becomes unable to continue making his payments. The mortgagee would then foreclose. Suppose that at foreclosure the property would bring only $16,000. The lender would then have lost $2,000 plus the expenses of the sale. F.H.A. would make up this loss to the lender.

Although the above example is vastly oversimplified from an administrative point of view, it explains simply the F.H.A. insuring process. This government insurance makes an investment in F.H.A. loans attractive to many lenders who would not otherwise be interested in such loans.

F.H.A. Mortgage Insurance Premiums. The F.H.A. requires that the borrower pay a mortgage insurance premium equal to $\frac{1}{2}$ of 1 percent of the average annual balance on the loan. This premium is paid in monthly installments as a part of the borrower's regular amortization payment.

Appraisal Requirements. F.H.A. requires that the subject property be appraised before it will commit to insure any loan. The appraisal must be requested by an approved lending institution, and may not be ordered by the buyer or seller directly. F.H.A.'s loan insurance amounts are based on a percentage of the appraised value of the property or sales price, whichever is lower. The formula for determining this maximum insurable value will be given later in this section. F.H.A. will accept appraisals made by the Veterans Administration.

Appraisal vs. Sales Price; Secondary Financing. F.H.A. has no requirement that the property sell at or below the appraised value. The sale price can be any price agreed upon by the buyer and seller. However, maximum insurable loan amounts are computed on the F.H.A. appraised value of the property or sales price, whichever is the lesser, and the difference between actual sale price and maximum loan amount must be paid in cash by the borrower as a down payment. No secondary financing of any kind is permitted on any F.H.A. insured loan. The difference between the sale price and maximum loan must be paid in cash at closing, and the buyer must demonstrate that he has the necessary cash available before F.H.A. will commit to insure the loan.

Maximum Loan Term and Amounts. The maximum term for F.H.A. insured loans is thirty-five years. However, F.H.A. discourages loans of this term, and for practical purposes, most F.H.A. loans are made for a maximum term of thirty years. Loans are available in multiples of five year terms from ten years to the maximum term. The maximum loan amounts available under Section 203 (the most frequently used type of loan) are: $33,000 on one-family dwelling; $35,750 on two-family or three-family dwellings; $41,250 on four-family dwellings. These amounts are subject to change by legislation from time to time.

Interest Rates; Monthly Payments. The maximum allowable interest rate on F.H.A. loans is subject to change by legislation from time to time. At the present time the maximum rate is 8.5 percent per annum on the outstanding principal balance. In addition, the borrower must also pay the $\frac{1}{2}$ percent mortgage insurance premium, but this is not an interest charge. The monthly payment on the loan must include a monthly mortgage insurance premium, hazard insurance premium, and one-twelfth of the annual taxes. Special miscellaneous items may also be included.

Veterans Administration Guaranteed Financing. The V.A. home financing guaranty program came into being as a result of the Servicemen's Readjustment Act of 1944. It was originally intended as a means of assistance to returning veterans of World War II. Through Congressional legislation, the program has been extended several times since and would now appear to be likely to remain in existence for an indefinite period. Loans guaranteed under this program are frequently called "G.I." loans.

The concept of the V.A. program is to guarantee lenders against loss by reasons of the veteran purchaser's default on the payment, in a fashion much like that of the F.H.A. program. In the event of a loss on a transaction by the lender, after the loan has been foreclosed and the property sold at auction, the Veteran's Administration will make up the loss suffered by the lender. However, the administrative processes employed by V.A. are much different than those of the F.H.A.

Although V.A. guarantees the lender against loss, the maximum amount of the guarantee is $12,500 or 60 percent of the purchase price, whichever should be lesser. If the $12,500 guarantee seems small when compared to the purchase price of a home today, remember that the guarantee covers a loss by the lender, after the foreclosure sale. The loss suffered by a lender will seldom exceed this amount after the partial recovery from a foreclosure sale.

V.A. Mortgage Insurance Premiums. V.A. does not insure the loans as does F.H.A., and there is no mortgage insurance premium for a V.A. loan.

Appraisal Requirements. V.A. requires that the property be appraised by the Veterans Administration. The appraisal is ordered usually through an approved lending source, in a manner similar to that used in ordering an F.H.A. appraisal.

Appraisal vs. Selling Price; Secondary Financing. V.A. does permit the veteran purchaser to pay more than the appraised value of the property; however, he must sign a statement to the effect that he has been made aware of the actual appraisal and is paying more than this amount of his own free will. In the event the purchaser does pay more than the appraised value, the maximum loan amount would be the appraised value, and all above this amount would have to be paid in cash at closing by the purchaser as a down payment. Secondary financing is allowed, provided the interest rate does not exceed that of the first mortgage, and the mortgage term is at least as long as that of the first mortgage. Since there is little advantage under these conditions, secondary financing is seldom used on V.A. loans.

Maximum Loan Terms and Amounts. The maximum term for V.A. residential loans is thirty years. Farm loans may run for a forty year amortization period. V.A. has no maximum loan ceiling. Since the maximum guarantee under any V.A. loan is $12,500, V.A. regulations do not place a ceiling on the maximum loan amount.

Interest Rates; Monthly Payments. The maximum allowable interest rate that may be charged a veteran purchaser on a V.A. guaranteed loan at present is 8.5 percent per annum on the outstanding principal balance. Monthly amortization payments are required, and such payments must include one-twelfth of the annual taxes and one month's hazard insurance premiums, as with a F.H.A. insured loan.

Ratio of Loan to Value; Down Payment Requirements. Since the maximum guarantee to the lender provided by V.A. is $12,500, there is no maximum loan amount and no down payment requirement on the part of V.A. However, many lenders will set their own down payment requirements and maximum loan amounts.

Eligibility for V.A. Guaranteed Loans. V.A. guaranteed loans require the borrower to have served in the armed services of the United States between September 16, 1940 and July 25, 1947; between June 27, 1950 and January 31, 1955; or, under the "cold war" program, after January 31, 1955, for a period of at least ninety days (181 days for cold war veterans) and to have received a discharge under conditions other than dishonorable. Also, persons who have been on active duty for at least two years are eligible. The period of eligibility is computed on the basis of ten years after discharge, plus one additional year for each three months of active service. The veteran, to be eligible for the loan, must apply to a V.A. regional office for a Certificate of Eligibility. This loan eligibility may generally be used only once by the veteran, except that in some cases of hardship nature it is possible to have the eligibility reinstated if the original loan has been paid off.

General Information; Restrictions on Loans. Following are some general requirements for V.A. loans not covered above.

1. Loans on property less than one year old may be made only on property which meets V.A. standards for construction and general acceptability.
2. V.A. may refuse to appraise properties built by certain builders who have previously failed to meet V.A. standards.
3. Veteran purchaser must sign a statement at closing that he intends to live in the subject property.
4. V.A. may refuse to guarantee loans for certain lenders who have in the past failed to meet V.A. requirements.
5. V.A. requires that on new construction the builder furnish the veteran purchaser certain warranties as to construction.

Conventional Loans. From the above it can be seen that F.H.A. and V.A. loans have one common characteristic; both provide insurance by the federal government for the lender against loss by reason of the borrower's default in repayment of the loan. For this reason, they are frequently referred to as "insured loans." A conventional loan is any loan which is not insured by the federal government. Since this loan is not insured by the federal government, there is less regulation by the government, and the lender is usually free to set his own lending policies, subject only to the limitations of his charter and the laws of the state. Conventional loans provide more flexibility in financing and leave more room for negotiation between borrower and lender. Outlined below are some general rules which are frequently applied in this type of lending.

Ratio of Loan to Value. Since the lender under a conventional loan is not insured by the government, he generally will offset somewhat the additional risk undertaken by requiring a higher down payment than would be required under government insured financing. There is no set pattern for ratio of loan to value, but, except in unusual cases, many lenders will not make loans in excess of 80 percent of value. Frequently, maximum loan to value ratios are set at 75 percent, and sometimes lower, depending on the policy of the lender.

Some conventional lenders insure their loans through private insurance companies. These companies offer insurance similar to F.H.A. mortgage insurance and afford the lender the same protection against default as would be provided by F.H.A. insurance.

Perhaps the best known of these companies is the Mortgage Guaranty Insurance Corporation, and the colloquial term for loans insured by this company is "magic loans." Loans which are insured by this company may in some instances be made up to 95 percent of the sale price of the property.

Loan Term. The maximum loan term for most lenders is set by their charter.

> Example: Thirty years for savings and loan associations, twenty-five years for commercial banks.

Most lenders will usually tend to hold their maximum term to periods somewhat shorter than those allowed by their charter. This is frequently done to diminish the risk, as faster amortization means faster buildup of borrower's equity in the property, thus reducing the probability of default.

Interest Rates. Except for state usury laws, there is no ceiling on interest rates that may be charged by conventional lenders, and interest rates are usually negotiable along with ratio of loan to value and amortization period. Generally, a buyer can get the lowest possible interest rate by making a larger than minimum down payment and taking a shorter than maximum amortization period. The lower the down payment, the longer the amortization period, the greater the interest rate is a good rule of thumb. The interest rates charged will also be influenced to some extent by the financial position of the borrower and the desirability of the property.

Assumption of Existing Financing. A final method of finance available to a real estate agent is to have the buyer assume the existing financing held by the seller. This method can be particularly advantageous in periods of "tight money," and whenever the interest rate on the seller's present financing is lower than that currently being charged in the investment market. It is particularly advantageous when the seller has a loan such as a F.H.A. or V.A. loan which has a high ratio of loan to value. Certain facts about assumption financing should always be brought out to both buyer and seller when a loan is assumed, however. Principal among these is the fact that the seller is not relieved of his liability for the loan when it is assumed. The buyer merely becomes a co-guarantor on the note of indebtedness, along with the seller, and the seller remains liable until the note is paid off. Should the buyer default on the note, the mortgagee can turn to the seller for the balance due. It is possible to have the seller relieved of liability on the note at the discretion of the mortgagee, but there is little incentive for the mortgagee to do so in most cases, and he will not always do so.

An agent should be aware of the difference in selling a property under an assumption of existing financing and selling "subject to" existing financing. When a loan is assumed, the buyer becomes a co-maker on the note of indebtedness along with the original maker. When a property is sold subject to existing financing, the buyer *does not* become a co-maker but merely takes over the payments. In the event of default under a sale subject to existing financing, the lender has recourse only to the original maker. Under assumption financing, the original maker and the assumee are mutually liable.

Secondary or Junior Financing.   Often a buyer will not have available sufficient cash to pay the difference between the maximum loan available or to be assumed, and the purchase price of the property. Except in the case of an original F.H.A. loan, it is often possible to make up the difference by means of secondary or junior financing. This financing is often referred to as a "second trust" or "second mortgage." Such secondary financing falls into two general types:

1. Deferred Purchase Money Mortgage (or Trust).
   This is accomplished by having the seller defer part of the purchase price, to be secured by a second deed of trust or mortgage, and having the buyer pay off this deferred balance in installments or in a lump sum at the end of a certain period. This second deed of trust is recorded following the lender's prior lien on the property and is in an inferior position in the event of the buyer's default in repayment. At foreclosure, the first note holder has first claim to any proceeds from the sale, and the second note holder will be paid only if there are sufficient proceeds from the sale. It is, of course, possible for the seller who owns the property free and clear to "take back" a first deed of trust (or mortgage) for the entire balance due after a purchaser's down payment. In this case the deferred purchase money deed of trust (or mortgage) would be first, rather than a second in lien.

2. Borrowed Money Second Mortgage (or Deed of Trust).

A borrowed money second deed of trust differs from a deferred purchase money deed of trust only in that the money is secured from a lender rather than through deferral of part of the purchase price. Because of the higher risk involved to the lender, such loans are usually made at higher interest rates than those employed on the first deed of trust, or at sizeable discounts (see *Discounts*). The amortization periods for secondary financing can be any terms agreed upon by the buyer and seller. A common practice is the "balloon" note. This is accomplished by having the buyer make payments on the second deed of trust lower than would be required to amortize the note in the desired period, and have the final payment on the note be for the entire balance then due.

Example: A $1,000 note at 6 percent per annum interest and five year term, paid off at the rate of $10 per month by the borrower, would at the end of five years be reduced by only about 35 percent of the original balance. The borrower would make fifty-nine payments of $10 and one payment of about $650 under this type of financing. (See *Amortization—How to Compute*.)

Discounts—Points

An often misunderstood method of increasing a lender's yield on a mortgage loan is the system of discounting, often called "points." Whenever government regulation or state usury laws prohibit the lender from charging a rate of interest which would make the real estate loan competitive with other fields of investment, he must, if he is to make the loan, seek some method of increasing his yield to that which he could secure from other investments. The only such method available to him is to discount the note to the borrower; in effect, this is to have the borrower sign a note for an amount greater than the actual cash advance from the lender. By this method, the lender secures additional income from the loan and increases his yield to an acceptable level. Following is an example of how discounting works.

Annual interest rate — 7%	
Face amount of note	$10,000
Lender's cash advance	9,400
Discount	$ 600
Percentage of discount — 6%	

One percent of discount equals one (1) *point*; thus, six (6) points discount. Borrower repays $10,000 plus interest on face amount of note.

Should the borrower repay the loan in one year, the lender's yield would be 12 percent (6 percent interest + 6 percent discount). However, if the loan ran for thirty years, the lender's yield would be 6 percent interest plus one-thirtieth of 6 percent per year, since the total discount must be divided by the term of the loan. From experience lenders have found that most residential loans are paid off by the sale of the property on an average of every eight years, and therefore, most lenders compute 1 percent of discount as equal to one-eighth percent interest. In the above example, the effective yield would then be 6 percent per annum interest plus six-eighths or .75 interest, or an effective yield of 6.75 percent on the loan.

Although discounts are not a pleasant method of increasing a lender's yield, they are the only method yet found by which it is possible to attract a lender to make real estate loans when allowable interest rates are set below the level of other investments. To the real estate agent, the greatest problem presented by discounting is that the government does not permit the borrower to pay the discount at the origination of an F.H.A. or V.A. loan. This leaves only the seller to pay the discount and places the seller in the position of paying a discount for the buyer to secure a loan. This is, of course, not pleasant to the seller, and he frequently feels that he is being taken advantage of when told that he must do so. Offsetting the disadvantage to the seller is the fact that he is often able to sell his property on much more favorable terms by paying such discounts.

On high risk loans such as second trust loans, the discounts frequently run 5 percent per year or more on the term of the loan. Although this may seem high to the layman, it should be remembered that the second trust lender is making loan with diminished security, since his lien on the property is inferior to that of the first deed of trust note holder. The old maxim of "the higher the risk the higher the yield" becomes apparent with this type of lending.

Amortization—How to Compute

Amortization is the process of reducing an indebtedness by means of a series of installment payments. It is common to most types of installment financing, and is today used in lieu of the straight mortgage for the repayment of more real estate loans. (A straight mortgage is one in which there is no payment on the principal balance until the note is due.) In computing a monthly amortization schedule, a fixed monthly payment in excess of the amount required to pay interest only is determined. Each month, when the payment is made, the interest due is then deducted from the payment, and the balance credited toward reduction of the principal balance. The following month, the principal will be a little lower and a smaller portion of the fixed payment will be required to pay the interest, leaving a greater portion to be credited toward the principal balance. An example follows:

EXAMPLE OF AMORTIZATION OF A LOAN

Terms of Loan: Original Balance $12,000.
                  Annual Interest   6 percent
                  Monthly Payment $100.

Amortization for first 2 months: 6 percent p/a $= \dfrac{.06}{12} = .005$ per month interest

1st month: (1) $12,000.   Balance
                     × .005   Interest Rate

                     $60.000   Interest Amount
               (2) $100.   Payment
                     − 60.   Interest Amount

                     $ 40.   To Principal
2nd month: (1) $12,000.   Original Balance
                     −   40.   Principal Reduction

                     $11,960.   Remaining Balance
                     × .005   Interest Rate

                     $ 59.80   Interest Payment
               (2) $100.00   Payment
                     − 59.80   Interest

                     $ 40.20   Principal Reduction

Repeat this process monthly to amortize loan.

Questions on Finance will be found in the Question Section, beginning on Page 185.

WORDS TO WATCH

Acceleration Clause	Deficiency Judgment
Amortization	Direct Reduction Mortgage
Annuity	Equity
Assumption Agreement	Equity of Redemption
Assumption of Mortgage	Escalator Clause
Attachment of Property	First Mortgage
Balloon Payment	Foreclosure
Beneficiary	Forfeiture
Blanket Mortgage	Hypothecate
Bond	Indorsement
Certificate of No Defense	Installment Note
Chattel Mortgage	Interest Rate
Collateral	Joint Note
Commitment	Judgment Creditor
Compound Interest	Judgment Debtor
Conditional Commitment	Junior Lien
Confession of Judgment	Junior Mortgage
Conventional Mortgage	Liability
Debenture	Lien
Default	Lis Pendens
Defendant	Mortgage
Deferred Payments	Mortgagee

Mortgagor

Negotiable

Negotiable Instrument

Note

Open End Mortgage

Prepayment Penalty

Purchase Money Mortgage

Redemption

Release

Release of Lien

Satisfaction of Mortgage

Secondary Financing

Security Agreement

Straight Mortgage

Subject to Mortgage

Subordinate

Subordination Clause

Subrogation

Surety

Trust Deed or Deed of Trust

Trustee

Usury

Voluntary Lien

Waiver

POINTS TO CHECK LOCALLY

1. Which type of security instrument—mortgages or trust deeds—is used in your community?
2. What interest rates are currently in effect in your community on:
   a. F.H.A. and V.A. loans.
   b. Conventional loans.
2. What are the current ratios of loan to value in effect on conventional loans in your community?
   a. Insured loans
   b. Uninsured loans

Sources of Information

1. Real estate brokers
2. Savings and loan associations
3. Banks
4. Mortgage loan correspondents

Chapter 7

Transfer of Title to Real Property

The final step in the real estate brokerage cycle is the transfer of the property title to the purchaser. This is sometimes referred to as *settlement* or *closing.* In some states it is referred to as *escrow.* Whatever it may be called, certain steps must be taken and certain documents prepared for a proper transfer of title to take place.

The principal document in this process will be the deed to the property, with which the seller (grantor) will transfer the property title to the purchaser (grantee). Perhaps the most important fact pertaining to deeds, to the real estate agent, is that he cannot prepare the deed for his client. The preparation of deeds is limited by law to attorneys at law and to the owner of the property. Under some circumstances a real estate broker may fill in the blank spaces in a form deed, but this is not a common practice in the industry. It is desirable, however, that a real estate agent be familiar with deed form and the laws related to the construction and preparation of deeds.

Deeds, Generally

A deed is a written instrument by which title to land and/or appurtenances is transferred from one person to another. Under common law it was necessary for a deed to be under seal, but most states no longer require this, if the signators are natural persons or partnerships. Corporate deeds, however, must be under seal in most states. The essential elements of a deed, in simplest form, are:

1. Competent parties, properly identified
2. Words of conveyance
3. Description of the property to be conveyed
4. Execution by the grantor

Competent Parties, Properly Identified.   Both the grantor and the grantee must be legally competent to pass and receive title to real property. In order to do this, the grantor must usually have reached majority and be of sound mind. In some instances a married minor may act as a grantor with a spouse. A minor can be named as grantee, and most others can receive title, the exceptions being felons or others who have been deprived by law of their civil rights. The parties must be adequately identified to the extent that their identity is clearly established.

Words of Conveyance.   Often called the "granting clause," these are the words which import the transfer of title to the grantee—the "action verbs" in the deed. Such words as "grant and convey," "grant and release," or "grant, bargain, sell, and convey" are common. In quitclaim deeds, the words "release, remise, convey, and quitclaim" may be used.

Description of the Property to be Conveyed.   Any description which adequately identifies the property is sufficient. If the identification is based on a recorded survey, this is done by lot, block, and subdivision. Government section and township descriptions are also used, and a description by metes and bounds is also adequate. Some description which identifies the property with certainty is essential.

Execution by the Grantor.   A deed is a unilateral contract and need be signed only by the grantor(s). In some states, the signatures of the grantor(s) must be witnessed. In order to make the instrument admissible to record, the signatures of the grantor(s) must be acknowledged by a notary public or other officer competent to administer oaths.

Types of Deeds

Although there are many types of deeds—executor's or administrator's deeds, gift deeds, sheriff's deed, guardian's deed, to name a few—there are two principal types of deeds which are likely to be used in conjunction with a brokerage transaction. These are *warranty deeds* and *quitclaim deeds.*

Warranty deeds contain a statement of warranty, or guarantee, as to the merchantability of the title to the property. These deeds include certain covenants to protect the grantee against a future claim against the title. Warranty deeds are usually regarded as the best possible deed from the point of view of the grantee.

The warranties in a deed may be either general or special in nature. In a general warranty deed the grantor assures the grantee of a merchantable title and agrees to defend the title against any possible future claim. With this deed the grantor agrees to protect the grantee against the world.

With a *special warranty deed* the grantor provides the grantee with the same guarantees of title as under a general warranty deed but limits the period of time covered to his own tenure in the property. He agrees to protect the grantee against any defect of title which had its origin in a condition which arose during the tenure of the grantor, but he has no responsibility for a historical defect which may be caused by a condition which existed prior to the grantor's tenure. The principal difference between a general warranty deed and a special warranty deed is the period of time covered by the warranty. A general warranty deed protects against all defects, immediate or historical, while the special warranty deed protects against only those defects which arose from conditions during the grantor's tenure.

A *quitclaim deed* contains no statement of warranty but merely conveys whatever interest the grantor possessed in the property. The grantee, in accepting this deed, takes title on an "as is" basis without any guarantee as to the condition of the title. This type of deed is often used as a release deed, when a mortgagor has paid off an encumbrance secured by a mortgage or deed of trust. The deed may be used for a simple conveyance of real estate but is not often used for this purpose. It is sometimes referred to as a *release deed.*

DIAGRAM OF WARRANTIES IN DEEDS

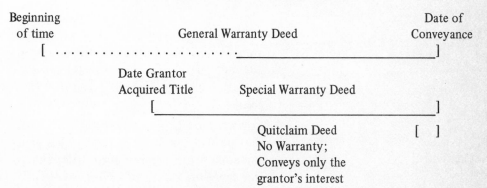

It should be noted that warranties to title can be relied upon only to the extent of the grantor's availability and/or financial capability.

A deed which is similar to a warranty deed, called a *grant deed,* is used in a few states. Certain warranties are implied but not written into this deed.

These implied warranties are:

1. that the grantor has not previously conveyed title to another.
2. a covenant against liens or other encumbrances of the grantor other than those set forth in the transaction.

Bargain and sale deed. This deed absolutely conveys the grantor's title but contains no guarantee of good title. In this respect it is similar to a quitclaim deed. The grantor does assert that he has the interest to be conveyed by the deed. This deed may also contain covenants of title.

Covenants of Title.   A covenant is a promise in a deed that some condition does not exist or will not exist in the future. Most warranty deeds contain the "English Covenants of Title." These covenants generally comprise the details of the grantor's warranty of title in warranty deeds. They are:

1. *Covenant of the Right to Convey.* This covenant assures that the grantor has the good right, full power, and absolute authority to convey title to the premises of the deed, according to the manner intended in the deed.

    Example: A joint tenant cannot alone convey a fee simple title to the property.

2. *Covenant of Seisin.* This covenant assures that the grantor is possessed of the title to be conveyed in the deed.

    Example: A grantor who held title as a life estate could not convey a fee simple title.

3. *Covenant Against Encumbrances.* This covenant assures that there are no encumbrances about which the grantee has not been advised, and that if any should later develop, the grantor would save the grantee harmless as far as the encumbrances were concerned.

4. *Covenant of Quiet Possession.* This covenant assures the grantee that he will not be disturbed in his enjoyment of the property by someone with a paramount title; that is, he will enjoy good title free from the claims of others.

5. *Covenant of Further Assurance.* This covenant assures that the grantor will execute any additional deeds necessary to perfect the title. This would usually be done by means of a quitclaim.

Although the English Covenants of Title would seem to give a grantee all possible assurance of a perfect title, it should be remembered that any guarantee is as good as the guarantor; and that if later the grantor were to die, could not be found, or were insolvent, he would not be in a position to act under his warranty.

Delivery and Acceptance

No deed is considered to be operative until it is delivered and accepted. It is not necessary for the grantor to make a manual delivery of the deed to the grantee. Generally, any act which would signify his intention to deliver will be regarded as if manual delivery had occurred. Acceptance of the grantee is considered to be automatic unless he takes some positive act indicating that he would not accept. Generally, it would be to the grantee's benefit to accept, and if so he is presumed to have accepted.

Recordation

All deeds must be recorded with the proper authority (county clerk, registrar, recorder) to be effective notice to the world of their existence. An unrecorded deed will pass title to real estate between the parties to the deed and as far as all others who have knowledge of its existence are concerned but will not be sufficient notice to future purchasers for value. Recordation is done on a chronological basis with the most recent recording being paramount. Thus, it is to the advantage of the grantee to record as soon as possible after delivery of the deed.

Title Examination

The title to real property is established from the recorded documents which affect the title. From a search of these records, a condensed history of the title is established showing all deeds, taxes, liens, and encumbrances affecting the property. This is known as an "abstract of title." The abstractor, in preparing his abstract, begins with the most recent recordation in the land records and takes note of, chronologically, all documents which affect the property title. These include checks of the lis pendens index, tax records, judgment records, probate court records, bankruptcy records, and, of course, the grantee-grantor records of deeds. The period of time covered by the abstract will vary, but generally covers from forty to sixty years. From this abstract, the examiner will form his certification as to the condition of the title. Some abstract companies issue a guarantee of title as shown in the abstract.

Title Insurance

When the title is not guaranteed by the abstract company, title insurance is often recommended. In many instances it will be required by the mortgagee as a condition of granting the loan.

Title insurance is a policy of insurance which protects the insured against a loss which might be occasioned by a defective title to the real estate. The title insurance company is obligated to defend the title against future claims from others, and to take necessary action to perfect the title, or to compensate the insured for his loss.

Title insurance is issued in three forms: Owner's policy, Mortgagee's policy, and Leasehold policy. Following is an explanation of the protections afforded by each of these policies:

Owner's Policy. This policy is issued in a face amount equal to the purchase price of the property, and the liability of the insurance company remains at this amount throughout the period of the grantee's tenure, or as long as he or his heirs retain an interest in the property. The policy insures the owner for any loss which he may sustain by reason of a defect or defects in the title to the property being insured.

Mortgagee's Policy. This policy insures the vested interest of the mortgagee in the premises of the policy. It protects him against any defects in the title, and against prior liens on the property. It is a policy of diminishing liability, with the liability of the title insurance company limited to the outstanding balance on the mortgage at any time. If the property is foreclosed, or if the property is voluntarily conveyed to the mortgagee in lieu of foreclosure, the policy becomes an owner's policy in favor of the mortgagee. Such a policy affords little or no protection for the owner, for the liability of the title insurance company is only to protect the interest of the mortgagee with no liability for the owner's interest in the property. Should the cost of defending the title exceed the outstanding balance on the mortgage at any time, the title insurance company may elect to pay off the mortgage, and the owner would still find himself with an imperfect title.

Leasehold Policy. This policy can be issued either to the tenant or leaseholder or to the mortgagee. The leaseholder's interest is written on a regular owner's policy, amended to show that the interest of the insured is a leasehold. The mortgagee policy is issued on a regular mortgagee policy form, amended to show that the title vested in the mortgagor is a leasehold rather than a fee simple title.

Questions on Transfer of Title to Real Property will be found in the Question Section, beginning on Page 189.

WORDS TO WATCH

A. L. T. A. Title Policy	Gift Deed
Abstract of Title	Grant
Acknowledgement	Grantee
Alienation	Grantor
Bargain and Sale Deed	Habendum Clause
Bequeath	Indenture
Bequest	Intestate
Bill of Sale	Involuntary Lien
Chain of Title	Marketable Title
Clear Title	Mechanic's Lien
Closing Statement	Offset Statement
Cloud on the Title	Quieting Title
Codicil	Quitclaim Deed
Color of Title	Restrictive Covenant
Constructive Notice	Sale-Leaseback
Conveyance	Sherriff's Deed
Covenant	Special Warranty Deed
Decedent	Tax Deed
Deed	Tax Sale
Deed Restriction	Testate
Defeasance	Testator
Devise	Title
Devisee	Title by Adverse Possession
Devisor	Title Insurance
Encumbrance	Torrens Land Titles
Escrow	Vested
Escrow Agreement	Will
General Warranty	

POINTS TO CHECK LOCALLY

1. What type of deed is customarily used in your state?
2. With whom are deeds recorded in your state?
3. Are abstracts or title insurance, or both, customarily employed in your state?

Sources of Information

1. Title companies.
2. Abstract companies.
3. Escrow companies.
4. Attorneys.
5. Real Estate Manual, if published by the Commission in your state.

Chapter 8

Plats and Land Descriptions

A real estate agent must be able to read and interpret information from plats and maps. It is not necessary that one be an expert in the technology and techniques of a surveyor, but one should be able to comprehend and generally interpret such information. An agent needs this knowledge in order to locate and identify properties and to properly advise his clients where needed.

Following is a review of the basic elements of plat construction and terminology. An understanding of the information in this section should enable an applicant to determine the proper answer to questions on typical examinations.

A plat, or map, uniquely describes a parcel of land. This may be a very small parcel, such as a residential lot, or a much larger tract of land. Each parcel of land is completely enclosed by boundary lines. These lines do not usually appear on the ground itself but are clearly identified on a plat of each lot or tract.

Bearings and Distances

These boundary lines have both length and direction, which are identified on the plat alongside each boundary line. The length of the line is usually shown in feet to the nearest hundredth of a foot (Ex: 124.08 ft. means 124 and 8/100ths of a foot, not 124′8″). The ends of a boundary line are marked by corners. Physical evidences of boundary lines are called monuments, which may consist of any physically identifiable object. Iron stakes, concrete markers, identifiable stones, or even trees can be monuments.

The direction of a boundary line is measured by its bearing. A bearing is defined as the situation or direction of one point or object with respect to another. Bearings on plats are measured with respect to either north or south on a compass and are the measurement of the acute angle between north or south and the bearing line. For example:

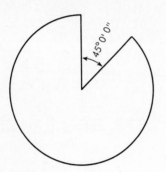

In Figure 1, the opening shown represents an angle of 45° 0'0".
° = degree (1/360th of a circle)
' = minute (1/60th of a degree)
" = second (1/60th of a minute)

Figure 1

If we superimpose on this circle the points of a compass, this angle can be measured from north on the compass, as an angle from north, as follows:

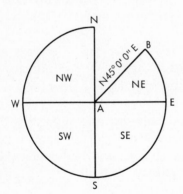

As shown in Figure 2, the circle can be divided into four quadrants (quarters), each identified according to the angle formed by its boundary lines as North-East; North-West; South-East; or South-West. The North-South line is identified as a meridian.

Figure 2

The bearing of any boundary line can be identified on a plat by showing its angle, measured from either north or south, and east or west of the north-south meridian, according to the compass quadrant in which it falls. The quadrant is identified by the prefix and suffix to the angle, as shown above. In this illustration, line AB is shown as N45°0'0"E, since it falls in the northeast quadrant.

These bearings can be measured in either a clockwise or counter-clockwise direction from north or south but never in both directions on the same plat.

The effect of a change of direction from clockwise to counter-clockwise will be to change the letter prefix and suffix on a boundary line but does not change its angular value. For instance, in the above illustration, if we measured from B to point A, instead of from A to B, the bearing would be shown as S 45° 0'0"W, since we changed the direction of our travel, and therefore measure in the opposite direction. For example, look at Figures 3 and 4:

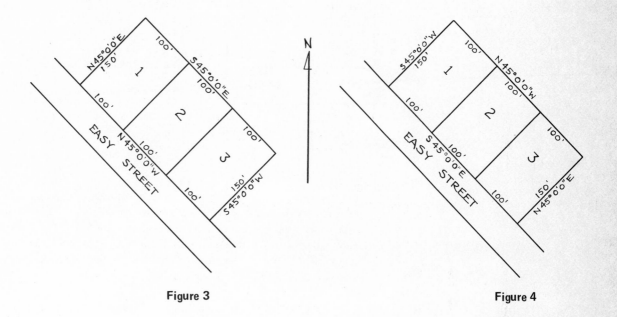

Figure 3   Figure 4

Each of these illustrations represents the same lots. However, in each illustration the prefix and suffix for the angular bearings are opposite, although the bearings remain the same. The difference in prefixes arises because in Figure 3 the angles are measured in a clockwise direction from the meridian, while those in Figure 4 are measured for a counter-clockwise direction of travel.

In summary, the description of any parcel of land should show:

1. The *angular bearing* of all boundary lines.
2. The *direction,* shown by angle and quadrant.
3. Any *monuments* that may be used as reference points.

Now, let's use this information to complete the description of a parcel of land. Figure 5 shows a parcel which is identified as Lot 3. A description of this lot would read as follows:

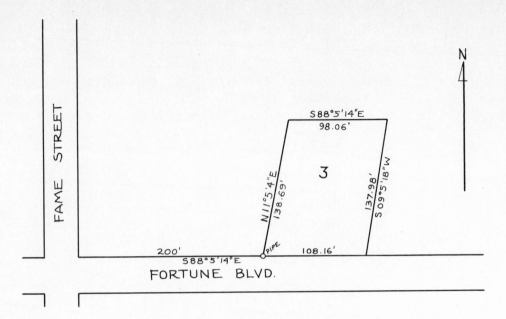

Figure 5

"Beginning at an iron pipe on the north side of Fortune Boulevard, 200′ from its intersection with the easterly boundary of Fame Street, on a bearing S88°5′14″E, and running on bearing N11°5′4″E for a distance of 138.69′; thence on bearing S88°5′14″E for a distance of 98.06′ thence for a distance of 137.98′ on bearing S09°5′18″W to the north side of Fortune Boulevard; thence 108.16′ on bearing S88°5′14″E to the beginning."

From such a description as this, any parcel of land can be identified on a plat.

Easements

Many times a lot or tract of land will have an easement on it. If the easement lies completely within the boundaries of the land, it will usually be shown by dotted lines, as in Figure 6. When it lies along the boundary of the property, the boundary line will be shown as a solid line and the other side of the easement will appear as a dotted line, as in Figure 7.

The purpose of the easement is shown within the lines as in Figure 6, or adjacent to it as in Figure 7.

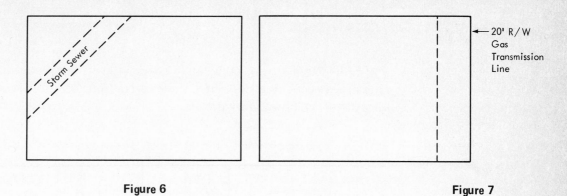

Figure 6   Figure 7

Arc, Radius, Delta

Not all boundaries are straight lines. Frequently, one or more boundaries will consist of an arc. To understand how these are shown, look at Figure 8.

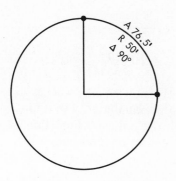

Arc: A portion of a curved line, as in a circle. Symbol A.

Radius: The distance from the center of a circle to its perimeter. Symbol R.

Delta: The angle between two intersecting lines, as with radii of a circle. Symbol Δ.

Figure 8

This data is shown on plats as in Figure 9.

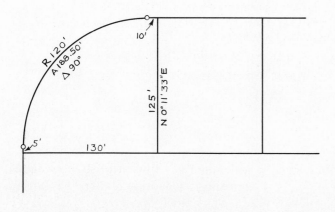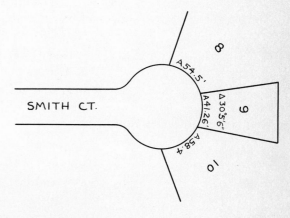

Figure 9

Continuations

If a plat does not completely cover a sheet, but would extend in one direction beyond the edge of a sheet, a continuation may be made on the same sheet, as shown in Figure 10.

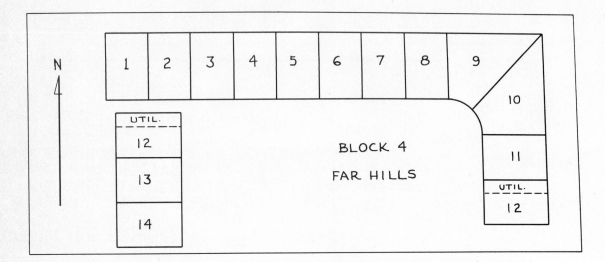

Figure 10

Note that Lot 12 is repeated on the continuation as a reference. The utility easement on Lot 12 is shown on each rendition of the lot, but *only one lot on this plat has an easement on it.*

Land Descriptions

In order to make it identifiable, each parcel of land must be accurately described in all records pertaining to the parcel. There are three accepted methods of land description.

1. Metes and bounds description.
2. Lot and block or recorded plat method.
3. Government rectangular survey system.

Metes and Bounds Description

This system describes land by a detailed description of its boundaries by courses and distances. The first requisite is a definite and stable starting point, such as a permanent marker or the intersection of the center line of two streets. From this point, the description recites the course and distance of each boundary line. These boundary lines are run continuously, running from one point or corner to another, always returning to the starting point so as to produce a closed area. A description which did not return to the starting point, or which left any part of the area not enclosed would be fatally defective. For example, see Figure 11.

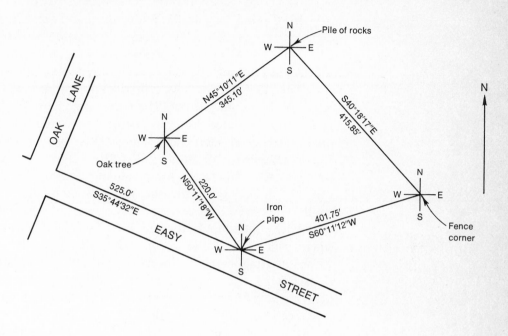

Metes and Bounds Description

That portion of land in the County of Misunderstanding; State of Confusion, described as follows:

Beginning at an iron pipe on the north side of Easy Street, which pipe is S35°44′32″E, 525′ from the northeast corner of the intersection of Easy Street and Oak Lane, and running on a line N50°11′18″W for a distance of 220′; thence on a line N45°10′11″E for a distance of 345.10′; thence on a line S40°18′17″E for a distance of 415.85′; thence on a line S60°11′12″W for a distance of 401.75′ to the point of beginning.

This description will usually end with a statement of the acreage or square feet in the parcel.

A metes and bounds description may also be based on general bearings and distances where no survey has been made of the property. For example, the property shown in Figure 11 could be described as follows:

Beginning at an iron pipe on the north side of Easy Street, northwest to an oak tree, thence northeast to a pile of rocks, thence southeast to a fence corner, thence southwest to the point of origin, and containing____acres, more or less.

This description always ends with the phrase "more or less" because the exact acreage cannot be determined without a survey.

Government Rectangular Survey System

Used principally in the midwestern and western states, the government rectangular survey system of land description is based on lines of latitude and longitude. Generally, the states lying west of the Ohio River, plus Florida, but not including Texas, employ this system.

The system is based on lines of longitude and latitude which form a huge checkerboard pattern. There are some 36 meridians (north-south lines) in the United States. Lines of latitude are called "base lines." On either side of the principal meridians, land is laid out in a huge checkerboard of approximately square units, called "townships." Each township is six miles long on each of its four sides. A line of townships running north and south is called a "range." Each township is identified by counting townships north or south of a named base line, and east or west of a principal meridian.

Each township is divided into 36 "sections" of approximately one square mile each. These sections are numbered within the township from 1 to 36, starting in the northeast corner and moving alternately right to left, then left to right, ending in the southeast section. Thus, each section is identifiable by its number, township, and range (See Figure 13).

Sections may be divided into quarter sections and quarter-quarter sections. Quarter sections measure one-half mile on each side and contain 160 acres. Quarter-quarter sections measure one-quarter mile on a side and contain 40 acres. Each quarter section is identified by its compass quadrant (NE, SE, SW, NW). Sections are normally marked on the ground by eight monuments, one at each corner and one midway between each corner monument. Because of the curvature of the earth, principal meridians converge as they extend north or south of the equator. To adjust for this, correction lines are run every 24 miles.

Under this system, each parcel of land can be easily identified. No two parcels will ever have the same identification.

In reading rectangular descriptions, one reads backwards from the general part of the description to the specific part at the beginning, or from the range and township to the section or part of a section. For example, in Figure 14, the shaded parcel would be described as follows:

> The Southeast ¼ of the Northwest ¼; Section 14; Township 2, South; Range 3, West. This description would ordinarily be abbreviated as follows, *SE ¼ of the NW ¼, S.14, T.2S, R.3W.*

In identifying this parcel, one would read from right to left, first identifying Range 3, West, then Township 2, South, then Section 14, then the Northwest ¼ Section 14, then the Southeast ¼ of the Northwest ¼ Section.

TOWNSHIP GRID
North
South
West
East
BASE
LINE
PRINCIPAL
MERIDAN
Initial Point
5
4
3
2
1
1
2
3
4
5
3
2
1
1
2
3

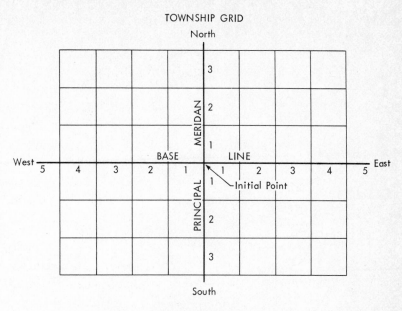

Figure 12

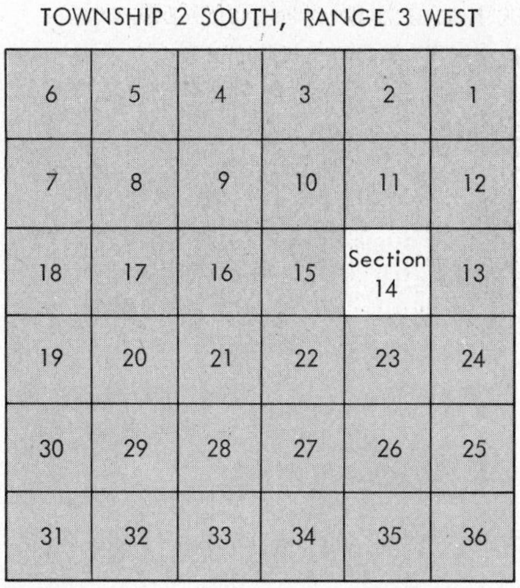

TOWNSHIP 2 SOUTH, RANGE 3 WEST
6 5 4 3 2 1
7 8 9 10 11 12
18 17 16 15 Section 14 13
19 20 21 22 23 24
30 29 28 27 26 25
31 32 33 34 35 36

Figure 13

SECTION 14
NW¼NW¼
NE¼NW¼
SW¼NW¼
SE¼NW¼
Northeast quarter (NE¼)
14
N½ SW¼
Lot 1
Lot 2
Lake
West Half of South-east quarter
E½ SE¼

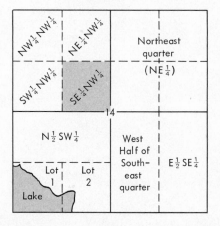

Figure 14

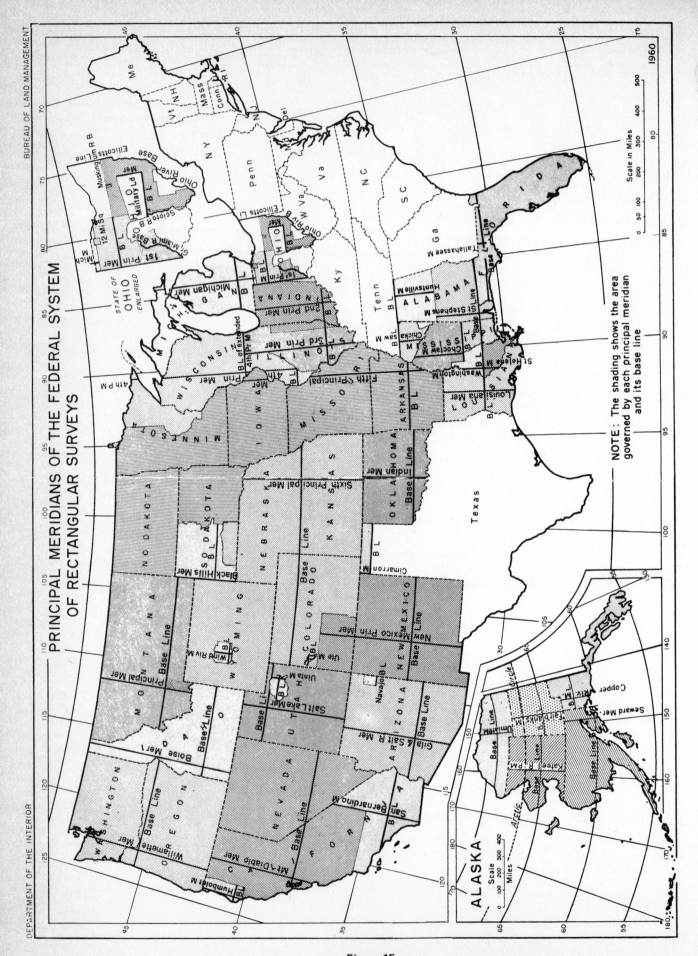

PRINCIPAL MERIDIANS OF THE FEDERAL SYSTEM OF RECTANGULAR SURVEYS

NOTE: The shading shows the area governed by each principal meridian and its base line

Figure 15

In the Question Section, you will find a sample plat and questions based on information in this chapter. These are typical of questions to be found on state examinations. Questions begin on page 194.

WORDS TO WATCH

Acre	Plat Book
Base and Meridian	Range
Chain	Rectangular Survey System
Contiguous	Section
Courses and Distances	Subdivision
Dedication	Survey
Legal Description	Topography
Metes and Bounds	Township
Monument	U. S. Government Survey System

POINTS TO CHECK LOCALLY

1. What system of land description is used in your state?

Sources of Information

1. Surveyors or civil engineers.
2. Real Estate Manual (if published by the Commission in your state).

Chapter 9

Fair Housing Laws and Ethics

Author's Note: In those states which utilize the examinations prepared by the Educational Testing Service, questions regarding fair housing laws are currently found only in the examination for real estate broker licensure. Because all licensees—both broker and salesmen—must be familiar with the laws governing fair housing, this digest of the federal laws is included in the salesman's license preparation course. Applicants for licensure as salesmen in those states which utilize the E.T.S. examinations, as they are constructed at the time of this publication, need not expect to be questioned on these laws.

Fair Housing Laws

A. The first and oldest of these is the Civil Rights Act of 1866, which prohibits discrimination on the basis of *race only*. This makes racial discrimination illegal anywhere in the United States by providing that "All citizens of the United States shall have the same right, in every State and Territory, as is enjoyed by white citizens thereof to inherit, purchase, lease, sell, hold, and convey real and personal property." This law was upheld by the U.S. Supreme Court on June 17, 1968, in the case of Jones vs. Meyer in their decision that ALL racial discrimination, whether private or public, in the sale or rental of property is prohibited by law.

B. The second of these laws is the Fair Housing Act of 1968, in Title VIII of which a national policy of fair housing was declared by Congress. This act goes further than the older one by making illegal any discrimination in connection with the sale or rental of *most* housing, as well as any vacant land offered for residential use, when such discrimination is based on race, color, religion, or national origin.

1. Prohibitions of the 1968 Fair Housing Law. Protection against the following acts is provided by this law, if these acts are based on race, color, religion, sex or national origin:
   a. Refusal to sell, rent to, negotiate, or deal with any person. (Section 804a)
   b. Differentiation in terms or conditions for buying or renting housing. (Section 804b)
   c. Discrimination by advertising housing as available only to persons of certain race, color, religion, or national origin. (Section 804c)
   d. Falsification of availability of housing for inspection, sale, or rent. (Section 804d)
   e. "Blockbusting"—using, for profit, threats of minority groups moving into neighborhood to persuade owners to sell or rent housing. (Section 804e)
   f. Presenting different terms or conditions for home loans, or denying same, by commercial lenders, as banks, savings and loan associations, and insurance companies. (Section 805)
   g. Prohibiting to anyone the use of or participation in any real estate services, as broker's organizations, multiple listing services, or other facilities related to the sale or rental of housing. (Section 806)
2. Types of Housing covered by the 1968 Fair Housing Law.
   a. Single Family Housing.
      (1) Privately-owned housing when: use is made of a broker or other person in the business of selling or renting dwellings, and/or discriminatory advertising is used.
      (2) Houses not privately owned.
      (3) Single family houses privately owned by an individual who owns three or more houses, or one who, in any two-year period, sells more than one of which he was not the most recent occupant.
   b. Multi-family Housing.
      (1) Multi-family dwellings containing five or more units.
      (2) Multi-family dwellings of four or less units, if none of these units is occupied by the owner.
3. Acts *not* covered by the 1968 Law. Certain acts as outlined below are not covered by the 1968 Fair Housing Law. HOWEVER, it is mandatory to remember that these acts ARE covered by the earlier 1866 Civil Rights Act when such discrimination is based on *race alone*.
   a. Single family houses owned by a private individual, owning three or less such houses and offering same for sale or rental:
      (1) Without use of a broker.
      (2) Without use of discriminatory advertising.
      (3) Not more than one house sold during any two-year period

in which the private owner was not the most recent occupant.

b. Renting of rooms or units in owner-occupied multi-dwellings for two to four families, provided no discrimination is shown.

c. Limiting the sale, rental, or occupancy of dwellings owned or operated by a religious organization for other than commercial purposes to persons of that same religion, provided that membership in such religion is not based on race, color, or national origin.

d. Limiting the rental or occupancy of lodgings owned by a private club to its own members, when such a club is operated for other than commercial purposes.

Enforcement

A. Enforcement of the Civil Rights Act of 1866. The fastest and most direct method of obtaining a remedy in cases of racial discrimination is provided by this law. The complainant takes his case directly to a federal court, which could:

1. Stop the sale or rental of desired housing to someone else.

2. Make it possible for the complainant to buy or rent the housing he wants.

3. Award damages and court costs and take other appropriate action of benefit to the complainant.

B. Enforcement of the Fair Housing Law of 1968, as provided in Title VIII. Discriminatory acts covered by the Federal Housing Law may be reported to:

Fair Housing   Fair Housing
Department of H.U.D.   or   c/o the nearest H.U.D.
Washington, D.C. 20410   regional office

1. A complaint form may be obtained from H.U.D., the nearest regional office, H.U.D., F.H.A. insuring offices, or the Post Office, or the complainant may state his complaint in letter form. In any case, the complaint should be notarized, if possible, and sent to H.U.D. within 180 days of the alleged discriminatory act. Upon receipt of the complaint, H.U.D. will forward a copy to the person charged with discrimination. This person may then file a written answer, which should also be notarized. H.U.D. will investigate the complaint and may do one of several things:

a. If it is covered by law, and the Secretary decides to resolve the complaint, H.U.D. may attempt informal, confidential conciliation to end the discriminatory practice.

b. H.U.D. may inform the complainant of his right to immediate court action.

c. In certain instances, H.U.D. may refer the complaint to the Attorney General.

d. H.U.D. may refer the complaint to a state or local agency which administers a law with rights and remedies substantially equivalent to the federal law. If this agency does not act within thirty days, and proceed with reasonable promptness, H.U.D. may require the case to be returned to the federal agency. In any case, the complainant will be notified of the action to be taken.

2. Court action by an individual.

    a. Within 180 days of the alleged act of discrimination, an individual may take his complaint directly to the U.S. District Court, or state or local court, regardless of whether he has filed a complaint with H.U.D. If circumstances warrant, an attorney may be appointed for the complainant, and waiver of costs, fees, or security obtained.

    b. If voluntary compliance is found to be unattainable at H.U.D., or the state or local agency, suit may be filed by the complainant in the appropriate U.S. District Court, provided this is done within thirty-one to sixty days after being filed with H.U.D. or after a complaint is returned to H.U.D. by the state or local agency under Section 810 of Title VIII. In certain states where equivalent judicial rights and remedies exist such suits would have to be brought in state court.

    c. Temporary restraining orders, temporary or permanent injunctions, or other appropriate relief may be granted by the court, which may also award actual damages and/or punitive damages not to exceed $1,000. They are directed to expedite cases under Section 812 and assign them for hearing at the earliest possible or practical date.

3. Court action by the Attorney General.

    a. The Attorney General's attention may be called to certain instances of discrimination in housing. If his investigation produces evidence of a pattern or practice of resistance to full enjoyment of rights granted under Title VIII, or the denial of such rights to a group of persons raises an issue of general public importance, he may bring court action to insure the correction of this practice.

Protecting Individual Rights

The Civil Rights Act of 1968, Section 817, Title VIII, makes provision for protection against interference with an individual's rights as well as the rights of persons who may have aided or encouraged him in the exercise of his rights under this law. Under these provisions, it is illegal to coerce, intimidate, threaten, or interfere with a person buying, renting, or selling housing, complaining of discrimination, or exercising his rights as set forth by this law. Furthermore, under Section 817 appropriate remedies are provided, and under Title IX criminal penalties are provided, and in case of threatened or actual violence, criminal prosecution may result.

Questions on Federal Fair Housing Laws will be found in the Question Section, beginning on Page 195.

Ethics

"Do unto others as you would have them do unto you."

Most state licensing authorities have no power or control over the ethics of licensees. Licensing statutes give to the Real Estate Commission the power to enforce only the licensing statutes, and to promulgate and enforce rules and regulations. Generally, the licensing statutes do not touch on matters of a purely ethical nature; hence, the Commission has no control over the ethics of licensees.

In a few states, licensing statutes do specifically charge the Real Estate Commission with the responsibility for adopting a code of ethics for licensees, and the enforcement of that code. In these states, the licensee is, of course, bound by ethical as well as legal considerations.

Enforcement of ethical codes is largely left up to the industry. Through trade associations such as the National Association of Realtors, the industry does police itself. Members of this and other associations, as a condition of their membership, subscribe to the association's code of ethics. Enforcement of the code is accomplished internally through grievance and ethics or professional standards committees.

Thus, the moral, ethical, and social conduct of a licensee in his business relations is to a large degree left up to his own discretion. The licensee's personal reputation in this regard is soon established.

As a practical matter, a licensee whose personal ethics were substandard would find the road to success to be a rocky one.

On the next several pages you will find the Code of Ethics of the Maryland Real Estate Commission.

CODE OF ETHICS
REAL ESTATE COMMISSION
STATE OF MARYLAND

Accepting this standard as his own, every licensee pledges himself to observe its spirit in all his activities and to conduct his business in accordance with the following Code of Ethics as adopted by the Real Estate Commission, State of Maryland:

PART I
RELATIONS TO THE PUBLIC

ARTICLE 1.

The licensee should keep himself informed as to movements affecting real estate in his community, so that he may be able to contribute to public thinking on matters of taxation, legislation, land use, and other questions affecting property interests.

ARTICLE 2.

It is the duty of the licensee to be well informed on current market conditions in order to be in a position to advise his clients as to the fair market price.

ARTICLE 3.

It is the duty of the licensee to protect the public against fraud, misrepresentation or unethical practices in the real estate field.

He should endeavor to eliminate in his community any practices which could be damaging to the public or to the dignity and integrity of the real estate profession. The licensee should assist the commission charged with regulating the practices of brokers and salesmen in this State.

ARTICLE 4.

The licensee should make a reasonable effort to ascertain all material facts concerning every property for which he accepts the agency, so that he may fulfill his obligation to avoid error, exaggeration, misrepresentation, or concealment of material facts.

ARTICLE 5.

The licensee shall not, acting as agent, discriminate in the sale, rental, leasing, trading, or transferring of property to any person or group of persons because of race, color, creed, religion, or national origin.

ARTICLE 6.

The licensee should not be a party to the naming of a false consideration in any document.

ARTICLE 7.

The licensee in his advertising should be especially careful to present a true picture and should neither advertise without disclosing his name, nor permit his salesmen to use individual names or telephone numbers, unless the salesman's connection with the licensee is obvious in the advertisement.

ARTICLE 8.

The licensee for the protection of all parties with whom he deals, should see that financial obligations and commitments regarding real estate transactions are in writing, expressing the exact agreement of the parties; and that copies of such agreements are placed in the hands of all parties involved within a reasonable time after they are executed.

PART II
RELATIONS TO THE CLIENT

ARTICLE 9.

In accepting employment as an agent, the licensee pledges himself to protect and promote the interests of the client. This obligation of absolute fidelity to the client's interest is primary, but it does not relieve the licensee from the obligation of dealing fairly with all parties to the transaction.

ARTICLE 10.

In justice to those who place their interests in his care, the licensee should endeavor always to be informed regarding laws, proposed legislation, governmental orders, and other essential information and public policies which affect those interests.

ARTICLE 11.

Since the licensee is representing one or another party to a transaction, he should not accept compensation from more than one party without the full knowledge of all parties to the transaction.

ARTICLE 12.

The licensee should not acquire an interest in or purchase for himself, any member of his immediate family, his firm or any member thereof, or any entity in which he has any ownership interest, property listed with him, or his firm, without making the true position known to the listing owner, and in selling or leasing property owned by him, or in which he has such interest, the facts should be revealed in writing to the to the purchaser or lessee.

ARTICLE 13.

When acting as agent in the management of property, the licensee should not accept any commission, rebate or profit on expenditure made for an owner, without the owner's knowledge and consent.

ARTICLE 14.

The licensee should not undertake to make an appraisal that is outside the field of his experience unless he obtains the assistance of an authority on such types of property, or unless the facts are fully disclosed to the client. In such circumstances the authority so engaged should be so identified and his contribution to the assignment should be clearly set forth.

ARTICLE 15.

When asked to make a formal appraisal of real property the licensee should not render an opinion without careful and thorough analysis and interpretation of all factors affecting the value of the property. His counsel constitutes a professional service.

The licensee should not undertake to make an appraisal or render an opinion of value on any property where he has a present or contemplated interest. Under no circumstances should he undertake to make a formal appraisal when his employment or fee is contingent upon the amount of his appraisal.

ARTICLE 16.

The licensee should not submit or advertise property without authority and in any offering, the price quoted should not be other than that agreed upon with the owners as the offering price.

ARTICLE 17.

In the event that more than one formal written offer on a specific property is made before the owner has accepted an offer, any other formal written offer presented to the licensee, whether by a prospective purchaser or another broker, should be transmitted to the owner for his decision.

PART III
RELATIONS TO HIS FELLOW-LICENSEE

ARTICLE 18.

The licensee should seek no unfair advantage over his fellow-licensees and should willingly share with them the lessons of his experience and study.

ARTICLE 19.

The licensee should not voluntarily disparage the business practice of a competitor, nor volunteer an opinion of a competitor's transaction. If his opinion is sought it should be rendered with strict professional integrity and courtesy.

ARTICLE 20.

The agency of a licensee who holds an exclusive listing should be respected. A licensee cooperating with a listing broker should not invite the cooperation of a third broker without the consent of the listing broker.

ARTICLE 21.

The licensee should cooperate with other brokers on property listed by him exclusively whenever it is in the interest of the client, sharing commissions on a previously agreed basis. Negotiations concerning property listed exclusively with one broker should be carried on with the listing broker.

ARTICLE 22.

The licensee should not solicit the services of an employee or licensee in the organization of a fellow-licensee.

ARTICLE 23.

Signs giving notice of property for sale, rent, lease or exchange should not be placed on any property by more than one licensee, and then only if authorized by the owner, except as the property is listed with and authorization given to more than one licensee.

POINTS TO CHECK LOCALLY

1. Does your state have fair housing laws that go beyond the requirements of the federal law?
2. If so, what are the requirements beyond those of the federal law?
3. Does your state's license law provide for the Real Estate Commission to adopt a Code of Ethics for licensees?

Sources of Information

1. Real estate board.
2. Consumer protection offices.
3. Local officials.
4. Real Estate License Law of your state.

PART II

LICENSE LAW
AND
OTHER EXAMINATION REQUIREMENTS

Chapter 10

Real Estate License Law

The history of real estate license laws in the United States began in 1919 when the first permanent set of statutes governing the actions of real estate brokers and salesmen was enacted by the California Legislature. Prior to this time, persons who acted as brokers or agents for others were governed to some extent by general laws which were quite similar to our present licensing statutes, but which did not define a real estate broker or salesman as such, and did not contain any provision for licensure as a prerequisite to doing business in this capacity.

Although there have been many challenges of the constitutionality of the license laws of various states, principally on the grounds that such laws violate the Fourteenth Amendment to the Constitution, over the years these challenges have usually been successfully met in the courts, and it is safe to say that the licensure of real estate brokers and salesmen is now established as a proper exercision of a state's police powers.

Following the successful enactment of licensing statutes in California, other states began to enact laws requiring licensure of real estate brokers and salesmen. On a nationwide basis, however, progress was slow. Several states at different times enacted laws which were wholly or in part declared unconstitutional, while other states took no action in this regard for quite some time. It was not until 1959, forty years after the California law was enacted, that all states in the union had enacted permanent legislation which required licensure for real estate brokers and salesmen.

Contents of Real Estate License Laws

As the license laws of various states have been enacted, there has evolved a pattern which can be discerned. Although the statutes of all states naturally do not always follow in the same order, a review of their provisions reveals considerable similarity in their approach to the subject. Details which deal with administrative matters, licensing fees, etc., do, of course, differ from state to state.

Generally, the pattern of licensing statutes is somewhat as follows:

1. General Provisions.

   The law defines a real estate broker and a real estate salesman and sets forth the requirement for licensure in either capacity. Often the statutes note exemptions from the need for licensure by certain categories of persons.

2. Real Estate Commission or Licensing Board.

   There is established a regulatory agency which is charged with the issuance of licenses and regulation of licensees within the state. This agency is usually administered by a group of appointed members, identified as the Real Estate Commission, Real Estate Licensing Board, or by some similar name. (The name of this agency varies from state to state. Henceforth, it will be referred to as the real estate commission, the most common designation.)

3. General Licensing Requirements.

   These statutes set forth the specific requirements of licensure for real estate brokers and real estate salesmen and establishes the conditions, such as educational requirements, for the granting of licenses. This section of the law provides for the issuance of licenses, control of licenses, and for the revocation or suspension of the licenses of those who violate the laws.

4. Administrative Statutes.

   These statutes establish procedures for the internal operation of the commission and its staff.

5. Nonresidents, Reciprocity, Bonding, Etc.

   Statutes governing the issuance of licenses to nonresidents, reciprocity with other states, bonding of licensees, and other related subjects are contained in this section.

Although the sequence in which these statutes appear will not be the same in all states, the individual statutes can usually be grouped under one of several general headings. Using these headings as a guide, let's take a look at the most frequently seen statutory provisions of each category.

I. General Provisions
   A. Definition of real estate broker.
   B. Definition of real estate salesman.
   C. Exemptions from license requirements.
   D. Penalties for violation of license law.
   E. Requirement for real estate broker to maintain office in the state.

II. Real Estate Commission
   A. Number of members.
   B. Qualifications required.
   C. Method of appointment.
   D. Length of term; reappointment upon expiration of term.
   E. Designation of chairman.
   F. General powers of commission.
   G. Compensation of members.
   H. Enforcement powers.
   I. Disposition of fees and charges.
   J. Provision for public inspection of records.
   K. Provision for real estate guaranty fund (if applicable).

III. General Licensing Requirements
   A. Necessity for license.
   B. Qualifications for license.
   C. Application procedures.
   D. Fees for license.
   E. Fees for examination.
   F. Refusal of license by commission.
   G. Provision for broker to maintain custody of salesman's license.
   H. Requirements for display of licenses.
   I. Expiration and renewal of licenses.
   J. Effect of revocation of broker's license on licenses of salesmen in his employ.
   K. Transfer of salesman's license.
   L. Duplicate licenses for branch offices.
   M. Change of location of broker's office.
   N. Discharge or termination of employment of salesmen.
   O. Grounds for suspension or revocation of licenses.
   P. Hearing required before refusal of license or revocation or suspension of license.
   Q. Procedures for hearings.
   R. Appeal from decisions of commission at hearings.
   S. Appeal bond requirements.
   T. Publication of list of licensees.
   U. Effect of contracts negotiated by unlicensed persons.
   V. Regulation of real estate schools.
   W. Provision for trust accounts.
   X. Fee splitting with unlicensed persons.
   Y. Blockbusting.
   Z. Fair housing.

IV. Administrative Statutes
   A. Executive officer.
   B. Staff.
   C. Office space, etc.
   D. Seal of commission.

V. Nonresidents, Reciprocity, Bonding, Etc.
   A. Provision for or prohibition of the granting of licenses to nonresidents.
   B. Provision for or prohibition of the granting of reciprocity to licensees from other states.
   C. Bonding requirements for licensees.
   D. Provision for certain rights or powers in regulating real estate brokers or salesmen to be vested in local jurisdictions.
   E. Any other statutes not covered above.

Some state codes may contain statutes not covered by these categories, but these will be few in number. In preparation for examination as an applicant for licensure, an applicant who is familiar with the requirements of his state in each of these categories can feel confident of an adequate knowledge in this part of the examination.

All state license laws make provision for the real estate commission to promulgate, in addition to the law, rules and regulations which govern the conduct of licensees. These rules and regulations have the effect of law upon the licensee, in that provision is made for revocation or suspension of licenses in the event of a violation. A knowledge of these rules and regulations is essential to any licensee. Because each state commission promulgates the rules as needed, no discernible pattern can be found by which to study. The only possible method of preparation is to read and study the rules for your state until you are thoroughly familiar with them.

Learning the Licensing Laws of Your State

The remainder of this chapter is devoted to assisting the applicant to learn the license laws of his state. To this end, a summary chart in which are enumerated each of the categories above is provided at the end of this chapter. Suggested study procedures are as follows:

1. Secure a copy of the license laws of your state. These can be obtained from the real estate commission, usually at no charge to applicants for licensure.
2. Beginning with the first statute, look to the heading in the summary chart which most nearly matches the subject of the statute. In the blank space opposite this heading, outline as briefly as possible a summary of the principal features of the statute.
3. Continue as above with all statutes in the license law. You will begin to learn the provisions of the law through this procedure.
4. After you have summarized all the statutes in this fashion, use the chart to review the provisions of the laws until you feel that you have learned all the laws.

When you have summarized the laws of your state on the chart, you will find questions on Page 200 in the Question Section. Because not all states have the same laws, the questions given are necessarily general in nature. It is possible that some questions may not be covered by the laws of your state, but the questions are typical of the type found on the E. T. S. and many other state examinations.

Example of the Use of Summary Chart of License Laws

In this illustration, the License Laws of Virginia are used as a basis for the illustration. The techniques which are employed can be adapted to the laws of any state.

Step One: From the summary chart, the first topic to be summarized is the definition of a real estate broker. The law of Virginia defines a real estate broker as follows:

> 54–730. Real estate broker defined.—A real estate broker within the meaning of this chapter is any person, partnership, association, or corporation who for a compensation or valuable consideration sells or offers for sale, buys or offers to buy, or negotiates the purchase or sale or exchange of real estate, or who leases or offers to lease, or rents or offers for rent, any real estate or the improvements thereon for others, as a whole or partial vocation.

Step Two: In analyzing this law, we find five pertinent features of the definition, as follows:

I. General Provisions

Summary

A. Definition of Real   A Real Estate Broker is:
    Estate Broker   —any person or business, who
                          —receives compensation
                          —for performing an act of
                            brokerage
                          —for others
                          —as a whole or partial vocation

Having summarized the features of this statute, we go to the next provision: Definition of a Real Estate Salesman.

> 54-731. Real estate salesman defined.—A real estate salesman within the meaning of this chapter is any person who for a compensation or valuable consideration is employed either directly or indirectly by a real estate broker, to sell or offer to sell, or to buy or offer to buy, or to negotiate the purchase or sale or exchange of real estate, or to lease,

to rent or offer for rent, any real estate, or to negotiate leases thereof, or of the improvements thereon, as a whole or partial vocation.

B. Definition of a Real
Estate
Salesman
	Any person (not a business)
	who is
	—employed by a real estate
	   broker
	—directly or indirectly
	—to perform an act of
	   brokerage
	—for others for compensation

Repeat this procedure throughout the entire license law of your state. Check off each law as you summarize it. When you have completed the summary chart, look through the entire law for any statutes which were not included in the summary. On a separate paper, make any necessary additions to the summary chart.

The results will be an orderly summation of the features of the laws of your state. In many instances this summary will be more coherent than the statutes in factual content and also in the order of presentation. State statutes are sometimes enacted in a chronological order and not always in the manner which is easiest to understand.

Using the techniques employed in the illustration, go on to complete the summary of your state's laws.

The summary chart begins on the next page.

SUMMARY OF LICENSE LAW PROVISIONS

STATE OF_____

Summary of Principal Features

I.   General Provisions

    A.   Definition of real estate
        broker

    B.   Definition of real estate
        salesman

    C.   Exemptions from license
        requirements

    D.   Penalties for violation
        of law

    E.   Broker to maintain office
        in state

II.   Real Estate Commission

    A.   Number of members

    B.   Qualifications

    C.   Method of appointment

Summary of Principal Features

III. Real Estate Commission (Contd.)

D. Length of term: reappointment upon expiration of term

E. Designation of chairman

F. General powers

G. Compensation of members

H. Enforcement powers

I. Disposition of fees and charges

J. Records open to public

K. Real estate guaranty fund provided for

III. General Licensing Requirements

A. Necessity for license

B. Qualifications for license

C. Application procedures

Summary of Principal Features

III. General Licensing Requirements
(contd.)

  D.   Fees for license

  E.   Fees for examination

  F.   Refusal of license by
commission

  G.   Broker to maintain custody
of salesman's license

  H.   Broker to display licenses

  I.   Expiration and renewal
of licenses

  J.   Effect of revocation of
broker license on licenses
of salesmen in his employ

  K.   Transfer of salesman's license

  L.   Duplicate licenses required
for branch offices

  M.   Change of location of
broker's office

  N.   Discharge or termination of
employment of salesmen

  O.   Grounds for suspension or
revocation of licenses

Summary of Principal Features

III. General Licensing Requirements
(Contd.)

O.   Grounds for suspension or
revocation of licenses
(contd.)

P.   Hearing required before
refusal or revocation of
license

Q.   Procedures for hearings

R.   Appeal from decision of
commission

S.   Appeal bond requirements

T.   Publication of list of
licensees

U.   Effect of contracts
negotiated by unlicensed
persons

Summary of Principal Features

III. General Licensing Requirements
      (contd.)

    V.   Regulation of real estate
      schools

    W.   Provision for trust accounts

    X.   Fee splitting with
      unlicensed persons

    Y.   Blockbusting

    Z.   Fair housing

WORDS TO WATCH

Administrator
Administratrix
Affidavit
Affirmation
Attest
Attorney-at-Law
Attorney-in-Fact
Broker
Code
Commingle
Corporation
Decree
Defendant
Escrow
Ethics
Executor
Executrix
Injunction

Irrevocable
Jurisdiction
License
Limited Partnership
N. A. R.
Ordinance
Partnership
Plaintiff
Power of Attorney
Prima Facie
Promulgate
Real Estate Board
Real Estate Trust
Realtor
Statute
Subpoena
Tort

Chapter 11

Truth in Lending

Many state license examinations have begun to include questions based on the Truth in Lending Laws. While real estate brokers and salesmen are not required to be expert in these laws, a general working knowledge of their provisions is required. This chapter provides an outline of the major provisions of the Consumer Credit Protection Act, commonly referred to as the Truth in Lending Law. Familiarization with the requirements of the act will enable license applicants to answer most questions employed on state license examinations.

DIGEST OF

CONSUMER CREDIT PROTECTION ACT

TRUTH IN LENDING

Effective July 1, 1969

I. PURPOSE OF THE ACT

To require that in credit transactions, certain information be disclosed to the borrower, such as finance charges and annual percentage rates of interest, and to allow the borrower the right to rescind the transaction in certain instances.

II.   *ENFORCEMENT OF THE TRUTH IN LENDING ACT*

The Federal Trade Commission is responsible for the administration and enforcement of the Truth in Lending Act, insofar as real estate licensees are concerned.

The Board of Governors of the Federal Reserve System have published Regulation Z to implement the Truth in Lending Act.

III.   *PENALTIES*

A. Criminal Liability

Violations are punishable by a fine of up to $5,000 or one year in jail, or both.

B. Civil Liability

Courts may award damages to the borrower for as much as twice the finance charge, but not to exceed $1,000. Action must be brought within one year.

C. Avoiding Liability

Liability may be avoided by correcting error within 15 days.

IV.   *THOSE WHO MUST COMPLY WITH THE TRUTH IN LENDING ACT*

A. Creditors

Definition: A person who in the ordinary course of business regularly extends or arranges for the extension of consumer credit.

B. Arrangers of Credit

Definition: A person who means to provide or offers to provide consumer credit which is or will be extended by another person under a business or other relationship pursuant to which the person arranging such credit receives or will receive a fee, compensation, or other consideration for such service, or has knowledge of the credit terms and participates in the preparation of the contract documents required with the extension of credit.

C. All Consumer Credit to Natural Persons.

D. Assumptions of Existing Mortgages and Trust Deeds, and Contracts From Creditors.

V. *FINANCING NOT SUBJECT TO TRUTH IN LENDING ACT*

    A. Business Loans

    B. Commercial Loans

    C. Installment Loans with Four or Less Installments

    D. No Financing Charges are Made

    E. Credit Extended to Corporations, Partnerships, Associations, Government Agencies, etc.

VI. *DISCLOSURE STATEMENT*

Purpose: To disclose to the consumer how much it is costing to borrow the money and the terms and conditions of said loan. The disclosure must be given by all creditors and arrangers of credit as defined in the Act. The Statement must be supplied before a PERMANENT contractual relationship is made between the borrower and creditor, therefore, an earnest money agreement would be exempt. The disclosure statement must contain:

    A. Date the Finance Charge Begins to Accrue.

    B. The Annual Percentage Rate.

    C. Number of Monthly Payments.

    D. Due Dates or Periods of Payments.

    E. Payoff Penalties.

    F. Balloon Payments.

    G. Default or Delinquency Charge.

    H. Description of the Property.

    I. Total Finance Charge.

    J. Method of Computing Any Unearned Portion of The Finance Charge in the Event of Prepayment.

    K. Any amount of Credit which will be made Available to the Borrower.

    L. Credit Sales, Cash Price, Total Down Payment and Unpaid Balance.

    M. Finance Charges.

    N. Total of All Payments.

NOTE: In the case of a FIRST Mortgage, Trust Deed, Land Sale Contract, to finance construction or acquisition of a DWELLING or an assumption of such first loan, the total of all payments and composition of finance charges need not be given.

VII. RECISION

The borrower-customer has the right to rescind the transaction until midnight of the third business day following the date of consummation of the transaction, or the date of delivery of the disclosure statement when all other material disclosures were made, whichever is later.

A. Transactions Exempt From Recision

1. First liens, i.e., mortgages, trust deeds, land contracts, etc. on dwellings in which the person resides or expects to reside.
2. Endanger the customer's property.

If no disclosure statement was given on the formal notice of the right to rescind, the borrower's right to rescind continues indefinitely as there is no statute of limitations on this right.

VIII. ADVERTISING

A. The Truth in Lending Act does not prohibit the advertising of credit terms, but it does determine how the credit terms may be advertised, and all real estate agents must comply.

Agents may advertise the cash price and the annual percentage rate only if stated as such. But, no other credit terms may be given unless a full disclosure is made which states the following:

1. Cash Price
2. Annual Percentage Rate
3. Down Payment
4. Monthly Payment
5. Finance Charge
6. Terms of the Loan
7. Number of Payments

B. If it is not a First Mortgage, Trust Deed, etc., on the sale of a private home, the total of all payments must be stated also.

Real Estate Agents are allowed to advertise in general terms, such as:

1. Excellent Loan for Assumption
2. Owner Will Finance
3. F.H.A. Financing Available
4. Reasonable Monthly Payments

Questions on Truth in Lending will be found in the Question Section, beginning on Page 198.

Chapter 12

How to Prepare
Listings and Contracts
From Narrative Problems

Many state license examinations require the applicant to prepare a listing agreement and a contract of sale from information furnished in a narrative problem. This chapter will provide basic instruction, sample listing and contract problems, and several problems for practice. Additionally, in the Question Section you will find a number of multiple choice questions which are based upon your solution to the listing and contract problems. This system of testing is employed on the E. T. S. examinations.

Although the listing and contract forms which are furnished may not be identical to those employed in your state's examinations, the essential elements of such forms are present, and once one is familiar with the procedures, a transition to another form should not present any insurmountable problem.

HOW TO PREPARE LISTINGS AND CONTRACTS FROM NARRATIVE PROBLEMS

Preliminary:

Read the Listing and Contract *Problems*. Be sure that you understand the problem. Make necessary mathematical calculations, such as price calculations, taxes, etc., prior to transferring information to the forms.

Step I:
Listing
Problem
Solution

Using the information in the listing problem, complete the listing by transferring the information to the listing form. The placement of the information on the listing form in any certain place is not especially important for purposes of the examination. *It is important that all information from the problem be transferred to the listing form.* One method of assuring that you have done this is to draw a line through each sentence on the listing problem sheet as you transfer the information.

Step II:
Contract
Problem
Solution

Complete the sale contract in the same manner as the listing. Remember that some information on the sale contract must be taken from your listing solution. As with the listing form, *where* you place the information on the form is not as important as being certain that you have employed all information from the contract problem in your solution.

The sample listing and contract problems on the next page are similar to problems employed on state examinations. Review these problems and the solutions which follow before going on to complete the problems in this section.

SAMPLE LISTING PROBLEM

You are a salesman employed by the Hitt and Runn Real Estate Corporation. On October 10, 1973, you secure a ninety day exclusive right to sell listing on a home which belongs to Titus Wadd, located at 16 E. Oak St., Alexandria, Virginia. The house is a 3 bedroom cape cod with a full basement. On the first floor is living room 12' × 17', dining room 11' × 12', kitchen with eating space, full bath, and one bedroom. The remaining bedrooms are on the second floor, plus one full bath on the second floor. Heating is oil hot air, and water is heated by electricity. There is a recreation room in the basement. House is of brick construction. There is a detached garage with side drive. Built in 1949, the house is connected to natural gas, city sewer, and water. Range and refrigerator are in the kitchen, and are included in the owner's asking price of $33,500. Your commission is to be 6 percent of the gross sales price. There is a washer in the basement, which is also included in the listing. Tax assessment is $5,500 on the land and $8,500 on improvements. Annual tax rate is $3.95, and taxes are $553 per year. Legal description is Lot 16, Block 5, Sec. 4, Rosemont Subd. Lot is 50' × 140'. The property is occupied by tenants, Knotts O. Bright and wife, Ubbetta B. Bright, whose lease expires on February 28, 1974. The rent is $275 per month. Schools are Maury Elementary and T. C. Williams High. Property is 1½ blocks from bus and 1 mile from downtown shopping. The house has been appraised at the listed price, and owner indicates that he will sell at that price. Mr. Wadd owns the property free and clear. He stipulates that the tenants must be called for an appointment to show the property. The house has no attic; roof is of composition shingle. The house contains 2,468 square feet of floor space.

SAMPLE CONTRACT PROBLEM

On November 1, 1973, you find purchasers, Ollie Z. Tyme and wife, Summer D. Tyme, who agree to purchase the home, but wish to make an offer of $32,500 for the property. Purchasers are to make a down payment of 25 percent and secure a conventional loan for the balance. Purchasers require that settlement be held on January 15, 1974, and the seller must furnish certificate of termite inspection with a five year guarantee from an approved exterminator. Purchasers make an earnest money deposit of $500 by check. You present this offer to the seller, who accepts the offer. Prepare a contract on these terms.

EXCLUSIVE AUTHORIZATION TO SELL

SALES PRICE: $33,500.00   TYPE HOME: Cape Cod   TOTAL BEDROOMS: 3   TOTAL BATHS: 2

ADDRESS: 16 East Oak Street   JURISDICTION OF: Alexandria

AMT. OF LOAN TO BE ASSUMED $ none   AS OF WHAT DATE: TAXES & INS. INCLUDED: YEARS TO GO   AMOUNT PAYABLE MONTHLY $ @   % TYPE LOAN

MORTGAGE COMPANY   2nd TRUST $

ESTIMATED EXPECTED RENT MONTHLY $ 275.00   TYPE OF APPRAISAL REQUESTED

OWNER'S NAME: Titus Wadd   PHONES (HOME)   (BUSINESS)

TENANTS NAME: Knotts O. Bright & wife, Ubetta B.   PHONES (HOME)   (BUSINESS)

POSSESSION: March 1, 1974   DATE LISTED: 10/10/73   EXCLUSIVE FOR 90 days   DATE OF EXPIRATION 1/10/74

LISTING BROKER: Hitt & Runn Real Estate Corp.   PHONE   KEY AVAILABLE AT

LISTING SALESMAN: Your name   HOME PHONE   HOW TO BE SHOWN: By appt.

(1) ENTRANCE FOYER ☐ CENTER HALL ☐	(18) AGE 1949 AIR CONDITIONING ☐	(32) TYPE KITCHEN CABINETS
(2) LIVING ROOM SIZE 12' x 17' FIREPLACE ☐	(19) ROOFING Comp. sh. TOOL HOUSE ☐	(33) TYPE COUNTER TOPS
(3) DINING ROOM SIZE 11' x 12'	(20) GARAGE SIZE Det. PATIO ☐	(34) EAT-IN SIZE KITCHEN x
(4) BEDROOM TOTAL: 3 DOWN 1 UP 2	(21) SIDE DRIVE x CIRCULAR DRIVE ☐	(35) BREAKFAST ROOM ☐
(5) BATHS TOTAL: 2 DOWN 1 UP 1	(22) PORCH ☐ SIDE ☐ REAR ☐ SCREENED ☐	(36) BUILT-IN OVEN & RANGE ☐
(6) DEN SIZE FIREPLACE ☐	(23) FENCED YARD OUTDOOR GRILL ☐	(37) SEPARATE STOVE INCLUDED x
(7) FAMILY ROOM SIZE FIREPLACE ☐	(24) STORM WINDOWS ☐ STORM DOORS ☐	(38) REFRIGERATOR INCLUDED x
(8) RECREATION ROOM SIZE Bsmt. FIREPLACE ☐	(25) CURBS & GUTTERS ☐ SIDEWALKS ☐	(39) DISHWASHER INCLUDED
(9) BASEMENT SIZE	(26) STORM SEWERS ☐ ALLEY ☐	(40) DISPOSAL INCLUDED ☐
NONE ☐ 1/4 ☐ 1/3 ☐ 1/2 ☐ 3/4 ☐ FULL x	(27) WATER SUPPLY City	(41) DOUBLE SINK ☐ SINGLE SINK ☐
(10) UTILITY ROOM SIZE	(28) SEWER x SEPTIC ☐	STAINLESS STEEL PORCELAIN ☐
TYPE HOT WATER SYSTEM: Elec.	(29) TYPE GAS: NATURAL x BOTTLED ☐	(42) WASHER INCLUDED x DRYER INCLUDED ☐
(11) TYPE HEAT Oil hot air	(30) WHY SELLING	(43) PANTRY ☐ EXHAUST FAN ☐
(12) EST. FUEL COST		(44) LAND ASSESSMENT $5,500
(13) ATTIC ☐ none	(31) DIRECTIONS TO PROPERTY	(45) IMPROVEMENTS $ 8,500
PULL DOWN STAIRWAY ☐ REGULAR STAIRWAY ☐ TRAP DOOR ☐		(46) TOTAL ASSESSMENT $ 14,000
(14) MAIDS ROOM ☐ TYPE BATH		(47) TAX RATE $3.95
LOCATION		(48) TOTAL ANNUAL TAXES 553.00
(15) NAME OF BUILDER		(49) LOT SIZE 50 x 140
(16) SQUARE FOOTAGE 2468		(50) LOT NO. 16 BLOCK 5 SECTION 4
(17) EXTERIOR OF HOUSE Brick	Rosemont Subd.	

NAME OF SCHOOLS: ELEMENTARY: Maury   JR. HIGH:
HIGH: T. C. Williams   PAROCHIAL:

PUBLIC TRANSPORTATION: 1 1/2 blocks

NEAREST SHOPPING AREA: 1 mile

REMARKS: Tenant's lease expires 2/28/74

Date: October 10, 1973

In consideration of the services of Hitt & Runn Real Est. Corp. (herein called "Broker") to be rendered to the undersigned (herein called "Owner"), and of the promise of Broker to make reasonable efforts to obtain a Purchaser therefor, Owner hereby lists with Broker the real estate and all improvements thereon which are described above (all herein called "the property"), and Owner hereby grants to Broker the exclusive and irrevocable right to sell such property from 12:00 Noon on October 10, 19 73 until 12:00 Midnight on January 10, 19 74 (herein called "period of time"), for the price of Thirty-three thousand five hundred & 00/100 Dollars ($ 33,500.00) or for such other price and upon such other terms (including exchange) as Owner may subsequently authorize during the period of time.

It is understood by Owner that the above sum or any other price subsequently authorized by Owner shall include a cash fee of 6 per cent of such price or other price which shall be payable by Owner to Broker upon consummation by any Purchaser or Purchasers of a valid contract of sale of the property during the period of time and whether or not Broker was a procuring cause of any such contract of sale.

If the property is sold or exchanged by Owner, or by Broker or by any other person to any Purchaser to whom the property was shown by Broker or any representative of Broker within sixty (60) days after the expiration of the period of time mentioned above, Owner agrees to pay to Broker a cash fee which shall be the same percentage of the purchase price as the percentage mentioned above.

Broker is hereby authorized by Owner to place a "For Sale" sign on the property and to remove all signs of other brokers or salesmen during the period of time, and Owner hereby agrees to make the property available to Broker at all reasonable hours for the purpose of showing it to prospective Purchasers.

Owner agrees to convey the property to the Purchaser by warranty deed with the usual covenants of title and free and clear from all encumbrances, tenancies, liens (for taxes or otherwise), but subject to applicable restrictive covenants of record. Owner acknowledges receipt of a copy of this agreement.

WITNESS the following signature(s) and seal(s):

Date Signed: October 10, 1973   _Titus Wadd_ (SEAL)
(Owner)

Listing Broker: Hitt & Runn Real Estate Corp.
Your name   (SEAL)
(Owner)

Address   Telephone

Go on to the Offer to Purchase Agreement.

114

OFFER TO PURCHASE AGREEMENT

This AGREEMENT made as of_____ November 1 , 19 73 ,

among Ollie Z. Tyme & wife, Summer D. Tyme _____ (herein called "Purchaser"),

and Titus Wadd _____ (herein called "Seller"),

and Hitt & Runn Real Estate Corp. _____ (herein called "Broker"),
provides that Purchaser agrees to buy through Broker as agent for Seller, and Seller agrees to sell the following described real estate, and all improvements
thereon, located in the jurisdiction of Alexandria, (Your State) _____ ,
(all herein called "the property"):
_____ Lot 16, Block 5, Section 4, Rosemont Subdivision _____

_____ Sale to include range, refrigerator, and washer. _____

_____ , and more commonly known as 16 East Oak Street, _____
_____ Alexandria, (Your State) _____ (street address).

1. The purchase price of the property is Thirty-two thousand five hundred and 00/100---------------
Dollars ($ 32,500.00), and such purchase price shall be paid as follows:
_____ $500.00 by deposit with contract.
_____ $7625.00 cash at settlement.
_____ $24,375.00 by 1st deed of trust loan to be secured by purchasers.

2. Purchaser has made a deposit of Five hundred & 00/100---------------------- Dollars ($ 500.00)
with Broker, receipt of which is hereby acknowledged, and such deposit shall be held by Broker in escrow until the date of settlement and then applied
to the purchase price, or returned to Purchaser if the title to the property is not marketable.

3. Seller agrees to convey the property to Purchaser by Warranty Deed with the usual covenants of title and free and clear from all encumbrances,
tenancies, liens (for taxes or otherwise), except as may be otherwise provided above, but subject to applicable restrictive covenants of record. Seller further
agrees to deliver possession of the property to Purchaser on the date of settlement and to pay the expense of preparing the deed of conveyance.

4. Settlement shall be made at the offices of Broker or at attorney selected by purchaser on or before
_____ January 15, 1974 , 19____ , or as soon thereafter as title can be examined and necessary documents prepared, with allowance of
a reasonable time for Seller to correct any defects reported by the title examiner.

5. All taxes, interest, rent, and F.H.A. or similar escrow deposits, if any, shall be prorated as of the date of settlement.

6. All risk of loss or damage to the property by fire, windstorm, casualty, or other cause is assumed by Seller until the date of settlement.

7. Purchaser and Seller agree that Broker was the sole procuring cause of this Contract of Purchase, and Seller agrees to pay Broker for services
rendered a cash fee of_____ per cent of the purchase price. If either Purchaser or Seller defaults under such Contract, such defaulting party shall
be liable for the cash fee of Broker and any expenses incurred by the non-defaulting party in connection with this transaction.
Subject to: Purchaser's ability to secure above financing. _____
_____ Seller to furnish certificate of termite inspection with 5 year guarantee _____
_____ from an approved exterminator. _____

_____ Sale subject to lease which expires February 28, 1974. _____

8. Purchaser represents that an inspection satisfactory to Purchaser has been made of the property, and Purchaser agrees to accept the property in
its present condition except as may be otherwise provided in the description of the property above.

9. This Contract of Purchase constitutes the entire agreement among the parties and may not be modified or changed except by written instrument
executed by all of the parties, including Broker.

10. This Contract of Purchase shall be construed, interpreted, and applied according to the law of the jurisdiction of (Your state) and shall
be binding upon and shall inure to the benefit of the heirs, personal representatives, successors, and assigns of the parties.

All parties to this agreement acknowledge receipt of a certified copy.

WITNESS the following signatures and seals:

_Titus Wadd_____ (SEAL)　　　_Ollie Z. Tyme_____ (SEAL)
　　　　　　　　　　　Seller　　　　_Summer D. Tyme_____ Purchaser
_____ (SEAL)　　　　　　　　　　　　　　(SEAL)
　　　　　　　　　　　Seller　　　　　　　　　　　　　　Purchaser
_____ (SEAL)
　　　　　　　　　　　Broker

Deposit Rec'd $ 500.00 _____
Check　　　　　　　　Cash

Sales Agent:
　　　　Your signature

Chapter 13

How to Prepare
Closing Statements

Introduction

Most state examinations require only broker license applicants to prepare closing statements. Salesman license applicants need not ordinarily be capable of this function. On broker examinations, the problems in closing are sequential; that is, the closing problems involve the use of previously completed listing and contract problems from the preceding chapter.

The training methods employed in this chapter are as follows:

1. Explanation of closing statements; their function and purpose.
2. Explanation of closing statement items on purchaser's and seller's statements.
3. Sample closing statement problems based on previously given listing and contract problems.
4. Proof of closing statement entries.
5. Practice problems.

Explanation of Closing Statements—Function and Purpose

The closing statement given to the buyer is an itemization of all charges to the buyer in the transaction, and a statement of how he paid these funds. The charges include the purchase price of the property, prepaid taxes, if any, insurance, legal fees, recording fees, loan service fees, and any other expenses of acquisition of the property. These will be followed by any credits to the buyer, such as earnest money deposits, loan proceeds, any credits due from seller, and finally, the cash paid by the buyer at closing.

The seller's statement begins with a statement of all credits to the seller, such as the sale price of the property, any credit for prepaid taxes, insurance, escrow accounts, etc., followed by a statement of all expenses of sale which are to be charged to the seller. These will include such items as balances on outstanding loans, sales commission, unpaid taxes, legal fees, etc. The final item on this statement will be the cash paid to the seller at closing.

Think of a closing statement as being similar to your monthly statement from your bank. It is a statement of account, in which the total of debits and credits must be equal in order to balance the account. The purpose of the statement is to provide all parties with an accurate record of the handling of all funds involved in the transaction. It is important to think of the statement as an accounting *after the completion of the transaction, rather than as a statement of funds due prior to the closing.* Although the statement may be prepared prior to the actual closing, *it is actually a statement of account following the end of the transaction.*

EXPLANATION OF CLOSING STATEMENT ITEMS

Purchaser's Statement; Debit Items, or "What did it cost"?

1. *Purchase price of property:* This is an item of expense to the purchaser. His primary obligation is to pay this amount to the seller.
2. *Taxes, paid in advance by seller:* If the seller has paid taxes in advance, the seller is due a refund of prorated taxes from closing date to the end of the tax year. Since the purchaser will benefit from these paid taxes, he is charged, pro rata, for the unused portion of the year's taxes. (*See also seller's credits.*)
3. *Insurance:*
   (a) Previously purchased by seller, to be assumed by purchaser. As in the case of prepaid taxes, the purchaser will benefit from this insurance and is to be charged pro rata for the unused portion of the policy. (*See also seller's credits.*)
   (b) New policy, purchased by purchaser. Here the purchaser will benefit from the entire policy and so is charged for the policy premium.
4. *Legal fees:*
   (a) Title examination: The examination of title is to the purchaser's benefit, and he is charged the legal fees for examination.

(b) Title insurance: Again this is to the purchaser's benefit, and therefore a charge to the purchaser.

(c) Recording fees: All instruments, the deed to the property, plus any deeds of trust or mortgages, must be recorded in the land records. These are benefits to the purchaser and the expenses of recordation are debits to his account. These fees vary in amounts in different states. Exam problem will give the rate for your jurisdiction.

(d) Preparation of deed(s) of trust on mortgages: These instruments are for the benefit of the purchaser, and legal fees charged for their preparation are a charge to the purchaser.

5. *Survey:* Usually required by a lender and often necessary for loan placement. Charge to purchaser unless otherwise instructed.

6. *Loan service fees:* Necessary for placement of the purchaser's loan, hence an expense to the purchaser.

7. *Appraisal fees:* Frequently required by lender. An expense to purchaser unless otherwise instructed.

8. *Assumption fees:* If purchaser is to assume a loan, there will often be an assumption fee charged by the lender. An expense to purchaser, usually a flat fee.

9. *Tax and insurance escrows:*
   (a) New loan: Sometimes required by lender on new loans. Charge to purchaser.

   (b) Assumed loans: Usually, a purchaser will be required to replace the seller's escrow funds on deposit with the lender, as the lender must return these funds to the seller. This amount will be a debit to the purchaser. (*See also seller's credits on seller's statement.*)

10. *Interest in advance:* Often when a settlement takes place other than on the first day of the month, the lender will require payment of interest on the loan from closing date to the first day of the next month in order to schedule future payments on the first day of the month. This interest payment is an expense to the purchaser.

11. *F.H.A. mortgage insurance premium:* On most sales involving new F.H.A. insured financing, it is customary to charge the first month's mortgage insurance premium in advance. This is an expense to the purchaser, charged at settlement, and remitted on the first of the month. F.H.A. and V.A. require that payments begin on first of month.

12. *Purchase of chattels by purchaser from seller:* When a purchaser has arranged to purchase some chattel (rugs, drapes, etc.) from seller under a separate bill of sale, this amount is shown as an expense to purchaser.

Purchaser's Statement; Credit Items, or "How did he pay for it"?

1. *Earnest money deposits:* Purchaser will have previously made a deposit with the signing of the contract of sale. This will be credited to his account and is shown as a credit to the purchaser.

2. *Loan proceeds:* Any loan proceeds, whether secured by a first or second trust, and whether new financing or assumed, are treated as cash and shown as credit to the purchaser. (*See also seller's debits, Item 2.*)

3. *Credits from seller:*
   (a) Tax credits: If the seller has not yet paid the taxes for the current year, he will owe the prorated taxes to the date of settlement. Since the purchaser, as the new owner of record, will receive the tax bill for the entire year, the seller will pay his pro rata share of the taxes to the purchaser who will pay the total annual taxes when due. Show as a credit to purchaser. (*See also seller's statement, debits to seller.*)

   (b) Miscellaneous credits from seller: Occasionally, there will exist some special condition which results in the seller's agreement to pay some expense for or allow credit to the purchaser. Show as a credit to the purchaser. (*See also seller's statement, debits to seller.*)(e.g., recordation fee)

4. *Rents, previously paid in advance:* If property is rented, and tenant has paid rent in advance of closing date, seller must pay to purchaser the prorated rent from closing date. Credit purchaser for this amount. (*See also seller's debits.*)

5. *Due from purchaser to close:* This item will be the total cash required from the purchaser at closing. It is determined by deducting from the purchaser's total debits the total of all other credits (deposit, loan proceeds, credits from seller). It represents the difference between total expense to the purchaser and the total of all other credits. Since the closing statement represents a statement of account after the completion of the closing, or after this amount has been paid, it becomes a credit to the purchaser.

Totals: The total debits and credits to the purchaser are shown as the last entry on the purchaser's statement. *These totals must balance.* The balance is actually "forced" by adjusting the amount due from purchaser to close.

Seller's Statement; Credit Items, or "What did he receive"?

1. *Purchase price of property:* This is the seller's principal benefit from the sale and it is a credit to his account. (*See also purchaser's debits.*)

2. *Taxes, previously paid in advance by seller:* The seller is due a refund of any taxes previously paid by him beyond the closing date. Show as a credit to seller. (*See also purchaser's debits.*)

3. *Insurance, assumed by purchaser:* As with previously paid taxes, any unused insurance premiums are credited to the seller. (*See also purchaser's debits.*)

4. *Tax and insurance escrow accounts:* If seller has on deposit with a lender monies in a tax and insurance escrow account, these funds must be returned to him. Show as a credit to seller. (*See also purchaser's debits.*)

5. *Purchase of chattels by purchaser:* If purchaser has agreed to purchase some chattels under a separate bill of sale, the purchase price will be shown as a credit to the seller. (*See also purchaser's debits.*)

Seller's Statement; Debit Items, or "What did he pay"?

1. *Taxes, not paid in advance:* If seller has not yet paid his taxes for the current tax year, his pro rata share of the taxes for the year will be a debit to him. (*See also purchaser's credits.*)

2. *Pay-off of loan balances, existing encumbrances:* If seller has outstanding indebtedness secured by first or second deeds of trust or mortgages, these must be paid off or assumed by purchaser in order for the seller to be able to transfer title. Show as a debit to seller, whether paid off or assumed. (*See also credits to purchaser.*)

   (a) Pay-off penalties, deed(s) of trust or mortgages: Occasionally, there will be a cash penalty to the seller for paying off a loan in advance of its due date. Show as a debit to seller.

3. *Agent's commission:* This is an item of expense to seller, and is shown as a debit to seller's account.

4. *Legal fees:*
   Preparation of deed: Seller usually pays the lawyer's charge for the preparation of the deed to the property. Debit seller for this amount.

5. *Loan placement discounts:* Any "points" to be paid by the seller are a debit to his account.

6. *Release fees on encumbrances:* Often there will be a charge by the lender for releasing deed(s) of trust or mortgages which seller is to pay off. Debit seller for this amount.

7. *Rents, previously paid in advance:* If property is rented, and the tenant has paid rent to seller in advance of closing date, seller must pay to purchaser the prorated rent from closing date. Debit seller for this amount.

8. *Satisfaction of liens necessary to transfer of title:* Occasionally, a

seller will have some indebtedness against his property which is secured by a lien (example: past due taxes, sewer or water charges, etc.). These liens must be satisfied before title can be transferred. Show as a debit to seller.

9. *Miscellaneous credits to purchaser:* Occasionally, there will exist some special agreement which requires the seller to pay some expense for, or allow credit to purchaser. Debit seller for this amount. (*See also purchaser's statement; credits to purchaser*).

10. *Due seller to close:* This item will be the total cash to be paid to the seller as proceeds from the sale. It is determined by deducting from seller's total credits the total of all other debit items. It represents the difference between expense to the seller and the total of all other credits. Since the closing statement is a statement of account after the completion of the closing, or after seller has been paid, this item becomes a *debit* to the seller.

Totals: The total debits and credits to seller are shown as the last entry on the seller's statement. *These totals must balance.* The balance is actually "forced" by adjusting the amount due seller to close.

Transfer Taxes: Most jurisdictions impose taxes on deeds. These may be referred to as excise tax, tax stamps, grantor tax, or simply transfer tax. The rates vary from jurisdiction to jurisdiction. Also, there is no universal rule as to who (grantor or grantee) pays such taxes. For this reason, these taxes are not included in the sample problems in this lesson. *They may be included in the exam problems.*

Prior to the examination, you should determine the designation (name) of such tax in your jurisdiction, the rate of taxation, and which party customarily (or by statute) must pay these taxes.

NOTE: It is possible, on some closings, for the total of the seller's debits to exceed his credits. This would occur on sales in which the seller had low equity in the property, or in which he held a large deferred purchase money trust. If his debits exceed his credits, the seller would have to pay out money to close. In this event, Item 10 of the seller's debits above, "Due seller to close," would become "Due from seller to close" and this would be a credit entry on the closing statement.

After you have studied and understand the information in this section, go on to Solution of Listing, Contract, and Closing Statement Problems.

SOLUTION OF CLOSING STATEMENT PROBLEM

The Closing Statement Problems in this lesson are based on Listing and Contract Problems 1 through 4 which were given earlier. The steps in their solution are as follows:

Step I: Read the Closing Statement Problem. Be sure that you under-stand all of its requirements before starting to work.

Step II: Using the numbered items on the closing statement as a guide, and taking each entry in turn, enter the dollar amount of each item. *Be certain that you enter the amount in the proper column(s).* In some instances no computation of amounts will be necessary, while others will require computation. Remember that the debits and credits to the purchaser, and also the debits and credits to the seller, must balance, and that the statement is not complete until these figures are shown in balance.

A sample closing statement follows. Study and understand it before going on to work the problems in this section. As an aid to your understanding of this statement, a list of the source of information for each entry in the sample statement follows.

Entry Number	*Source of Information*
1. Purchase price	Contract of Sale
2. Hazard insurance policy	Settlement Problem
3. Taxes, 1973, plus interest and penalty	Listing and Math Computation Sheet
4. Taxes, 1-1-74 to 1-15-74	Listing and Math Computation Sheet
5. Title examination	Settlement Problem
6. Title insurance	Settlement Problem
7. Preparation of deed	Settlement Problem
8. Preparation of 1st D/T	Settlement Problem
9. Recording fee	Math Computation Sheet
10. Loan origination fee	Math Computation Sheet
11. Earnest money deposit	Contract
12. Agent's commission	Math Computation Sheet
13. Proceeds, 1st D/T loan	Contract of Sale
14. Rent adjustment	Math Computation Sheet
15. Termite inspection	Settlement Problem
16. Survey	Settlement Problem
17. Recording fee, D/T	Math Computation Sheet
18. Due from purchaser to close	Math Computation Sheet
19. Due seller to close	Math Computation Sheet

CLOSING STATEMENT PROBLEM—BROKER COURSE SAMPLE PROBLEM

Using the data contained in the listing and contract problems, close the Wadd to Tyme sale. To save time, do not compute interest on loans or monthly payments if involved. Clerk's fees, notary fees, etc., are purposely omitted. The following information is given to assist you: buyer to purchase new fire insurance policy at a cost of $90; taxes for first half of 1973 have been paid, but taxes for last 6 months of 1973, plus 5 percent penalty and 6 percent interest from 1-1-74 have not been paid. Also, taxes for 1974 have not been paid. Title examination, $175; title insurance, $95; preparation of deed, $25; preparation of D/T, $20; recording fees, 20 cents per $100; loan origination fee, 1 percent; tenant's rent is paid until 1-31-74. Termite inspection, $25; survey, $45.

	Purchaser		Seller	
	Debit	Credit	Debit	Credit
1. Purchase price	$32,500.00			$32,500.00
2. Hazard insurance policy	90.00			
3. Taxes, 1973, plus interest & penalty			$ 291.05	
4. Taxes, 1-1-74 to 1-15-74			23.04	
5. Title examination	175.00			
6. Title insurance	95.00			
7. Preparation of deed			25.00	
8. Preparation of 1st D/T	20.00			
9. Recording fees, deed of B & S	65.00			
10. Loan origination fee	243.75			
11. Earnest money deposit		$ 500.00		
12. Agent's commission			1,950.00	
13. Proceeds, 1st D/T loan		24,375.00		
14. Rent adjustment, 1-15-74 to 1-31-74		137.50	137.50	
15. Termite inspection			25.00	
16. Survey	45.00			
17. Recording fees, deed of trust	48.80			
18. Due from purchaser to close		8,270.05		
19. Due seller to close			30,048.41	
20. TOTALS	$33,282.55	$33,282.55	$32,500.00	$32,500.00
21.				
22.				
23.				
24.				
25.				
26.				
27.				

PROOF OF CLOSING STATEMENT ENTRIES

Cash In–Cash Out Method

The determination of the accuracy of closing statement entries can be determined by the Cash In–Cash Out Method. This method involves the addition of all cash dollars received in the transaction and deducting from these dollars all cash disbursements from the sale. The resulting balance should leave no funds left over and should be exactly enough to meet all cash requirements. That is, the total cash in should balance with the cash paid out. As an example, let's look at the sample closing statement problem:

The following cash items were received:

Cash In

From Purchaser's Statement:

Earnest money deposit	$ 500.00	
Proceeds, 1st D/T loan	24,375.00	
Cash from purchaser at closing	8,270.05	
Total of cash received		$33,145.05

The following cash disbursements were made:

Cash Out

From Purchaser's Statement:

Hazard insurance policy	$ 90.00
Title examination	175.00
Title insurance	95.00
Preparation of 1st D/T	20.00
Record deed	65.00
Loan origination fee	243.75
Survey	45.00
Record D/T	48.80

From Seller's Statement:

Taxes, 1973, plus interest and penalty	$ 291.05	
Taxes, 1-1-74 to 1-15-74	23.04	
Preparation of deed	25.00	
Agent's commission	1,950.00	
Termite inspection	25.00	
Due seller to close	30,048.41	
Total of cash paid out		$33,145.05

It should be noted that on the sample problems there are two entries each on the purchaser's and seller's statements which do not appear in the Cash In–Cash Out Statement (purchase price and taxes, paid in advance). These items do not appear on this statement, as they are offsetting debit and credit entries in the two statements. Any such offsetting entries do not appear on the Cash In–Cash Out Statement.

MATH COMPUTATIONS FOR SAMPLE PROBLEM

3. Taxes, 1973, plus interest and penalty.

   Annual tax $\dfrac{\$553.00}{2}$ = $276.50 last half of year

   $276.50 + .05% penalty = $290.33 + .0025 (1/2 mo. interest
   @ 6% p/a) = $291.05

4. Taxes, 1974 = $\dfrac{\$553.00}{12} = \dfrac{\$46.08/mo.}{2}$ = $23.04

9. Record deed
   Sale price, $32,500 = 325 $\times$ .20 = $65.00

10. Loan origination fee: Loan amount, $24,375 $\times$ .01 = $243.75

12. Agent's commission: $32,500 $\times$ .06 = $1,950

14. Rent adjustment:

    Rent $\dfrac{\$275.00/mo.}{2}$ = $137.50

17. Record deed of trust: D/T amount, $24,375 $\times$ .20/$100 =
    244 $\times$ .20 = $48.80

18. Due from buyer to close:
    Total debits: $33,282.55
    Total credits: 25,012.50
    Due to close: $ 8,270.05

19. Due seller to close:
    Total credits: $32,500.00
    Total debits: 2,451.59
    Due to close: $30,048.41

Chapter 14

Improved Property
Summary Card

Examinations prepared by the Educational Testing Service for real estate salesman license applicants, as presently constructed, contain a segment entitled "Improved Property Summary Card." Essentially, this section is a test of an applicant's reading skills and comprehension. It consists of a narrative description of a situation, property, contract, or other document. The applicant is required to read and interpret the information, and then answer questions based on his interpretation of what he has read.

An example, in part, might read somewhat as follows:

> The house is two story, of brick construction, located in a new residential subdivision of similar homes, built by the same builder at about the same time. There are four large bedrooms on the second floor, plus two bathrooms .... Owners have added a large below ground swimming pool, plus bath house containing a sauna, and have had the grounds professionally landscaped at a cost of several thousand dollars ....

QUESTIONS:

1. From the above information, you can determine that all bedrooms contain more than 90 square feet.
   A. True
   B. False

2. You may assume that the house is over-improved for the neighborhood.
   A. True
   B. False.

The answer to question 1 would be "True." A bedroom containing 90 square feet or less would be only approximately 9 × 10 feet in size, a small bedroom by any standard. The information given describes the bedrooms as large. Therefore, one would be safe in assuming that they each contained more than 90 square feet.

The answer to question 2 is "False." While the additions and improvements to the property would have been expensive, no information is given that would indicate over-improvement for the neighborhood.

Hints On Solving Improved Property Summary Card Problems

1. Read carefully. This is one instance where "skimming" can fail to discern a key word that can alter the idea or facts. Those who prepare these problems are expert in the use of such words.

2. Read the entire passage and all questions through one time before attempting to answer any questions. Then go back and read the passage again, looking for the answers to the questions.

3. Read the questions as carefully as you read the passage. Many wrong answers come from not understanding the questions.

4. Watch for limiting words such as **must, all, none, never, always,** etc. These words can so limit the thought that a statement is made incorrect when it otherwise might be true.

5. Words such as **usually, many, few, often, sometimes,** etc. often can change an otherwise false statement to true.

6. Double negatives can change the meaning of a statement or question. Suppose Question 2 had read

   "From the information furnished, it cannot be determined that the property is not over-improved for the neighborhood."

   The answer to the question as stated here would be "True," rather than "False" as stated in the example.

7. Watch for words of similar spelling but different meaning, such as "**demise–devise**," "**mortgagee–mortgagor**," etc. Careless reading can be costly where such words are concerned.

SAMPLE PROBLEM

The problem which follows is illustrative of the type of problem found on a typical license examination for real estate salesmen.

A house and lot were listed at a price equivalent to 100 percent of fair market value. The house is valued at $25,000 and the adjoining lot at $4,000. The buyer wants to purchase the house at the listed price and wants an option on the vacant lot for $3,000. Taxes for both parcels of property were $1,100, paid in advance the first of the calendar year.

The improved lot has a 2 story home with three large bedrooms and a two car garage with driveway. The lot is 150' × 180'. It is connected to the city water system and sewer is also connected. Gas and electrical lines are in the street. Telephone lines run across the rear of the lot. The landscaping is nicer than the rest of the homes in the neighborhood. The lot has a zoned 50' setback from the street.

There is an existing first mortgage of $22,000 at $7\frac{1}{2}$ percent which can be assumed by a 1 percent assumption fee. There is also a second mortgage of $2,800 at 10 percent. The buyers want the deal closed on August 15th and want to take occupancy on August 1st. The sellers accept the offer. The broker will be paid a 6 percent commission on the transaction at closing.

1. Can you deduce that all utility lines are underground?
   A. Yes
   B. No

2. Can you assume that on August 15th the buyers paid a $220 mortgage assumption fee?
   A. Yes
   B. No

3. The ad valorem tax rate on the property is approximately
   A. $4.40/$100
   B. $3.80/$100
   C. $5.00/$100
   D. Neither

4. You can assume that the garage contains at least 200 square feet.
   A. True
   B. False

5. The driveway is at least 50 feet long.
   A. True
   B. False

Practice problems on Property Improvement Cards will be found in the Question Section beginning on page 235.

PART III

ARITHMETIC

Chapter 15

Arithmetic Review

This chapter is constructed so as to provide basic review and instruction in those areas of mathematics needed and used by real estate brokers and salesmen. It is based on the kinds of problems likely to be found on most state license examinations. Practice problems are provided in the Question Section for each area of review, and a number of review problems are furnished, beginning on Page 241.

A Look at Percentages

Many of the day to day functions of a real estate agent involve the computation of problems which are based upon percentages. Determination of interest rates, appraisals, loan amortization, taxes, insurance, and commissions are but a few of the uses of percentage computation. No real estate agent can satisfactorily perform his duties without the ability to solve certain percentage problems.

The Arithmetic of Percentages

There are three basic types of percentage problems. Before reviewing the methods of solution of these problems, let's learn how to analyze any problem which involves the use of percent.

First . . . . What does *percentage* mean?

(Def.) A proportion or part of a whole.

. . . . How does *percent* relate to decimal and common fractions?

> (**Ans.**) Percent may be expressed by the
> percent sign (%), as a decimal fraction,
> or as a common fraction. **Ex:** 10%, .10,
> and $\frac{1}{10}$, all have the same value.

In solving a percentage problem, we will have to express all factors in the same fashion. If one factor is shown as a percent (%), one as a decimal fraction, and perhaps another as a common fraction, we must change all factors to one common means of expression. Let's review the methods of doing this.

1. Percent (%) means *per hundred,* so change percent to decimal form by changing to hundredths. (Divide by 100)

    $$50\% = .50 \qquad 6\% = .06 \qquad 110\% = 1.10$$

    (To divide by 100, move the decimal point 2 places to the left.)

2. Change decimal fractions to percent by doing the opposite.

    $$.65 = 65\% \qquad .02 = 2\% \qquad 1.05 = 105\%$$

    (Move decimal point 2 places to the right.)

3. Change percent to a common fraction by showing as hundredths and reducing to lowest terms.

    $$50\% = \frac{50}{100} = \frac{1}{2} \qquad 25\% = \frac{25}{100} = \frac{1}{4} \qquad 80\% = \frac{80}{100} = \frac{4}{5}$$

4. Change common fractions to percent by changing to decimal fraction (hundredths) then showing as percent.

    $$\frac{1}{4} = \frac{25}{100} = .25 = 25\% \quad \frac{2}{5} = \frac{40}{100} = .40 = 40\% \quad \frac{3}{4} = \frac{75}{100} = .75 = 75\%$$

    The above can be accomplished very quickly by dividing the numerator by the denominator.

    $$\frac{1}{4} = 4\overline{)1.00}^{\,.25} = 25\% \qquad \frac{1}{8} = 8\overline{)1.000}^{\,.125} = 12.5\%$$

    $$\qquad\qquad\qquad\qquad \frac{8}{20}$$

    $$\frac{3}{5} = 5\overline{)3.00}^{\,.60} = 60\% \qquad\qquad \frac{16}{40}$$

    $$\qquad\qquad\qquad\qquad\qquad\qquad \frac{40}{}$$

DIVISION, MULTIPLICATION, ADDITION, AND SUBTRACTION OF DECIMALS

Division

When dividing by a decimal number, change the divisor to a whole number, then move the decimal point in the dividend a corresponding number of places to the right:

$$3.21.\overline{)\,9.63.}$$ gives $3.$

$$17.25.\overline{)\,6.90.0}$$ gives $.4$

When dividing a decimal number by a whole number, place the decimal point in your answer directly above the decimal point in the dividend:

$$23\overline{)4.6}$$ gives $.2$

$$402\overline{)12.06}$$ gives $.03$

Multiplication

When multiplying decimal numbers, count the total number of places to the right of the decimal point in *both* numbers to be multiplied, then count off the same number of places in your answer:

$$
\begin{array}{r}
400 \\
\times \ \ .02 \ \ \text{(2 places)} \\
\hline
8.00 \ \ \text{(2 places)}
\end{array}
$$

$$
\begin{array}{r}
.02 \ \ \text{(2 places)} \\
\times \ \ .03 \ \ \text{(2 places)} \\
\hline
.0006 \ \ \text{(4 places)}
\end{array}
$$

Addition

When adding decimal numbers, place the decimals in the numbers to be added directly over one another, and the decimal point in the solution directly underneath that in the numbers to be added, and add as a whole number.

$$
\begin{array}{r}
2.25 \\
3.5 \\
+ \ 4.175 \\
\hline
9.925
\end{array}
$$

$$
\begin{array}{r}
1.00 \\
3.83 \\
+ \ 4.725 \\
\hline
9.555
\end{array}
$$

Subtraction

When subtracting decimal numbers, place the decimals in the numbers to be subtracted directly over one another, and the decimal point in the solution directly underneath. Subtract as whole numbers.

$$
\begin{array}{r}
5.25 \\
-\ 3.25 \\
\hline
2.00
\end{array}
\qquad\qquad
\begin{array}{r}
7.5 \\
-\ 4.75 \\
\hline
2.75
\end{array}
$$

Solving Percentage Problems

In any problem involving percentage we will have to find one of the following:

(P) percentage   (R) rate   (B) base

Let's look at some problems in percentages.

1. A house is listed for $22,000. If the salesman's share of the commission is 3 percent of the sales price, how much will he receive for selling the house at the listed price?

   In this problem you are given the rate (3%) and the base (selling price of $22,000) and will have to determine the percentage (amount of salesman's commission).

2. The annual net income from an apartment house is $12,300. If this represents a return of 15 percent annually on the investment, what did the property cost?

   In this problem we are given the percentage ($12,300) and the rate (15%) and must find the base (cost of the property).

3. If the investor in Problem 2 above had paid $102,500 for the same apartment house, what would the annual rate of return on his investment be?

   In this problem we know the base ($102,500) and the percentage ($12,300) and must determine the rate.

We will use the equation $P = R \times B$ to solve each problem. The problems can be resolved as follows:

1. What is 3% of 22,000?

$$\frac{(P)}{?} \quad = \quad \frac{(R)}{.03} \quad X \quad \frac{(B)}{22,000}$$

Multiply rate times base to find percentage.

$$P \quad = \quad \$660.00$$

2. 12,300 is 15% of what number?

$$\frac{(P)}{12,300} \quad = \quad \frac{(R)}{.15} \quad X \quad \frac{(B)}{?}$$

Divide percentage by rate to find base.

$$\frac{12,300}{.15} \quad = \quad \$82,000$$

3. 12,300 is what percent of 102,500?

$$\frac{(P)}{12,300} \quad = \quad \frac{(R)}{?} \quad X \quad \frac{(B)}{102,500}$$

Divide percentage by base to find rate.

$$\frac{12,300}{102,500} \quad = \quad .12 \quad or \quad 12\%$$

Setting up the Equation

1. To identify base, rate, and percentage, think of the word "equals" as meaning "is" and the multiplication symbol as meaning "of." For example:

   $P = R \times B$ becomes

   Percentage is what percent of base?
   Substituting numbers, in an equation where
   Percentage = 10, Rate = 20%, and Base = 50, we find:

   10 is 20% of 50

   If any factor were unknown, the equation would look like this:

   Percentage unknown: What is 20% of 50?
   Rate unknown: 10 is what % of 50?
   Base unknown: 10 is 20% of what number?

2. To find Percentage, you *multiply;* to find Base or Rate, you *divide;* if Percentage is given, it is always the *dividend.*

3. *Percentage* is a unitary number—dollars, cents, apples, acres, etc.

   Percent is a fractional number, shown as decimal fraction, %, or common fraction. *Rate* is always shown as a percent.

4. If *percent* (Rate) is less than 100%, the Base will be larger than Percentage; if percent is more than 100%, Percentage will be larger than Base.

5. Use these rules to determine whether you are to find Percentage, Rate, or Base in the following:

8 is 5% of what number _____

What is 5% of 160? _____

8 is what % of 160? _____

Tax and Insurance Problems

Problems which involve tax and insurance premium computation are forms of percentage problems. The formula for their solution is the same as the standard percentage problem with other designations for the factors. The factors are as follows:

Tax: *Percentage* is the same as *Tax*
Rate is the same as *Rate*
Base is the same as *Assessment*
thus, our formula P = R × B becomes
T = R × A

Insurance: *Percentage* is the same as *Premium*
Rate remains the same − *Rate*
Base is the same as *Amount of Insurance*
thus, our formula P = R × B becomes
P = R × A

Tax Rates

Tax rates are normally given in terms of a certain number of dollars and cents of tax *per hundred* dollars of assessed valuation. Therefore, in any problems which involve assessments, we must always work in terms of the number of hundreds of dollars in the assessment. To do this, we move the decimal two places to the left in the assessment.

1. If assessed valuation is $18,000 and tax rate is $3.50 per hundred,
   a. 18,000 divided by 100 = 180
   b. Multiply 3.50 × 180 to determine taxes of $630.

2. Determine taxes if assessed valuation is $14,750, and tax rate is $2.75 per hundred.
   a. 14,750 divided by 100 = 147.5
   b. Multiply 2.75 × 147.5 to determine taxes of $405.63.

Formulae for determining tax, tax rate, or assessment when only two of these factors are given:

1. Tax = Rate × Assessment.
   a. Tax rate is $3 and assessment is $10,000.
   b. 10,000. divided by 100 = 100 × $3 rate = $300 tax.
2. Tax divided by Assessment = Tax Rate
   a. Tax is $300 and assessment is $10,000.
   b. $300 divided by 100 (assessment divided by 100) = $3 tax rate.
3. Tax divided by tax rate equals assessment
   a. Tax is $300 and tax rate is $3.00.
   b. $300 divided by $3 = 100 × 100 = $10,000 assessment.

Insurance rates may be given per hundred or per thousand.

1. If insurance in the amount of $15,000 is purchased at the rate of $.55 per hundred, what is the cost of the premium?
   a. 15,000 divided by 100 = 150
   b. Multiply .55 times 150 to determine cost.
2. If rate is given per thousand, simply divide by 1000 instead of 100 before multiplying by the insurance rate. (To divided by 1000, move decimal 3 places to the left.)
   a. 24,000 divided by 1000 = 24
   b. 28,600 divided by 1000 = 28.6
   c. Multiply by rate per thousand to determine cost.
3. Problems
   (a) If insurance in the amount of $15,000 is purchased at the rate of $5.50 per thousand dollars, what is the cost of the premium?
       (1) 15,000 divided by 1000 = 15
       (2) Multiply 5.50 × 15 to determine cost of $82.50.
   (b) A house is insured for $13,500 at the rate of $3.50 per thousand. What is the cost of the insurance premium?
       (1) 13,500 divided by 1000 = 13.5
       (2) Multiply 3.50 × 13.5 to determine cost of $47.25.

Proration of Taxes or Insurance

1. If taxes or insurance have been prepaid by the seller through some date beyond the date of settlement, a refund will be due the seller (and a charge made to the buyer) for the unexpired portion.

2. If taxes for the year have not been paid by the seller at the time of settlement, the seller will be charged for that part of the year up to the settlement date.

3. Computing proration of taxes and insurance.

   a. Determine from the problem whether you must figure the used or unused portion of a given period of time.

   b. Find the number of months in the period of time you are figuring. Figure parts of months on the basis of a 30-day month:

   $$10 \text{ days} = \tfrac{1}{3} \text{ of a month}$$
   $$15 \text{ days} = \tfrac{1}{2} \text{ of a month}$$
   $$20 \text{ days} = \tfrac{2}{3} \text{ of a month}$$

   c. Figure taxes or insurance premium per month.

   (1) Divide total by 12 if paid by the year.

   (2) Insurance premium may be paid for a 3-year period. If so, divide total by 36.

   d. Multiply the monthly tax or insurance amount by the number of months you have figured in "b" above.

4. Example of Proration Problem:

   Mr. Black has paid his taxes of $300 in advance for the year 1969. He sells his house and settlement takes place on June 10, 1969. What refund should he receive?

   a. Figure the number of months remaining in the year—that portion of the year during which Mr. Black will not be the owner of the house:

   20 days left in June $= \tfrac{2}{3}$ of a month.

   July through December = 6 months.

   Total months remaining: $6\tfrac{2}{3}$.

   b. Figure tax amount per month:

   $300 divided by 12 = $25.

   c. Multiply: $6\tfrac{2}{3} \times 25$

   $$\tfrac{2}{3} \times 25 = \$\ \ 16.67$$
   $$6 \times 25 = \$150.00$$

   Refund due $166.67
   Seller

Computing Proration Periods

The period of time involved in a proration period can be computed by setting down the beginning date in terms of years, months, and days. For example, June 15, 1968 would be shown as follows: 68-6-15. Repeat this process with the second date, placing the later calendar date above the earlier date. Subtract the lower number from the upper number. The result will be the number of years, months, and days to be used in the proration.

Example: Beginning Date   June 15, 1968
           Ending Date   May 10, 1969

Solution:
$$
\begin{array}{ccc}
 & 16 & \\
8 & 4 & 40 \\
\cancel{69} & - \quad \cancel{5} \quad - & \cancel{10} \\
- \quad 68 & - \quad 6 \quad - & 15 \\
\hline
\end{array}
$$

0 yrs.   10 mos. 25 days

In this problem, we could not subtract 15 days from 10 days, so we "borrowed" 30 days from the months column, making 40 days, from which we subtracted 15 days. In the months column, we could not subtract 6 months from 4 months, so we "borrowed" 12 months from the years column, making 16 months, leaving 68 in the years column. The time involved in our proration period is 0 years, 10 months, 25 days.

Problems on percentage will be found in the Question Section, beginning on Page 241.

SOLVING MEASUREMENT PROBLEMS

The solution of problems involving measurements is an integral part of the work of a real estate agent. Computation of acreage, square feet in a building, cubic feet in a room are only a few of these needs. Let's take a look at the method of solution of some of these problems.

Units of Measurement

1. *Familiar Units:* These units of measure with which we will ordinarily deal are the familiar ones of inches, feet, and yards.
2. *Less Familiar Units:* In dealing with real estate, we will sometimes encounter less familiar units. Some of these units are:

         1 chain = 66 feet
         1 rod   = $16\frac{1}{2}$ feet
         1 mile   = 5,280 feet

Linear Measurement

The measurements which we will use are those of linear measurement—the distance from one point to another. This is normally, but not necessarily, expressed in a straight line and may be expressed in any of the units above.

Area Measurement

1. *Area measurement* is the measurement of a surface, a two dimensional figure; a plane surface. Some examples are:

   > acres of land
   > square feet of land
   > square yards of carpet

2. *Units of measurement and their equivalents:*
   Some of the more common units of measurement are:

   > 1 square foot = 144 square inches
   > 1 square yard = 9 square feet
   > 1 acre = 160 square rods
   > 1 acre = 43,560 square feet
   > 1 square mile = 640 acres

3. *Formulae for determination of area.*
   a. The area of any square or rectangular plane surface is easily determined by one simple formula:

   > Area = Length times Width
   > (A = L $\times$ W)

   Problem: A room measures 12 feet by 15 feet. How many square feet of floor space does it contain?

   > A = 12′ (L) $\times$ 15′ (W)
   > A = 180 square feet

   b. The formula for determination of the area of a triangle is:

   > Area = $\frac{1}{2}$ Base $\times$ Altitude
   > (A = $\frac{1}{2}$ B $\times$ Alt.)

   Altitude: The perpendicular distance from the base of a figure to its summit.

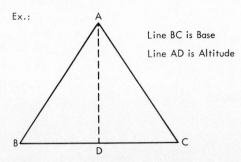

Ex.:

Line BC is Base
Line AD is Altitude

Problem: A triangular lot has a base of 150′ and an altitude of 80′. How many square feet are in the lot?

$$A = \tfrac{1}{2} B \times Alt.$$
$$A = \frac{150}{2} \times 80$$
$$A = 75 \times 80$$
$$A = 6,000 \text{ square feet}$$

c. The formula for determination of the area of a circle is:

$$Area = \pi \times Radius, \text{ squared}$$
$$(A = \pi R^2)$$
(π is Pi, which is numerically expressed as 3.1416)

Problem: A circular room measures 10′ in diameter. How many square feet does it contain?

$$A = \pi R^2$$
$$A = 3.1416 \times 25 \text{ (Diameter 10′-Radius 5′)}$$
$$A = 78.54 \text{ square feet}$$

Volume Measurement

1. *Volume measurement* adds a third dimension to area measurement, that of height (or depth).

    Some examples are: cubic inches
    cubic feet
    cubic yards

2. *Units of measurement and their equivalents.*
    Some of the more common units of measurement are:

    1 cubic foot = 1728 cubic inches
    1 cubic yard = 27 cubic feet

Formulae for Determination of Volume

1. To determine the volume of a rectangle or a cube, the formula is

    $$Volume = Length \times Width \times Height$$
    $$(V = L \times W \times H)$$

Problem: A room measures 12′ × 15′ and has a ceiling height of 8′. How many cubic feet are in the room?

$$V = 15(L) \times 12(W) \times 8(H)$$
$$V = 1440 \text{ cubic feet}$$

2. To determine the volume of a triangular or cylindrical object, the *area* is multiplied by the height (or depth).

$$\text{Volume} = \text{Area} \times \text{Height}$$
$$(V = A \times H)$$

Problem: The triangular attic of a building has an altitude of 6′, a width of 20′, and a length of 40′. How many cubic feet are in the attic?

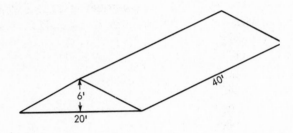

$$V = \frac{20}{2} \times 6 \times 40$$
$$V = 240 \text{ cubic feet}$$

Problem: A circular silo measures 12 feet in inside diameter and is 30 feet in height. How many cubic feet does it contain?

$$V = \pi \times 6^2 (R) \times 30$$
$$V = 3,392.928 \text{ cubic feet}$$

Square Root

Some problems will require the determination of the square root of a number. This is one of the more complicated of the mathematical processes we will need to know. Two methods of determining square root follow. The first, and most difficult method, is necessary if the number of which you seek the square root is either a fractional number or the product of a fractional number. The second, and simpler method, is easier to use if the number is a whole number or the product of a whole number.

METHOD A

Note: Be sure to actually do each step as you read it. Do not merely follow through the solution as it is given here, but get a sheet of paper and put down yourself each figure and step of the process as it occurs in the solution. Only in this way will you be able to learn the method of finding square root. No attention need be given to the principles underlying the process or the reasons for using the various steps. Just take these for granted and memorize the process itself.

Step 1: Separate the number into *periods* of two figures each beginning *at the right*, and place a curved line over each as shown. The number of periods thus formed will be the same as the number of figures in the answer.

$$\overparen{92}\overparen{16}$$

Step 2: Next, draw a line straight up and down at the left of the number, and an "L" shaped line to the right of the number, as shown in the illustration.

$$\Big|\,\overparen{92}\overparen{16}\,\underline{}$$

Step 3: Look at the first *period* at the left with the little curve over it and see if you can decide what number when multiplied by itself (or squared) will equal it or be a little less, *but not more*. In this case the *period* is 92 and the next smallest square below 92 is 81 which is 9 times 9. This number 81 is smaller than 92, so 9 is the number to be used as the first figure of the *root*. Square this number and place the result (81) under the first *period* and subtract. The square of 9 is 81 and you place 81 under the 92. Now subtract 81 from 92 which is eleven and bring down the next *period* 16 and place it beside the remainder 11 as shown. This gives 1116.

$$\begin{array}{r|l} \overparen{92}\overparen{16} & 9 \\ 81 & \\ \hline 1116 & \end{array}$$

Step 4: Take 9, the first figure of the root and multiply it by 2 and put the product 18 to the left of 1116 back of the up and down line. The 18 is called the *trial divisor.*

$$\begin{array}{r|r|l} & \overparen{92}\overparen{16} & 9 \\ & 81 & \\ & \hline \\ 18 & 1116 & \end{array}$$

Step 5: Find out how many times 18 is contained in 111, the first 3 figures of 1116. It is contained 6 times. This 6, then is the second figure in the *root*. Place this figure in the root and also at the right of the 18 (or trial divisor) giving 186 which is called the *complete divisor*, back of the up and down line. Now multiply 186 by the 6 just put in the *root* and write the product 1116 under the number 1116. Since there is no remainder, the square root of 9216 is 96. To check your work, square the root, 96 times 96 equals 9216.

$$\overset{\frown}{92}\overset{\frown}{16}\ \underline{\big|96}$$

$$81$$

$$186\ \big|\ \underline{1116}$$

$$1116$$

Step 6: If there had been a remainder at *Step 5*, you would proceed as in *Step 6* of this new problem (compute this problem through *Step 5*), multiply the figures now in the root (52) by 2 and put the product 104 to the left of 3129 back of the up and down line as the *new trial divisor*.

$$\overset{\frown}{27}\overset{\frown}{35}\overset{\frown}{29}\ \underline{\big|52}$$

$$25$$

$$102\ \big|\ 235$$

$$204$$

$$104\ \big|\ 3129$$

Step 7: Find out how many times 104 is contained in 312 (the first three figures of 3129). It is contained 3 times. So put 3 as the third figure of the root and also place it at the right of the 104, giving 1043 as the complete divisor. Multiply 1043 by the 3 just put in the root and put the product 3129 under the 3129. There is no remainder. The required square root is 523.

$$\overset{\frown}{27}\overset{\frown}{35}\overset{\frown}{29}\ \underline{\big|523}$$

$$25$$

$$102\ \big|\ 235$$

$$204$$

$$1043\ \big|\ \begin{matrix}3129\\3129\end{matrix}$$

If there is an odd number of digits in the whole number mark them off as shown and proceed as above.

$$\overset{\frown}{5}\overset{\frown}{31}\overset{\frown}{76}\overset{\frown}{36}$$

If there is a decimal in the number mark them as follows:

$$\overset{\frown}{5}\overset{\frown}{70}.\overset{\frown}{73}\overset{\frown}{21}$$

METHOD B

Step 1: Take the first two digits of the numbers and ask yourself "What numbers, multiplied by themselves, are close to this number?" For example, suppose the number were 7569. The first two digits are 75. 8 × 8 = 64, and 9 × 9 = 81.

Step 2: Multiply these numbers by 10, then by themselves. For example, 80 × 80 = 6400, and 90 × 90 = 8100. We now know that the number we seek is more than 80, but less than 90.

Step 3: Look at the last digit in the number for which we seek to determine the square root. In the example, this digit is 9. Now ask yourself, "What numbers, multiplied by themselves, end in 9?" The answer is either 3 × 3 = 9 or 7 × 7 = 49.

Since 7569 is closer to 8100 than 6400, the last digit in our solution is 7, the larger of the two choices. Therefore, the square root of 7569 is 87.

Proof: 87 X 87 = 7569

Problem in Square Root:

Area Problem: A square building contains 1024 sq. ft. of interior floor space. What is the length of each wall?

a. 30 X 30 = 900
40 X 40 = 1600

Hence, the square root is more than 30′ and less than 40′.

b. 2 X 2 = 4
8 X 8 = 64

One thousand twenty-four is closer to 900 than to 1600. Hence, each wall is 32′ long.

Proof: 32 X 32 = 1024

Volume Problem: The ceiling height of the building in the above problem is 8 feet. How many cubic feet are there in the building?

V = Area X Height
V = 1024 X 8
V = 8192 cu. ft.

COMMON DENOMINATORS

Some volume problems will give the dimensions in mixed units of measurement. Before arriving at a solution, we must resolve these units to a common denominator. Usually, the chances of error can be reduced by using the largest unit as a common denominator, thus reducing the figures with which we will work to the smallest possible figures.

Problem: How many cubic yards are in a platform measuring 15 feet long, 4 yards wide, and 9 inches deep?

The largest unit given is the *yard*.

$$15' = 5 \text{ yards} \qquad = \text{(Length)}$$
$$4 \text{ yards} \qquad = \text{(Width)}$$
$$\frac{36'' \text{ (1 yard)}}{9'' \text{ depth}} = .25 \text{ yd.} = \text{(Depth or Height)}$$
$$V = 5 \times 4 \times .25$$
$$V = 5 \text{ cu. yards.}$$

CIRCLE FORMULAE

The formulae, which we have learned, can be simplified by the use of "circle" formulae. To understand these formulae, we must remember that in algebra, when numbers are separated by a horizontal line, we must divide upward (divide the numerator by the denominator); and when numbers appear on the same line, we multiply these numbers.

In the circle formula, the basic formula for determination of percentage appears as follows:

To apply this formula, we cover the unknown factor, and do what the remaining factors tell us to do.

Example: Percentage unknown: cover P. The formula tells us to multiply R × B to find P.

Rate unknown: cover R. The formula tells us to divide P by B to find R.

Base unknown cover B. The formula tells us to divide P by R to find B.

These same rules can be applied to any of the following formulae:

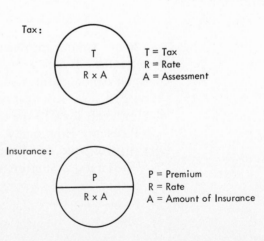

Tax:

T = Tax
R = Rate
A = Assessment

Insurance:

P = Premium
R = Rate
A = Amount of Insurance

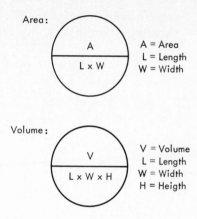

Area:

A

L x W

A = Area
L = Length
W = Width

Volume:

V

L x W x H

V = Volume
L = Length
W = Width
H = Heigth

Other formulae, such as those for profit or loss, depreciation, capitalization, etc., can also be set up in this manner.

Ratios and Proportion

Some examination problems involve the use of ratios and proportions. For example, a problem may appear as follows:

> If 30 air conditioners pump 9000 gallons of water in 6 hours, how many air conditioners would it take to pump 6000 gallons in 3 hours?

If you already understand the algebraic method of solving this problem, it is simple. However, if you do not understand this method, it can easily be solved by logic and simple arithmetic. Let's look at it this way:

Step 1: $\dfrac{9000 \text{ gallons}}{6 \text{ hrs.}}$ = 1500 gallons per hr. by 30 A/C

Step 2: $\dfrac{1500 \text{ gallons per hr.}}{30 \text{ hrs.}}$ = 50 gallons per hr. per A/C

Step 3: $\dfrac{6000 \text{ gallons}}{3 \text{ hrs.}}$ = 2000 gallons per hr. by ? A/C

Step 4: $\dfrac{2000 \text{ gallons}}{50 \text{ gallons per hr. per A/C}}$ = 40 A/C

Any problem involving ratio or proportion can be solved in this manner.

SPECIAL EXAMINATION PROBLEMS

Some problems which are used on license examinations do not fall into any of the categories mentioned and do not lend themselves easily to classification. One such problem which is frequently seen may be stated something like this:

> Brown is going to fence an enclosed area of land which measures 80 feet by 120 feet. The fence will be in 8 foot sections. How many fence posts will be required?

$$\text{Solution: } \begin{array}{l} \text{2 sides @ 80 feet } = 160 \text{ feet} \\ \text{2 sides @ 120 feet} = \underline{240 \text{ feet}} \\ \phantom{\text{2 sides @ 120 feet} = } 400 \text{ feet} \end{array}$$

$$400' \div 8' = 50 \text{ sections, also 50 posts}$$

A similar problem, but with a different solution, might appear as follows:

> The property line between Brown's farm and that of his neighbor is 400 feet long. How many fence posts would be required to fence along this line in 8 foot sections?

$$400' \div 8' = 50 \text{ sections, } \textit{plus one extra post}$$

The rules to be applied here are:

    a. If the area to be fenced is an enclosure, the number of fence posts will be equal to the number of sections in the fence.

    b. If the area to be fenced is not enclosed, the number of fence posts will be equal to the number of sections in the fence, *plus one post*.

If this is not readily apparent, draw a diagram of the two problems above, and it will become clear.

Problems on Area and Volume will be found in the Question Section, beginning on Page 243.

Supplemental arithmetic problems will be found in the Question Section, beginning on Page 244.

WORDS TO WATCH

Acre

Assessed Valuation

Assessment

Chain

Front Foot

Mill

PART IV

SUPPLEMENT

Chapter 16

Glossary of
Real Estate Terms

A.L.T.A. TITLE POLICY: A type of title insurance policy issued by title insurance companies which expands the risks normally insured against under the standard type policy to include unrecorded mechanic's liens, unrecorded physical easements, facts a physical survey would show, water and mineral rights, and rights of parties in possession, such as tenants and buyers under unrecorded instruments.

ABSTRACT OF TITLE: A condensed history of the title, consisting of a summary of the various links in the chain of title, together with a statement of all liens, judgments, or taxes, or encumbrances affecting a particular property.

ACCELERATION CLAUSE: A clause in a contract by which the time for payment of a debt is advanced, usually making the obligation immediately due and payable, because of the breach of some condition, such as failure to pay an installment when due.

ACCEPTANCE: The indication or manifestation by the offeree that he is willing to be bound by the terms of the offer.

ACCRETION: Addition to one's real estate by the gradual deposition of soil through the operation of natural causes.

ACCRUED DEPRECIATION: The difference between the cost of replacement new, as of the date of the appraisal, and the present appraised value.

ACKNOWLEDGMENT: A declaration made by a person to a notary public, or other public official authorized to take acknowledgments, that the instrument was executed by him and that it is his free and voluntary act.

ACRE: A measure of land equaling 160 square rods, or 4,840 square yards, or 43,560 square feet, or a tract about 208.71 feet square.

ADMINISTRATOR: A person appointed by a Court to manage and settle the estate of a deceased person who has left no will.

ADMINISTRATRIX: A woman appointed to perform the duties of an administrator.

AD VALOREM: Designates an assessment of taxes against property. Literally, according to value.

ADVERSE POSSESSION: The open and notorious possession and occupancy under an evident claim or right, in denial or opposition to the title of another claimant.

AFFIDAVIT: A statement or declaration reduced to writing, and sworn to or affirmed before some officer who has authority to administer an oath or affirmation.

AFFIRMATION: A solemn declaration in the nature of an oath made by persons who have religious scruples against taking oaths.

AGENCY: A contract by which one person with greater or less discretionary power undertakes to represent another in certain business relations.

AGENT: One who represents another from whom he has derived authority.

AGREEMENT OF SALE: A written agreement; whereby the purchaser agrees to buy certain real estate and the seller agrees to sell upon terms and conditions set forth therein.

AIR RIGHTS: The rights vested by a grant (fee simple, lease agreement, or other conveyance) of an estate in real property to build upon, occupy, or use, in the manner and degree permitted, all or any portion of space above the ground or any other stated elevation within vertical planes, the basis of which corresponds with the boundaries of the real estate described in the grant.

ALIENATION: The transferring of property to another; the transfer of property and possession of lands, or other things, from one person to another.

ALLUVION (ALLUVIUM): Soil deposited by accretion. Increase of earth on a shore or bank of a river.

AMENITIES: In real estate amenities refer to such circumstances in regard to location, outlook, or access to a park, lake, highway, view, or the like which enhance the pleasantness or desirability of real estate and which contribute to the pleasure and enjoyment of the occupants.

AMORTIZATION: The liquidation or gradual retirement of a financial obligation by periodic installments.

ANNUITY: A sum of money or its equivalent that constitutes one of a series of periodic payments. Any advantage that may be interpreted in terms of money and answers the requirements of regularity may be considered as an "annuity."

APPRAISAL: An estimate and opinion of value; a conclusion resulting from the analysis of facts.

APPRAISER: One qualified by education, training, and experience who is hired to estimate the value of real and personal property based on experience, judgment, facts, and use of formal appraisal processes.

APPRECIATION: An increased conversion value of property or mediums of exchange due to economic or related causes which may prove to be either temporary or permanent.

APPURTENANCE: A right, privilege, or improvement belonging to and passing with a principal property.

ASSESSED VALUATION: Assessment of real estate by a unit of government (assessor) for taxation purposes.

ASSESSMENT: An official valuation of taxable property.

ASSIGNMENT: A transfer to another of rights, interest, or claim in or to real or personal property.

ASSIGNOR: The party who assigns or transfers an interest in property to another.

ASSIGNEE: One to whom an assignment is made.

ASSUMPTION AGREEMENT: An undertaking of a debt or obligation primarily resting upon another person.

ASSUMPTION OF MORTGAGE: The taking of title to property by a grantee, wherein he assumes liability for payment of an existing note secured by a mortgage or deed of trust against the property. He becomes a co-guarantor for the payment of said mortgage or deed of trust along with the original maker of the note who is not released from his responsibility.

ATTACHMENT OF PROPERTY: A writ issued at the institution or during the progress of an action commanding the Sheriff or other proper officer to attach the property, right, credit, or effects of the Defendant to satisfy the demands of the Plaintiff.

ATTEST: To affirm to be true or genuine; an official act establishing authenticity.

ATTORNEY-AT-LAW: A lawyer; an officer in a court of justice who is employed by a party in a cause to manage the same for him.

ATTORNEY-IN-FACT: One who is authorized to perform certain acts for another under a power of attorney; power of attorney may be general or limited to a specific act or acts.

AVULSION: Removal of land from one owner to another when a stream suddenly changes its channel.

BALLOON PAYMENT: When the final installment payment on a note is greater than the preceding installment payments and it pays the note in full, such final installment is termed a balloon payment.

BARGAIN AND SALE DEED: Any deed that recites a consideration and purports to convey the real estate; a bargain and sale deed with a covenant against the grantor's acts is one in which the grantor warrants that he himself has done nothing to harm or cloud the title.

BASE AND MERIDIAN: Imaginary lines used by surveyors to find and describe the location of private or public lands.

BENEFICIARY: (1) One entitled to the benefit of a trust; (2) One who receives profit from an estate, the title to which is vested in a trustee; (3) The lender on the security of a note and deed of trust.

BEQUEATH: To give or hand down, by will; to leave by will.

BEQUEST: That which is given by the terms of a will.

BILL OF SALE: A written instrument transferring right, title, and interest in personal property to another.

BINDER: An agreement to cover a down payment for the purchase of real estate as evidence of good faith on the part of the purchaser.

BLANKET MORTGAGE: A single mortgage which covers more than one piece of real estate.

BONA FIDE: In good faith, without fraud.

BOND: Any obligation under seal. A real estate bond is a written obligation, usually issued on security of a mortgage or a trust deed.

BREACH: The violation of an obligation, engagement, or duty.

BROKER: One employed by another, for a fee, to carry on any of the activities listed in the license law definition of the word.

BUILDING CODE: Regulations established by local governments setting forth the structural requirements for building.

BUILDING LINE: A line fixed at a certain distance from the front and/or sides of a lot, beyond which no building can project.

BUNDLE OF RIGHTS: Beneficial interests or rights.

CAPITALIZATION: In appraising, determining value of property by considering net income and percentage of reasonable return on the investment.

CAPITALIZATION RATE: In real estate, capitalization rate can be defined as the relationship or ratio between the net income from an investment and the value of an investment. This ratio is usually expressed as a percentage.

CERTIFICATE OF NO DEFENSE: An instrument, executed by the mortgagor, upon the sale of the mortgage, to the assignee, as to the validity of the full mortgage debt.

CAVEAT EMPTOR: Let the buyer beware. The buyer must examine the goods or property and buy at his own risk.

CHAIN: Unit of land measurement—66 feet.

CHAIN OF TITLE: A history of conveyances and encumbrances affecting the title from the time the original patent was granted or as far back as records are available.

CHATTEL MORTGAGE: A personal property mortgage.

CHATTEL REAL: An estate related to real estate, such as a lease on real property.

CHATTELS: Are things movable which may be carried about by the owner; such as animals, household furnishings, money, jewels, etc., and everything else that can be put into motion and transferred from one place to another.

CLEAR TITLE: A title free and clear of all encumbrances.

CLOSING STATEMENT: An accounting of funds in a real estate sale made by a broker to the seller and buyer, respectively.

CLOUD ON THE TITLE: An outstanding claim or encumbrance, which, if valid, would affect or impair the owner's title; a deed of trust or judgment.

CODE: A systematic body of law which is given statutory force. Generally, the term is used to describe the entire body of laws which have been established by the legislature.

CODICIL: In law, an addition to a will, to change or explain some provision or to add new ones. An appendix or supplement.

COLLATERAL: The property subject to the security interest.

COLLUSION: An agreement between two or more persons to defraud another of his rights by the forms of law or to obtain an object forbidden by law.

COLOR OF TITLE: That which appears to be good title but which is not title in fact.

COMMINGLE: To combine, join, or mix.

COMMISSION: An agent's compensation for performing the duties of his agency; in real estate practice, a percentage of the selling price of property, or percentage of rentals.

COMMITMENT: A pledge or a promise or firm agreement.

COMMON LAW: The principles and rules of law, originating from usage and custom, sanctioned by the courts and which are not dependent upon legislative expression or enactment for their authority; also that body of law, based on custom and usage, developed and formulated by the old English courts.

COMMUNITY PROPERTY: Property accumulated through joint efforts of husband and wife.

COMPETENT: Legally qualified.

COMPOUND INTEREST: Interest paid both on the original principal and on interest accrued from the time it fell due.

CONDEMNATION: In real property law, the process by which property of a private owner is taken for public use, with just compensation to the owner, under the right of eminent domain.

CONDITIONAL COMMITMENT: A commitment of a definite loan amount for some future unknown purchaser of satisfactory credit standing.

CONDITIONAL SALE CONTRACT: A contract whereby the owner retains title to the property until the purchaser has met all of the terms and conditions of contract.

CONDOMINIUM: A system of individual fee ownership of units in a multi-family structure, combined with joint ownership of common areas of the structure and the land. (Sometimes referred to as a vertical subdivision.)

CONFESSION OF JUDGMENT: An entry of judgment upon the debtor's voluntary admission or confession.

CONSIDERATION: One of the essential elements of a contract; a promise or an act of legal value bargained for and received in return for a promise.

CONSTRUCTIVE NOTICE: Often called "legal notice," the conclusive presumption that all persons have knowledge of the contents of a recorded instrument.

CONSTRUCTIVE EVICTION: Breach of a covenant of warranty or quiet enjoyment; for example, the inability of a purchaser or lessee to obtain possession by reason of a paramount outstanding title.

CONTIGUOUS: Adjoining.

CONVENTIONAL MORTGAGE: A mortgage securing a loan made by private investors without governmental participation, that is, which is not F.H.A. insured or G.I. guaranteed.

CONTRACT: An agreement, either written or oral, to do or not to do certain things.

CONTRACT OF SALE: A written agreement whereby the purchaser agrees to buy certain real estate and the seller agrees to sell upon terms and conditions set forth therein.

CONVEYANCE: An instrument in writing by which some estate, interest, or title in real estate is transferred from one person to another, such as a deed or mortgage.

CORPORATION: A group of persons established and treated by law as an individual or unit with rights and liabilities, or both, distinct from those of the persons composing it.

COST OF REPRODUCTION: The normal cost of exact duplication of a property with the same or closely similar materials as of a certain date or period.

COURSES AND DISTANCES: A method of describing or locating real property; this description gives a starting point and the direction and lengths of lines to be run; practically indistinguishable from a metes and bounds description.

COVENANT: Agreements written into deeds and other instruments promising performance or nonperformance of certain acts or stipulating certain uses or nonuses of the property.

CURTESY: An estate for life which a husband takes at the death of his wife in one-third of those lands of which she was seized during coverture.

CURTILAGE: Area of land occupied by a building and its yard and outbuildings, actually enclosed or considered enclosed.

DEBENTURE: Bonds issued without security.

DECEDENT: A deceased person.

DEDICATION: An appropriation of land by an owner to some public use together with acceptance for such use by or on behalf of the public.

DECREE: The judgment of a court of equity.

DEED: A legal instrument in writing, duly executed and delivered, whereby the owner of real property (grantor) conveys to another (grantee) some right, title, or interest in or to real estate.

DEED RESTRICTION: A provision in a deed controlling or limiting the use of the land.

DEFAULT: The nonperformance of a duty.

DEFEASANCE: An instrument which nullifies the effect of some other deed or of an estate.

DEFEASANCE CLAUSE: The clause in a mortgage that gives the mortgagor the right to redeem his property upon the payment of his obligations to the mortgagee.

DEFEASIBLE FEE: Sometimes called a base fee or qualified fee; a fee simple absolute interest in land that is capable of being defeated or terminated upon the happening of a specified event.

DEFENDANT: The party sued or called to answer in any suit, action, or proceeding.

DEFERRED MAINTENANCE: Existing but unfulfilled requirements for repairs and rehabilitation.

DEFERRED PAYMENTS: Money payments to be made at some future date.

DEFICIENCY JUDGMENT: The difference between the indebtedness sued upon and the sale price of the mortgaged property at foreclosure where the sale price is less than the indebtedness.

DEMISE: The conveyance of an estate, chiefly by lease.

DETERIORATION: Impairment of condition. One of the causes of depreciation and reflecting the loss in value brought about by wear and tear, disintegration, use in service, and the action of the elements.

DEVISE: A gift of real estate by will or last testament.

DEVISEE: One who receives a bequest made by will.

DEVISOR: One who bequeaths by will.

DIRECT REDUCTION MORTGAGE: An amortized mortgage; one which is repaid by a series of installment payments, with each payment credited first to interest, and then to principal.

DISPOSSESS: To deprive a person of possession and/or use of real property.

DOMICILE: The place where a man has his true, fixed, and permanent home, and principal establishment, and to which whenever he is absent he has the intention of returning.

DOWER: A common law estate in land given to the wife in her husband's real property upon his death, consisting of a life estate in one-third of all the real estate owned by the husband during the marriage.

DURESS: Forcing action or inaction against a person's will.

EARNEST MONEY: Down payment made by a purchaser of real estate as evidence of good faith.

EASEMENT: A privilege or right of use or enjoyment which one person may have in the lands of another, i.e., a right of way.

ECONOMIC LIFE: The period over which a property will yield a return on the investment, over and above the economic or ground rent due to land.

ECONOMIC OBSOLESCENCE: Impairment of desirability or useful life arising from economic forces, such as changes in optimum land use, legislative enactments which restrict or impair property rights, and changes in supply-demand relationships.

EJECTMENT: A form of action to regain possession of real property, with damages for the unlawful retention.

EMBLEMENTS: Things which grow on the land and require annual planting and cultivation.

EMINENT DOMAIN: The right of a government to take private property for public use upon the payment of just compensation. The legal proceeding by which the government exercises this right is called "condemnation proceedings."

ENCROACHMENT: Trespass, the building of a structure or any improvements partly or wholly intruding upon the property of another.

ENCUMBRANCE: Anything which affects or limits the fee simple title to property, such as mortgages, easements, or restrictions of any kind. Liens are special encumbrances that make the property security for the payment of a debt or obligation, such as mortgages and taxes.

EQUITY: In real estate, the interest or value of the real estate over and above the amount of the indebtedness thereon.

EQUITY OF REDEMPTION: Right of original owner to reclaim property sold through foreclosure proceedings, by payment of debt, interest, and cost.

ESCALATOR CLAUSE: A clause in a contract providing for the upward or downward adjustment of certain items to cover specified contingencies.

ESCHEAT: The reverting of property to the state by reason of failure of persons legally entitled to hold or when heirs capable of inheriting are lacking.

ESCROW: In real estate, it is the state or condition of a deed which is conditionally held by a third party, called the escrow agent, pending the performance or fulfillment of some act or condition.

ESCROW AGREEMENT: A written agreement between two or more parties whereby the grantor, promisor, or obligor delivers certain instruments or property into the hands of a third party, the escrow agent, to be held by said third party until the happening of a contingency or performance of a condition, and then to be delivered to the grantee, promisee, or obligee.

ESTATE: In real estate, it refers to the degree, quantity, nature, and extent of interest which a person has in real property; such as a fee simple absolute estate, an estate for years.

ESTATE AT SUFFERANCE: An estate in land arising when the tenant wrongfully holds over after the expiration of his term; the landlord has the choice of evicting the tenant as a trespasser or accepting such tenant for a similar term and under the conditions of the tenant's previous holding; often called a tenancy at sufferance.

ESTATE FOR LIFE: A freehold estate, not of inheritance, but which is held by the tenant for his own life or the life or lives of one or more other persons, or for an indefinite period that may extend for the life or lives of persons in being, and beyond the period of life.

ESTATE FOR YEARS: An interest in land for a fixed period of time, whether for a day or ninety-nine years; often called a tenancy for years.

ESTATE FROM PERIOD TO PERIOD: An interest in land where there is no definite termination date but the rental period is fixed at a certain sum per week, month, or year; often called a periodic tenancy.

ESTATE IN REVERSION: The residue of an estate left in the grantor to commence in possession after the termination of some particular estate.

ESTOPPEL: A doctrine which bars one from asserting rights that are inconsistent with a previous position or representation.

ESTOVERS: Wood which a tenant is allowed to take from the landlord's premises for the necessary fuel, implements, repairs, etc., of himself and his (resident) servants.

ET AL.:   Abbreviation for et alius, meaning "and another."

ETHICS: That branch of moral science which treats of the duties which a member of a profession or craft owes to the public, to his client, and to other members of the profession.

ET UX: Abbreviation for et uxor, meaning "and wife."

EVICTION: Dispossession by process of law; the act of depriving a person of the possession of lands in pursuance of the judgment of a court.

EXCLUSIVE AGENCY: The appointment of one real estate broker as the sole agent for the sale of a property for a designated period of time. Owner may sell without obligation to pay the agent a commission.

EXCLUSIVE AUTHORIZATION TO SELL LISTING: A written agreement between owner and agent giving agent the right to collect a commission if the property is sold by anyone during the term of his agreement.

EXECUTOR: One to whom another man commits by his last will the execution of that will and testament.

EXECUTRIX: A woman appointed to perform the duties of an executor.

FEE: When applied to property, an inheritable estate in land.

FEE SIMPLE: The largest possible estate which a man can have in real estate.

FEE SIMPLE ABSOLUTE: Often called a fee or fee simple; the most comprehensive ownership of real property known to the law; the largest bundle of ownership rights possible in real estate.

FEE TAIL: An estate or interest in land which cannot be conveyed but which must descend to the heirs of the holder; abolished in most states.

FIDUCIARY: A person in a position of trust and confidence, as principal and broker; broker as fiduciary owes certain loyalty which cannot be breached under rules of agency.

FIRST MORTGAGE: A mortgage which has priority as a lien over all other mortgages.

FIXTURE: A chattel affixed or attached to a building and used in connection with it, movable or immovable.

FORECLOSURE: Procedure whereby property pledged as security for a debt is sold to pay the debt in event of default in payments or terms.

FORESHORE: Land between high-water mark and low-water mark.

FORFEITURE: Loss of money or anything of value due to failure to perform.

FRAUD: The intentional and successful employment of any cunning, deception, collusion, or artifice, used to circumvent, cheat, or deceive another person, whereby that person acts upon it to the loss of his property and to his legal injury.

FREEHOLD: An estate in fee simple or for life.

FRONT FOOT: Property measurement for sale or valuation purposes; the property measures by the front foot on its street line—each front foot extending the depth of the lot.

FUNCTIONAL OBSOLESCENCE: Impairment of functional capacity or efficiency.

GENERAL WARRANTY: A covenant in the deed whereby the grantor agrees to protect the grantee against the world.

GIFT DEED: A deed for which the consideration is love and affection and where there is no material consideration.

GRADUATED LEASE: Lease that provides for a varying rental rate, often based upon future determination; sometimes rent is based upon result of periodical appraisals; used largely in long-term leases.

GRANT: A generic term applicable to all transfers of real property; a technical term made use of in deeds of conveyance of lands to import a transfer.

GRANTEE: A person to whom real estate is conveyed; the buyer of real estate.

GRANTOR: A person who conveys real estate by deed; the seller of real estate.

GROSS INCOME: Total income from property before any expenses are deducted.

GROSS LEASE: A lease of property whereby lessor is to meet all property charges regularly incurred through ownership.

GROUND LEASE: An agreement to use land for a stated period, which may be secured by improvements which the tenant will provide.

HABENDUM CLAUSE: The "To Have and To Hold" clause which defines or limits the quantity of the estate granted in the premises of the deed.

HEREDITAMENTS: Every sort of inheritable property, such as real, personal, corporeal, and incorporeal.

HIGHEST AND BEST USE: That use of, or program of utilization of, a site which will produce the maximum net land returns over the total period which comprises the future. The optimum use for a site.

HOLDOVER TENANT: A tenant who remains in possession of leased property after the expiration date of the lease term.

HOMESTEAD: The place of a home or house; that part of a man's land or property which is about and contiguous to his dwelling house; the land or town, or city lot upon which the family residence is situated.

HOMESTEAD EXEMPTION: Often called "homestead" or "homestead right"; a right given by statute to a householder or head of a family to designate real estate as his homestead and said homestead is exempt, up to a stated amount, from execution by his creditors.

HYPOTHECATE: To give a thing as security without the necessity of giving up possession of it.

INCREMENT: An increase. Most frequently used to refer to the increase of value of land that accompanies population growth and increasing wealth in the community. The term "unearned increment" is used in this connection, since values are supposed to have increased without effort on the part of the owner.

INDENTURE: A formal written instrument made between two or more persons in different interests; name comes from practice of indenting or cutting the deed on the top or side in a waving line.

INDORSEMENT: The act of signing one's name on the back of a check or a note, with or without further qualification.

INJUNCTION: A writ or order of the court to restrain one or more parties to a suit or proceeding from doing an inequitable or unjust act in regard to the rights of some other party in the suit or proceeding.

INSTALLMENT CONTRACT: Purchase of real estate upon an installment basis; upon default, payments are forfeited.

INSTALLMENT LAND CONTRACT: Often called a land contract or an installment contract; an agreement for the purchase of real estate upon an installment basis, the deed to the property is not given to the purchaser until either all or a certain portion of the purchase price is paid.

INSTALLMENT NOTE: A note which provides that payments of a certain sum be paid on the dates specified in the instrument.

INSTRUMENT: A written legal document created to effect the rights of the parties.

INTEREST RATE: The percentage of a sum of money charged for its use.

INTESTATE: A person who dies having made no will, or one defective in form, in which case, his estate descends to his heirs at law or next of kin.

INVOLUNTARY LIEN: A lien imposed against property without consent of an owner; example: taxes, special assessments, and federal income tax.

IRREVOCABLE: Incapable of being recalled or revoked; unchangeable.

JOINT NOTE: A note signed by two or more persons who have equal liability for payment.

JOINT TENANCY: A type of co-ownership of real property, held by two or more persons, with all co-owners being equally entitled to the use, enjoyment, control, and possession of the land and with the right of survivorship.

JUDGMENT: The final determination of the rights of the parties by a court in an action before it.

JUDGMENT CREDITOR: One who has obtained a judgment against his debtor under which he can enforce execution.

JUDGMENT DEBTOR: One against whom a judgment has been obtained.

JUNIOR LIEN: A lien placed on property after previous lien has been made and recorded.

JUNIOR MORTGAGE: A mortgage second in lien to a previous mortgage.

JURISDICTION: The authority by which judicial officers take cognizance of and decide causes.

LAND: Real property; the surface of the earth and that which is affixed to it permanently, that which is below it, and the space above it; synonymous with "real property," "realty," and "real estate." Sometimes used to mean only the unimproved surface of the earth.

LAND CONTRACT: A contract for the purchase of real estate upon an installment basis; upon payment of last installment deed is delivered to purchaser.

LANDLORD: One who rents property to others.

LEASE: A contract between owner and tenant, setting forth conditions upon which tenant may occupy and use the property, and the term of the occupancy.

LEASEHOLD: The interest or estate which a lessee has in real estate by virtue of his lease.

LEGAL DESCRIPTION: A statement containing a designation by which land is identified according to a system set up by law or approved by law.

LESSEE: The person who leases property from another.

LESSOR: The party who leases property to a tenant or lessee. He is often referred to as the landlord.

LIABILITY: Responsibility; the state of one who is bound in law and justice to do something which may be enforced by action.

LICENSE: A privilege or right granted to an individual by the State to operate as a real estate broker or salesman. An authority to go upon or use another person's land or property without possessing any estate therein.

LIEN: A hold or claim which one person has upon the property of another as a security for some debt or charge.

LIFE ESTATE: An estate or interest in real property which is held for the duration of the life of some certain person.

LIMITED PARTNERSHIP: A partnership with some partners whose contribution and liability are limited.

LIS PENDENS: A public notice, filed against specific lands, that an action at law is pending that may affect the title to the land.

LISTING: A record of property for sale by a broker who has been authorized by the owner to sell. Also used to denote the property so listed.

LITIGATION: A contest, authorized by law, in a court of justice, for the purpose of enforcing a right.

M.A.I.:   Designates a person who is a member of the American Institute of Appraisers of the National Association of Realtors.

MARKET PRICE: The price paid regardless of pressures, motives, or intelligence.

MARKET VALUE: The price at which a willing seller would sell and a willing buyer would buy, neither being under abnormal pressure.

MARKETABLE OR MERCHANTABLE TITLE: A title which is free from reasonable doubt of defect which can be readily sold or mortgaged to a reasonably prudent purchaser or mortgagee; a title free from material defects or grave doubts and reasonably free from possible litigation.

MECHANIC'S LIEN: A lien created by statute which exists against real property in favor of persons who have performed work or furnished materials for the improvement of the real estate.

MEETING OF MINDS: A mutual intention of two persons to enter into a contract affecting their legal status based on agreed-upon terms.

MERIDIANS: Imaginary north-south lines that intersect base lines to form a starting point for the measurement of land.

METES AND BOUNDS: A method of describing or locating real property; metes are measures of length and bounds are boundaries; this description starts with a well-marked point of beginning and follows the boundaries of the land until it returns once more to the point of beginning.

MILL: One-tenth of one cent; the measure used to state the property tax rate. That is, a tax rate of one mill on the dollar is the same as a rate of one-tenth of one percent of the assessed value of the property.

MINOR: A person who has not reached the legal age of majority.

MONUMENT: A fixed object and point established by surveyors to establish land locations.

MORTGAGE: An instrument recognized by law by which property is hypothecated to secure the payment of a debt or obligation; procedure for foreclosure in event of default is established by statute.

MORTGAGEE: One to whom a mortgage is made; the lender.

MORTGAGOR: One who makes a mortgage; the borrower.

MULTIPLE LISTING: The arrangement among real estate boards or exchange members whereby each broker brings his listings to the attention of the other members so that if a sale results, the commission is divided between the broker bringing the listing and the broker making the sale, with a small percentage going to the board or exchange.

MUTUAL ASSENT: One of the essential elements of a contract, often called Meeting of the Minds; the agreement of the parties to the contract, mutually consenting to be bound by the exact terms thereof.

NATIONAL ASSOCIATION OF REALTORS: A national trade association of real estate brokers and salesmen. The copyrighted term Realtor designates membership in this organization.

NEGOTIABLE: Capable of being negotiated; assignable or transferable in the ordinary course of business.

NEGOTIABLE INSTRUMENT: A written instrument signed by a maker or drawer containing an unconditional promise to pay a certain sum of money, which can be passed freely from one person to another.

NET INCOME: In general, synonymous with net earnings, but considered a broader and better term; the balance remaining, after deducting from the gross income all operating expense, maintenance, taxes, and losses pertaining to operating properties excepting interest or other financial charges on borrowed or other capital.

NET LEASE: A lease where, in addition to the rental stipulated, the lessee assumes payment of all property charges such as taxes, insurance, and maintenance.

NET LISTING: A price below which the owner will not sell the property or at which price the broker will not receive a commission; the broker receives the excess over and above the net listing as his commission.

NOTE: A written instrument acknowledging a debt and promising payment.

NOTICE TO QUIT: A notice to a tenant to vacate rented property.

OBSOLESCENCE: As applied to real estate it is the loss of value due to structural, economic, or social changes—becoming outmoded.

OFFER: A promise by one party to act in a certain manner provided the other party will act in the manner requested.

OFFEREE: One to whom an offer is made.

OFFEROR: One who makes an offer.

OFFSET STATEMENT: Statement by owner of property or owner of lien against property, setting forth the present status of liens against said property.

OPEN-END MORTGAGE: A mortgage containing a clause that permits the mortgagor to borrow additional money after the loan has been reduced without rewriting the mortgage.

OPEN LISTING: An authorization given by a property owner to a real estate agent wherein said agent is given the nonexclusive right to secure a purchaser; open listings may be given to any number of agents without liability to compensate any except the one who first secures a buyer ready, willing, and able to meet the terms of the listing, or secures the acceptance by the seller of a satisfactory offer.

OPTION: A privilege, acquired for a consideration, of demanding within a specified time the carrying out of a transaction upon stipulated terms.

OPTIONEE: One to whom an option has been granted.

OPTIONOR: One who has granted an option to another.

ORAL CONTRACT: A verbal agreement; one which is not reduced to writing.

ORDINANCE: A law enacted by the governing body of the city or county.

PAROL: Oral, as distinguished from written.

PARTITION: A division made of real property among those who own it in undivided shares.

PARTNERSHIP: The relation existing between two or more competent persons who have contracted to join in business and share the profits.

PERSONAL PROPERTY: Property of a temporary or movable nature; all articles, things, and property which are not real estate.

PERSONALTY: A term sometimes used as a collective noun for personal property.

PLAINTIFF: The complaining party in an action or suit.

PLAT BOOK: A public record of various recorded plans in the municipality or county.

PLEDGE: The depositing of personal property by a debtor with a creditor as security for a debt or engagement.

POLICE POWER: The inherent right of a government to enact such legislation as may be deemed necessary to protect and promote the health, safety, and general welfare of the public.

POWER OF ATTORNEY: An instrument authorizing a person to act as the agent or attorney of the person granting it.

PREPAYMENT PENALTY: Penalty for the payment of a mortgage or trust deed note before it actually becomes due.

PRESCRIPTION: The securing of title to property by adverse possession by occupying it for the period determined by law barring action for recovery.

PRIMA FACIE: From Latin and meaning first view. Prima Facie evidence of fact is in law sufficient to establish the fact unless rebutted.

PRINCIPAL: Any person, partnership, association, or corporation who authorizes or employs another, called the agent, to do certain acts on his behalf.

PROCURING CAUSE: That cause originating from series of events that, without break in continuity, results in the prime object of an agent's employment producing a final buyer.

PROMULGATE: To make known by open declaration, as a decree.

PROPERTY: The rights of ownership; the right to use, possess, enjoy, and dispose of a thing in every legal way and to exclude everyone else from interfering with these rights. Property is generally classified into two groups; personal property and real property.

PURCHASE MONEY MORTGAGE: A mortgage given by a grantee to the grantor in part payment of the purchase price of real estate.

QUIET ENJOYMENT: The right of an owner to the use of property without interference of possession.

QUIETING TITLE: The removal of a cloud from a title by proper action in a court of competent jurisdiction.

QUITCLAIM DEED: A deed in which the grantor warrants nothing; it conveys only the grantor's present interest in the real estate, if any.

RANGE: A strip of land six miles wide determined by government survey running in a north-south direction.

REAL ESTATE: Land and hereditaments or rights therein, and whatever is made part of or is attached to it by nature or man.

REAL ESTATE BOARD: An organization whose membership consists primarily of real estate brokers and salesmen.

REAL ESTATE TRUST: A special arrangement under federal and state law whereby investors may pool funds for investments in real estate and mortgages, yet escape corporation taxes.

REALTOR: A copyrighted word used to designate an active member of a real estate board affiliated with the National Association of Realtors.

REALTY: A term sometimes used as a collective noun for real property or estate.

RECTANGULAR SURVEY SYSTEM: Often called the United States Governmental Survey System; a method of describing or locating real property by reference to the governmental survey.

REDEMPTION: The right to redeem property during the foreclosure period; the right of an owner to redeem his property after a sale for taxes. Often referred to as Equity of Redemption.

RELEASE: The giving up or abandoning a claim or right to the person against whom the claim exists or the right is to be exercised or enforced.

REMAINDER: An estate which vests after the termination of the prior estate, such as a life estate.

REMAINDER ESTATE: An estate in property created at the same time and by the same instrument as another estate and limited to arise immediately upon the termination of the other estate.

RELEASE OF LIEN: The discharge of certain property from the lien of a judgment, mortgage, or claim.

RENT: A compensation, either in money, provisions, chattels, or labor, received by the owner of real estate from the occupant thereof.

RESCISSION OF CONTRACTS: The abrogating or annulling of contracts; the revocation or repealing of contract by mutual consent by parties to the contract, or for cause by either party to the contract.

RESERVATION: A right reserved by an owner in the grant (sale or lease) of a property.

RESTRICTION: A limitation upon the use or occupancy of real estate, placed by covenant in deeds or by public legislative action.

RESIDUARY ESTATE: That which remains of a testator's estate after deducting the debts, bequests, and devises.

RESTRICTIVE COVENANT: A clause in a deed limiting the use to which the property may be put.

REVERSION: The residue of an estate left in the grantor to commence in possession after the determination of some particular estate granted out by him. The return of land to the grantor and his heirs after the grant is over.

REVERSIONARY INTEREST: The interest that a person has in lands or other property upon the termination of the preceding estate.

REVOCATION: The recall of a power or authority conferred, or the vacating of an instrument previously made.

RIGHT OF SURVIVORSHIP: Right to acquire the interest of a deceased joint owner; distinguishing feature of a joint tenancy.

RIGHT OF WAY: The term has two significances; as a privilege to pass or cross, it is used to describe that strip of land which railroad companies use for a roadbed; or as dedicated to public use for roadway, walk, or other way.

RIPARIAN OWNER: One who owns lands bounding upon a river or water course.

RIPARIAN RIGHTS: The right of a landowner to water on, under, or adjacent to his land.

SALES CONTRACT: A contract by which buyer and seller agree to terms of a sale.

SALE-LEASEBACK: A situation where the owner of a piece of property wishes to sell the property and retain occupancy by leasing it from the buyer.

SATISFACTION OF MORTGAGE: An instrument for recording and acknowledging payment for an indebtedness secured by a mortgage.

SEAL: An impression made to attest the execution of an instrument.

SECONDARY FINANCING: A loan secured by a second mortgage or trust deed on real property.

SECTION: One of the portions of one square mile each (640 acres), into which the public lands of the United States are divided; one thirty-six part of a township.

SECURITY AGREEMENT: An agreement between the secured party and the debtor that creates the security interest.

SEISIN: The possession of real estate with intent, on the part of the holder, to claim at least a life estate therein.

SEPARATE PROPERTY: Property owned by a husband or wife which is not community property; property acquired by either spouse prior to marriage or by gift or devise after marriage.

SETBACK: The distance from curb or other established line within which no buildings may be erected.

SETBACK ORDINANCE: An ordinance prohibiting the erection of a building or structure between the curb and the setback line.

SEVERALTY OWNERSHIP: Sole ownership. Owned by one person only.

SINKING FUND: Fund set aside from the income from property which, with accrued interest, will eventually pay for replacement of the improvements.

SHERIFF'S DEED: An instrument drawn under order of court to convey title to property sold to satisfy a judgment of law.

SPECIAL WARRANTY DEED: A deed in which the grantor warrants or guarantees the title only against defects arising during his ownership of the property and not against defects existing before the time of his ownership.

SPECIFIC PERFORMANCE: A remedy which the court will grant, in certain cases, compelling the defendant to perform or carry out the terms of a valid, existing agreement or contract.

SQUATTERS' RIGHTS: The rights to occupancy of land created by virtue of long and undisturbed use but without legal title or arrangement; in the nature of right at common law.

STATUTE: A law established by the act of the legislative power. An Act of the Legislature. The written will of the legislature, solemnly expressed according to the forms necessary to constitute it the law.

STATUTE OF FRAUDS: State law which provides that certain contracts must be in writing in order to be enforceable at law.

STRAIGHT LINE DEPRECIATION: Definite sum set aside annually from income to pay cost of replacing improvements without reference to interest it earns.

STRAIGHT MORTGAGE: A mortgage wherein there is no reduction of the principal balance during the term of the mortgage. Payments to interest are usually made on an annual, semi-annual, or quarterly basis; a non-amortized mortgage.

SUBJECT TO MORTGAGE: The taking of title to property by a grantee, wherein he is not responsible to the holder of the promissory note for the payment of any portion of the amount due. In the event of foreclosure the most that he can lose is his equity in the property. The original maker of the note is not released from his responsibility.

SUBDIVISION: A tract of land divided into lots suitable for home building purposes.

SUBLETTING: A leasing by a tenant to another, who holds under the tenant.

SUBORDINATE: To make subject to, or junior to.

SUBORDINATION CLAUSE: A clause in a mortgage or lease stating that rights of the holder shall be secondary or subordinate to a subsequent encumbrance.

SUBPOENA: A process to cause a witness to appear and give testimony.

SUBROGATION: The substitution of another person in place of the creditor, to whose rights he succeeds in relation to the debt. The doctrine is used very often when one person agrees to stand surety for the performance of a contract by another person.

SURETY: One who guarantees the performance of another. The guarantor.

SURRENDER: The cancellation of a lease by mutual consent of lessor and lessee.

SURVEY: The act by which the quantity and boundaries of a piece of land is ascertained; the paper containing a statement of the courses, distance and quantity of land is also called a survey.

TAX DEED: A deed given where property has been purchased at a sale to the public of property for nonpayment of taxes.

TAX SALE: A sale of property, usually at auction, for nonpayment of taxes assessed against it.

TENANT AT SUFFERANCE: One who comes into possession of lands by lawful title and keeps it afterwards without any title at all.

TENANCY AT WILL: A license to use or occupy lands and tenements at the will of the owner.

TENANCY FOR YEARS: A tenancy of a definite duration.

TENANCY IN COMMON: A type of co-ownership of real property; a holding of an estate in land by two or more persons, each being entitled to possession of the property according to his proportionate share; distinct from a joint tenancy in that there is no right of survivorship in a tenancy in common.

TENANT: One who holds or possesses lands or tenements by any kind of title, either in fee, for life, for years, or at will. In a popular sense, he is one who has the temporary use and occupation of lands or tenements which belong to another, the duration and other terms of whose occupations are usually defined by an agreement called a lease, while the parties thereto are placed in the relationship of landlord and tenant.

TENURE IN LAND: The mode or manner by which an estate in lands is held.

TESTATE: The condition of one who leaves a valid will at his death.

TESTATOR: One who leaves a will in force at his death.

TIME IS OF THE ESSENCE: One of the essential requirements to forming of a binding contract; contemplates a punctual performance.

TITLE: The union of all the elements which constitute proof of ownership.

TITLE BY ADVERSE POSSESSION: Acquired by occupation and recognized as against the paper title owner.

TITLE INSURANCE: A policy of insurance which indemnifies the holder for any loss sustained by reason of defects in the title.

TOPOGRAPHY: Nature of the surface of land; topography may be level, rolling, mountainous.

TORRENS LAND TITLES: A state operated land title system based upon registration of titles.

TORT: A wrongful act; wrong, injury; violation of a legal right.

TOWNSHIP: A territorial subdivision, six miles long, six miles wide, and containing thirty-six sections, each one mile square.

TRADE FIXTURES: Articles of personal property annexed to real property but which are necessary to the carrying on of a trade and are removable by the owner.

TRUST DEED OR DEED OF TRUST: A deed conveying land to a trustee as collateral security for the payment of a debt; upon payment of a debt secured thereby the Deed of Trust is released; upon default the trustee has power to sell the land and pay the debt.

TRUSTEE: One who holds property in trust for another to secure the performance of an obligation.

UNDUE INFLUENCE: Taking any fraudulent or unfair advantage of another's weakness of mind, distress, or necessity.

UNEARNED INCREMENT: An increase in value of real estate due to no effort on the part of the owner; often due to increase in population.

UNIFORM COMMERCIAL CODE: Effective January 1, 1965. Establishes a unified and comprehensive scheme for regulation of security transactions in personal property, superseding the existing statutes on chattel mortgages, conditional sales, trust receipts, assignment of accounts receivable, and others in this field.

USURY: On a loan, claiming a rate of interest greater than that permitted by law.

UNITED STATES GOVERNMENTAL SURVEY SYSTEM: Often called the rectangular survey system; a method of describing or locating real property by reference to the governmental survey.

VALID: Having force, or binding force; legally sufficient and authorized by law.

VALUATION: The act or process of estimating value; the amount of estimated value.

VALUE: Ability to command goods, including money, in exchange; the quantity of goods, including money, which should be commanded or received in exchange for the thing valued; utility; desirability. As applied to a property—value may be broadly defined as "the present worth of all the rights to future benefits arising from ownership."

VENDEE: A purchaser; a buyer; the person to whom a thing is rendered or sold.

VENDOR: The seller; one who disposes of a thing for a consideration.

VESTED: Bestowed upon someone; secured by someone, such as title to property.

VOID: That which is unenforceable; having no force or effect.

VOIDABLE: That which is capable of being adjudged void but is not void unless action is taken to make it so.

VOLUNTARY LIEN: Any lien placed on property with consent of, or as a result of, the voluntary act of the owner.

WAIVER: The renunciation, abandonment, or surrender of some claim, right, or privilege.

WARRANTY DEED: One that contains a covenant that the grantor will protect the grantee against any claimant.

WASTE: Willful destruction of any part of the land which would injure or prejudice the landlord's reversionary right.

WILL: A legal declaration of a person's wishes as to the disposition of his property after his death.

ZONING: Act of city or county authorities specifying type of use to which property may be put in specific areas.

ZONING ORDINANCE: The valid execution of the police power of a municipality in controlling and regulating character and use of property.

Chapter 17

Question Section

QUESTIONS ON CONTRACTS

B
1. A written agreement in which a purchaser agrees to buy and a seller agrees to sell is
    I. an agency.
    II. a contract.
A. I only   B. II only   C. Both I and II   D. Neither I nor II

A
2. A woman who has reached the age of legal majority is legally
    I. an adult.
    II. an adulteress.
A. I only   B. II only   C. Both I and II   D. Neither I nor II

B
3. The person to whom an assignment is made is
    I. the assignor.
    II. the assignee.
A. I only   B. II only   C. Both I and II   D. Neither I nor II

B
4. Money paid as evidence of good faith by the vendee under a contract is
    I. the consideration.
    II. earnest money.
A. I only   B. II only   C. Both I and II   D. Neither I nor II

C
5. A valid contract is one which is
    I. legally sufficient and authorized by law.
    II. binding upon all parties.
A. I only   B. II only   C. Both I and II   D. Neither I nor II

B

6. Brown lists his property for sale and receives an offer to purchase from Smith. Brown, in this circumstance, is the
   - I. offeror.
   - II. offeree.

   A. I only   B. II only   C. Both I and II   D. Neither I nor II

B

7. The term "consideration," as applied to contracts, means
   - I. careful thought has been given to the agreement.
   - II. that which is given in exchange for something from the other party.

   A. I only   B. II only   C. Both I and II   D. Neither I nor II

D

8. A voidable contract is one which is
   - I. legally insufficient, not recognized by law.
   - II. not binding upon either party.

   A. I only   B. II only   C. Both I and II   D. Neither I nor II

A

9. The law upon which contracts are based is known as the
   - I. Statute of Frauds.
   - II. Law of Agency.

   A. I only   B. II only   C. Both I and II   D. Neither I nor II

B

10. When the consideration in a contract is a promise given in exchange for a promise, the contract is a
    - I. binary contract.
    - II. bilateral contract.

    A. I only   B. II only   C. Both I and II   D. Neither I nor II

A

11. Contracts entered into with an adult by a minor are usually
    - I. voidable by the minor.
    - II. voidable by either party.

    A. I only   B. II only   C. Both I and II   D. Neither I nor II

D

12. The Statute of Frauds requires that
    - I. all contracts for the sale of real estate be in writing.
    - II. all contracts for the leasing of real estate be in writing.

    A. I only   B. II only   C. Both I and II   D. Neither I nor II

C

13. A contract of sale cannot be valid and enforceable unless
    - I. there is an offer and acceptance.
    - II. the object of the contract is legal.

    A. I only   B. II only   C. Both I and II   D. Neither I nor II

B

14. A contract based on fraud is
    - I. void on its face.
    - II. voidable by the party upon whom the fraud was committed.

    A. I only   B. II only   C. Both I and II   D. Neither I nor II

B

15. The act of threatening physical injury to force someone to sign a contract is
    - I. undue influence.
    - II. duress.

    A. I only   B. II only   C. Both I and II   D. Neither I nor II

B

16. An executory contract is one which is
  I. entered into by the executor of an estate.
  II. one for the performance of an act in the future.
  A. I only   B. II only   C. Both I and II   D. Neither I nor II

C

17. Contracts for the sale of real estate are
  I. executory in nature.
  II. contracts for the performance of a future act.
  A. I only   B. II only   C. Both I and II   D. Neither I nor II

C

18. Should a seller renege on a contract of sale, and the purchaser stood ready, willing, and able to perform according to the terms of the contract, the purchaser
  I. may sue for specific performance.
  II. may rescind the contract.
  A. I only   B. II only   C. Both I and II   D. Neither I nor II

A

19. Should a property under contract for sale be damaged by fire after the contract was completed
  I. the loss falls upon the purchaser.
  II. the loss falls upon the seller.
  A. I only   B. II only   C. Both I and II   D. Neither I nor II

C

20. Which of the following are essential to a contract?
  I. Legal object
  II. Offer and acceptance
  A. I only   B. II only   C. Both I and II   D. Neither I nor II

QUESTIONS ON AGENCY AND LISTINGS

C

1. The employment contract between an agent and a principal creates
  I. an agency.
  II. a fiduciary relationship.
  A. I only   B. II only   C. Both I and II   D. Neither I nor II

D

2. Under an exclusive authorization to sell listing,
  I. the seller may sell of his own efforts without obligation for a commission.
  II. the broker receives a commission regardless of whether the property is sold.
  A. I only   B. II only   C. Both I and II   D. Neither I nor II

C

3. A real estate broker is
  I. a fiduciary to the owner of property which he lists.
  II. appointed by the owner to act for and in his stead.
  A. I only   B. II only   C. Both I and II   D. Neither I nor II

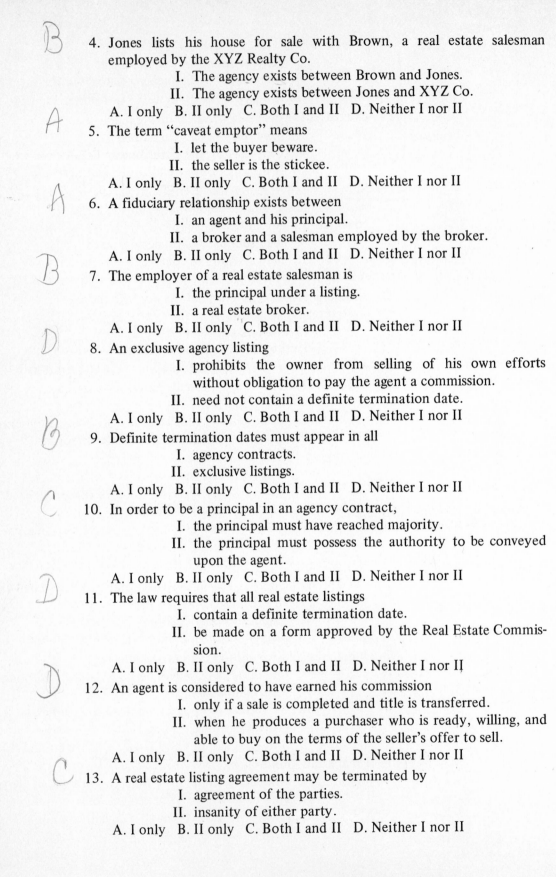

B 4. Jones lists his house for sale with Brown, a real estate salesman employed by the XYZ Realty Co.
       I. The agency exists between Brown and Jones.
      II. The agency exists between Jones and XYZ Co.
A. I only B. II only C. Both I and II D. Neither I nor II

A 5. The term "caveat emptor" means
       I. let the buyer beware.
      II. the seller is the stickee.
A. I only B. II only C. Both I and II D. Neither I nor II

A 6. A fiduciary relationship exists between
       I. an agent and his principal.
      II. a broker and a salesman employed by the broker.
A. I only B. II only C. Both I and II D. Neither I nor II

B 7. The employer of a real estate salesman is
       I. the principal under a listing.
      II. a real estate broker.
A. I only B. II only C. Both I and II D. Neither I nor II

D 8. An exclusive agency listing
       I. prohibits the owner from selling of his own efforts without obligation to pay the agent a commission.
      II. need not contain a definite termination date.
A. I only B. II only C. Both I and II D. Neither I nor II

B 9. Definite termination dates must appear in all
       I. agency contracts.
      II. exclusive listings.
A. I only B. II only C. Both I and II D. Neither I nor II

C 10. In order to be a principal in an agency contract,
       I. the principal must have reached majority.
      II. the principal must possess the authority to be conveyed upon the agent.
A. I only B. II only C. Both I and II D. Neither I nor II

D 11. The law requires that all real estate listings
       I. contain a definite termination date.
      II. be made on a form approved by the Real Estate Commission.
A. I only B. II only C. Both I and II D. Neither I nor II

D 12. An agent is considered to have earned his commission
       I. only if a sale is completed and title is transferred.
      II. when he produces a purchaser who is ready, willing, and able to buy on the terms of the seller's offer to sell.
A. I only B. II only C. Both I and II D. Neither I nor II

C 13. A real estate listing agreement may be terminated by
       I. agreement of the parties.
      II. insanity of either party.
A. I only B. II only C. Both I and II D. Neither I nor II

C

14. A listing agreement may be terminated by law if
    I. the subject property is destroyed.
    II. the property is sold at mortgage foreclosure.
    A. I only   B. II only   C. Both I and II   D. Neither I nor II

A

15. An agent will usually be entitled to a commission if he
    I. is the procuring cause of sale.
    II. presents a written offer to purchase during the term of the listing.
    A. I only   B. II only   C. Both I and II   D. Neither I nor II

C

16. An agent owes his principal the duty of
    I. loyalty to the principal's interest.
    II. obedience to the principal's instructions.
    A. I only   B. II only   C. Both I and II   D. Neither I nor II

C

17. A general listing may be terminated by
    I. the expiration of a reasonable time.
    II. either party's giving notice to the other of his intention to terminate.
    A. I only   B. II only   C. Both I and II   D. Neither I nor II

D

18. In his dealings with a principal's property, an agent should
    I. treat the principal's interest as paramount to all other considerations.
    II. place his own interests ahead of those of the principal.
    A. I only   B. II only   C. Both I and II   D. Neither I nor II

B

19. The first agent to show a property to a prospect
    I. is always entitled to a commission even though the prospect may later purchase the property through another agent.
    II. is not necessarily entitled to the commission if the prospect later purchases from another agent.
    A. I only   B. II only   C. Both I and II   D. Neither I nor II

B

20. If a property under a listing agreement is destroyed by a flood,
    I. the agent is entitled to a commission.
    II. the agency may be terminated by law.
    A. I only   B. II only   C. Both I and II   D. Neither I nor II

QUESTIONS ON REAL PROPERTY INTERESTS

A

1. The right or interest which an individual has in lands and chattels to the exclusion of all others is called
   I. property.
   II. a freehold.
   A. I only   B. II only   C. Both I and II   D. Neither I nor II

C 2. An interest in real property of not less than a life estate is
   I. a freehold.
   II. seisin.
   A. I only   B. II only   C. Both I and II   D. Neither I nor II

B 3. When more than one person has an interest in real property, this is
   I. severalty ownership.
   II. concurrent ownership.
   A. I only   B. II only   C. Both I and II   D. Neither I nor II

B 4. A right, privilege, or improvement which belongs to and passes with a property is
   I. a fixture.
   II. an appurtenance.
   A. I only   B. II only   C. Both I and II   D. Neither I nor II

A 5. The removal of land from one owner to another when a stream suddenly changes its channel is
   I. avulsion.
   II. accretion.
   A. I only   B. II only   C. Both I and II   D. Neither I nor II

B 6. Things which grow on land and require annual planting and cultivation are treated by law as
   I. real property.
   II. personal property.
   A. I only   B. II only   C. Both I and II   D. Neither I nor II

A 7. The act of the state in taking private property for public use is
   I. condemnation.
   II. eminent domain.
   A. I only   B. II only   C. Both I and II   D. Neither I nor II

C 8. An interest in property for the term of a life is
   I. a life estate.
   II. a freehold.
   A. I only   B. II only   C. Both I and II   D. Neither I nor II

B 9. All property which is inheritable is known as a
   I. tenement.
   II. hereditament.
   A. I only   B. II only   C. Both I and II   D. Neither I nor II

A 10. Joint tenants may divide their interests in property by
   I. partition.
   II. subdivision.
   A. I only   B. II only   C. Both I and II   D. Neither I nor II

A 11. The right to acquire the interest of a deceased joint tenant is
   I. the right of survivorship.
   II. the homestead right.
   A. I only   B. II only   C. Both I and II   D. Neither I nor II

B

12. An interest in real property for less than a lifetime is
       I. realty.
      II. personalty.
  A. I only B. II only C. Both I and II D. Neither I nor II

A

13. Ownership of real property by an individual, without any limitations,
       I. is not possible.
      II. is possible.
  A. I only B. II only C. Both I and II D. Neither I nor II

A

14. Zoning laws are the utilization of a state's
       I. police power.
      II. power of eminent domain.
  A. I only B. II only C. Both I and II D. Neither I nor II

B

15. The reversion of property to the state when no legal owner can be found is
       I. an estate in remainder.
      II. escheat.
  A. I only B. II only C. Both I and II D. Neither I nor II

A

16. The degree, quantity, nature, and extent of a person's interest in real property is
       I. an estate in land.
      II. a freehold.
  A. I only B. II only C. Both I and II D. Neither I nor II

D

17. The right of survivorship cannot exist among
       I. tenants by the entirety.
      II. joint tenants.
  A. I only B. II only C. Both I and II D. Neither I nor II

D

18. Tenancy in common and joint tenancy are
       I. estates in severalty.
      II. life estates.
  A. I only B. II only C. Both I and II D. Neither I nor II

B

19. A fee simple estate is
       I. an estate held by a minor.
      II. an inheritable estate.
  A. I only B. II only C. Both I and II D. Neither I nor II

A

20. An estate which may be held only by husband and wife is
       I. a tenancy by the entireties.
      II. joint tenancy.
  A. I only B. II only C. Both I and II D. Neither I nor II

B

21. The unities of time, interest, title, and possession are essential to
       I. tenancy in common.
      II. joint tenancy.
  A. I only B. II only C. Both I and II D. Neither I nor II

C   22. A fee simple estate is
             I. the largest possible estate in land.
             II. the least limited estate in land.
      A. I only   B. II only   C. Both I and II   D. Neither I nor II

C   23. A life estate may be
             I. an estate in reversion.
             II. an estate in remainder.
      A. I only   B. II only   C. Both I and II   D. Neither I nor II

D   24. An estate held as tenancy by the entireties
             I. may be sold by either party without the consent of the other.
             II. may exist between parent and child.
      A. I only   B. II only   C. Both I and II   D. Neither I nor II

C   25. There is no right of survivorship among
             I. tenants in common.
             II. tenants for years.
      A. I only   B. II only   C. Both I and II   D. Neither I nor II

C   26. A leasehold estate is
             I. an estate less than a freehold.
             II. personal property.
      A. I only   B. II only   C. Both I and II   D. Neither I nor II

A   27. A tenancy from year to year is
             I. a tenancy of indefinite duration.
             II. a tenancy of definite duration.
      A. I only   B. II only   C. Both I and II   D. Neither I nor II

B   28. A tenancy from year to year may be created by
             I. a holdover.
             II. express contractual agreement.
      A. I only   B. II only   C. Both I and II   D. Neither I nor II

B   29. Whenever either party has the right to terminate at his own pleasure, the estate is
             I. a tenancy by sufferance.
             II. a tenancy at will.
      A. I only   B. II only   C. Both I and II   D. Neither I nor II

A   30. A tenant who retains possession of the premises after the termination of his legal rights is
             I. a tenant by sufferance.
             II. a trespasser.
      A. I only   B. II only   C. Both I and II   D. Neither I nor II

C   31. An easement may be created by
             I. prescription.
             II. implied grant.
      A. I only   B. II only   C. Both I and II   D. Neither I nor II

C 32. A right of way may be
> I. an easement.
> II. an appurtenance.
A. I only   B. II only   C. Both I and II   D. Neither I nor II

B 33. To the owner of land across which it runs, an easement is
> I. an appurtenance.
> II. an encumbrance.
A. I only   B. II only   C. Both I and II   D. Neither I nor II

D 34. Dower, in states where it is recognized, is
> I. the right of the wife to receive, upon the death of the husband, not less than a fee simple estate in one-third of the land which he owned during the marriage.
> II. a gift from the bride's parents to the groom's parents.
A. I only   B. II only   C. Both I and II   D. Neither I nor II

A 35. A built-in range and wall oven are
> I. fixtures.
> II. emblements.
A. I only   B. II only   C. Both I and II   D. Neither I nor II

QUESTIONS ON APPRAISING

C 1. An appraisal is
> I. an estimate of value.
> II. an appraisal of value.
A. I only   B. II only   C. Both I and II   D. Neither I nor II

A 2. The price for which property should sell if placed on the market and sold in normal fashion is
> I. market value.
> II. market price.
A. I only   B. II only   C. Both I and II   D. Neither I nor II

A 3. The lessening of value from any cause is
> I. depreciation.
> II. obsolescence.
A. I only   B. II only   C. Both I and II   D. Neither I nor II

B 4. An official valuation of property for tax purposes is
> I. an appraisal.
> II. an assessment.
A. I only   B. II only   C. Both I and II   D. Neither I nor II

D 5. The act of the state in exercising its right of eminent domain is
> I. escheat.
> II. police power.
A. I only   B. II only   C. Both I and II   D. Neither I nor II

6. The power of a commodity to command other commodities in exchange is
   - I. price.
   - II. value.
   - A. I only   B. II only   C. Both I and II   D. Neither I nor II

7. Loss of value because of social change is
   - I. obsolescence.
   - II. physical deterioration.
   - A. I only   B. II only   C. Both I and II   D. Neither I nor II

8. Market value considers
   - I. only the present worth of the property.
   - II. not only the present, but also the past worth of a property.
   - A. I only   B. II only   C. Both I and II   D. Neither I nor II

9. The amount, expressed in terms of money, actually paid for a property is its
   - I. market price.
   - II. market value.
   - A. I only   B. II only   C. Both I and II   D. Neither I nor II

10. The value of a property can be affected by
    - I. zoning laws.
    - II. neighborhood changes.
    - A. I only   B. II only   C. Both I and II   D. Neither I nor II

11. The acquisition cost of a property is
    - I. an accurate indication of present market value.
    - II. important to the income approach to appraising.
    - A. I only   B. II only   C. Both I and II   D. Neither I nor II

12. Capitalization is employed in the
    - I. cost approach to appraising.
    - II. income approach to appraising.
    - A. I only   B. II only   C. Both I and II   D. Neither I nor II

13. A factor by which the appraiser multiplies the total rental income from a property as an estimate of its value is the
    - I. gross rent multiplier.
    - II. land residual process.
    - A. I only   B. II only   C. Both I and II   D. Neither I nor II

14. The comparison of a property with like properties of known value is employed in the
    - I. income approach.
    - II. market data approach.
    - A. I only   B. II only   C. Both I and II   D. Neither I nor II

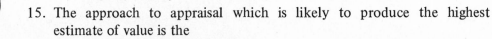

15. The approach to appraisal which is likely to produce the highest estimate of value is the
    - I. income approach.
    - II. market data approach.
    - A. I only   B. II only   C. Both I and II   D. Neither I nor II

16. The most widely used approach to appraisal is
    I. the market data approach.
    II. the cost approach.
    A. I only B. II only C. Both I and II D. Neither I nor II

17. Obsolescence may be
    I. functional.
    II. economic.
    A. I only B. II only C. Both I and II D. Neither I nor II

18. Functional obsolescence arises from factors
    I. inside the property.
    II. outside the property.
    A. I only B. II only C. Both I and II D. Neither I nor II

19. A four bedroom home with one bathroom suffers from
    I. functional obsolescence.
    II. economic obsolescence.
    A. I only B. II only C. Both I and II D. Neither I nor II

20. In the cost approach to appraising, the appraiser
    I. calculates the value of the land.
    II. estimates the value of the land.
    A. I only B. II only C. Both I and II D. Neither I nor II

QUESTIONS ON REAL ESTATE FINANCING

1. The act of liquidating an indebtedness by a series of periodic payments
   is
    I. annuitization.
    II. amortization.
    A. I only B. II only C. Both I and II D. Neither I nor II

2. When a mortgage is assumed,
    I. the grantee becomes a co-maker on the original note of
       indebtedness.
    II. both grantee and grantor may be held responsible for the
        repayment of the loan.
    A. I only B. II only C. Both I and II D. Neither I nor II

3. A blanket mortgage covers
    I. more than one parcel of real estate.
    II. household goods.
    A. I only B. II only C. Both I and II D. Neither I nor II

4. The transfer of property or valuables to guarantee the performance of
   an agreement is
    I. collateral security.
    II. amortization.
    A. I only B. II only C. Both I and II D. Neither I nor II

D

5. Interest paid on accrued interest is
   - I. add-on interest.
   - II. simple interest.
   - A. I only   B. II only   C. Both I and II   D. Neither I nor II

C

6. A mortgage which is paid off in a series of installments, with each payment credited first to interest, then to principal, is
   - I. an amortized mortgage.
   - II. a direct reduction mortgage.
   - A. I only   B. II only   C. Both I and II   D. Neither I nor II

B

7. Property which is mortgaged as security for a loan on real estate, upon default of the loan, may be sold
   - I. at a trustee's sale.
   - II. through foreclosure.
   - A. I only   B. II only   C. Both I and II   D. Neither I nor II

A

8. To give a thing as security without giving up possession of it is
   - I. to hypothecate.
   - II. to amortize.
   - A. I only   B. II only   C. Both I and II   D. Neither I nor II

B

9. Under a deed of trust, the borrower is the
   - I. grantee.
   - II. grantor.
   - A. I only   B. II only   C. Both I and II   D. Neither I nor II

B

10. The right of an owner to redeem his property during the foreclosure period is known as
    - I. repossession.
    - II. redemption.
    - A. I only   B. II only   C. Both I and II   D. Neither I nor II

A

11. An instrument which conveys land to a trustee as collateral security for the payment of a debt is
    - I. a deed of trust or trust deed.
    - II. a mortgage.
    - A. I only   B. II only   C. Both I and II   D. Neither I nor II

A

12. A legal remedy to collect a debt secured by a mortgage on real property is
    - I. foreclosure.
    - II. a trustee's sale.
    - A. I only   B. II only   C. Both I and II   D. Neither I nor II

B

13. The lending of money at a rate of interest above the legal rate is
    - I. discounting.
    - II. usury.
    - A. I only   B. II only   C. Both I and II   D. Neither I nor II

D

14. The "prime" interest rate is that which is charged to
    - I. the average borrower.
    - II. a high-risk borrower.
    - A. I only   B. II only   C. Both I and II   D. Neither I nor II

A

15. Real estate loans are usually made at interest rates
    I. higher than the prime rate.
    II. lower than the prime rate.
    A. I only   B. II only   C. Both I and II   D. Neither I nor II

C

16. In standard money-lending practices
    I. risk is directly proportional to gain.
    II. the probability of default is regarded as being inversely proportioned to equity.
    A. I only   B. II only   C. Both I and II   D. Neither I nor II

C

17. Loans from savings and loan associations may be secured by mortgages on
    I. real estate.
    II. mobile homes.
    A. I only   B. II only   C. Both I and II   D. Neither I nor II

B

18. Most Federally chartered savings and loan associations are
    I. stock associations.
    II. mutual associations.
    A. I only   B. II only   C. Both I and II   D. Neither I nor II

A

19. A person or firm appointed by an investor to originate and service loans for him is known as
    I. a mortgage loan correspondent.
    II. a trustee.
    A. I only   B. II only   C. Both I and II   D. Neither I nor II

A

20. Real estate mortgages and deeds of trust are
    I. negotiable securities.
    II. non-negotiable securities.
    A. I only   B. II only   C. Both I and II   D. Neither I nor II

A

21. Conventional loans are
    I. negotiable securities.
    II. non-negotiable securities.
    A. I only   B. II only   C. Both I and II   D. Neither I nor II

B

22. The Federal Housing Administration
    I. makes loans from government funds.
    II. insures loans made by private lenders.
    A. I only   B. II only   C. Both I and II   D. Neither I nor II

D

23. When a loan is approved by F.H.A.,
    I. the appraised value must not be less than the sale price.
    II. the government guarantees the value of the property.
    A. I only   B. II only   C. Both I and II   D. Neither I nor II

C

24. Loans insured by F.H.A. must be
    I. made in increments of $50.00.
    II. made at an interest rate approved by F.H.A.
    A. I only   B. II only   C. Both I and II   D. Neither I nor II

B

25. When a F.H.A. insured loan is originated,

    I. the seller may hold a second mortgage for part of the sale price.

    II. there must not be any secondary financing.

A. I only B. II only C. Both I and II D. Neither I nor II

26. Before securing a V.A. guaranteed loan, the borrower must

    I. sign a statement that he intends to live on the property.

    II. secure a certificate of eligibility.

A. I only B. II only C. Both I and II D. Neither I nor II

27. The maximum V.A. guarantee on a loan is

    I. $12,500, or 60 percent of the purchase price, whichever is less.

    II. $33,000.

A. I only B. II only C. Both I and II D. Neither I nor II

28. Second mortgages or deed of trust

    I. are permitted on V.A. loans.

    II. are never permitted on V.A. loans.

A. I only B. II only C. Both I and II D. Neither I nor II

29. The borrower under a V.A. loan

    I. may not pay more than the appraised value of the property.

    II. must sign a statement that he intends to live on the property.

A. I only B. II only C. Both I and II D. Neither I nor II

30. Under a deferred purchase money mortgage, the seller is the

    I. mortgagee.

    II. mortgagor.

A. I only B. II only C. Both I and II D. Neither I nor II

31. A purchaser who takes title to real property subject to a mortgage

    I. does not become legally responsible for the repayment of the debt.

    II. becomes a co-maker on the note of indebtedness.

A. I only B. II only C. Both I and II D. Neither I nor II

32. Discount "points" on loans are computed on

    I. the selling price of the property.

    II. the amount of the loan.

A. I only B. II only C. Both I and II D. Neither I nor II

33. The monthly rate of interest on a loan made at a 6 percent annual rate is

    I. .005.

    II. one-half of 1 percent.

A. I only B. II only C. Both I and II D. Neither I nor II

34. When "points" are charged on F.H.A. or V.A. loans,

    I. the purchaser may not pay the discount.

    II. the purchaser may be charged a 1 percent loan origination fee.

A. I only B. II only C. Both I and II D. Neither I nor II

QUESTIONS ON TRANSFER OF TITLE TO REAL PROPERTY

1. Possession which is inconsistent with the right of the true owner is
   I. undue influence.
   II. adverse possession.
   A. I only   B. II only   C. Both I and II   D. Neither I nor II

2. Title to real property may pass by
   I. deed.
   II. bill of sale.
   A. I only   B. II only   C. Both I and II   D. Neither I nor II

3. Real property title may be conveyed by
   I. adverse possession.
   II. inheritance.
   III. deed.
   IV. all of the above.

4. A warranty deed protects the grantee against a loss by
   I. casualty.
   II. defective title.
   A. I only   B. II only   C. Both I and II   D. Neither I nor II

5. Property conveyed by will is conveyed by
   I. demise.
   II. devise.
   A. I only   B. II only   C. Both I and II   D. Neither I nor II

6. The clause in a deed which defines or limits the quantity of the estate being granted is the
   I. habendum.
   II. granting clause.
   A. I only   B. II only   C. Both I and II   D. Neither I nor II

7. Deeds may be prepared by
   I. the owner of the property.
   II. an attorney.
   A. I only   B. II only   C. Both I and II   D. Neither I nor II

8. A quitclaim deed
   I. can be used to convey real property title.
   II. conveys whatever interest the grantor possesses in the property.
   A. I only   B. II only   C. Both I and II   D. Neither I nor II

9. A deed which protects the grantee against the world is
   I. a general warranty deed.
   II. a special warranty deed.
   A. I only   B. II only   C. Both I and II   D. Neither I nor II

10. A deed of conveyance must be signed by
    I. grantee and grantor.
    II. only by the grantee.
    A. I only   B. II only   C. Both I and II   D. Neither I nor II

11. A quitclaim deed
       I. does not contain any warranty of title.
      II. may be used to release a mortgagor from a mortgage upon its satisfaction.
  A. I only B. II only C. Both I and II D. Neither I nor II

12. A deed is not operative until it is
       I. delivered.
      II. accepted.
  A. I only B. II only C. Both I and II D. Neither I nor II

13. Deeds are recorded
       I. to provide constructive notice of their existence.
      II. because the law requires it.
  A. I only B. II only C. Both I and II D. Neither I nor II

14. Title to real property may be conveyed
       I. to a minor.
      II. by a quitclaim deed.
  A. I only B. II only C. Both I and II D. Neither I nor II

15. An unrecorded deed is valid and binding
       I. between the parties to the deed.
      II. upon a bona fide purchaser for value.
  A. I only B. II only C. Both I and II D. Neither I nor II

16. In order to claim title by adverse possession, a claimant must
       I. have maintained continuous possession for the statutory period.
      II. have possessed the property openly and notoriously.
  A. I only B. II only C. Both I and II D. Neither I nor II

17. The covenant in a deed by which the grantor assures the grantee that he will not be disturbed in his enjoyment of the property by someone with a paramount title is
       I. the covenant of seisin.
      II. the covenant of quiet possession.
  A. I only B. II only C. Both I and II D. Neither I nor II

18. Recordation of a deed is the responsibility of the
       I. grantor.
      II. grantee.
  A. I only B. II only C. Both I and II D. Neither I nor II

19. Deeds should be recorded
       I. as soon as possible after delivery.
      II. within thirty days of delivery.
  A. I only B. II only C. Both I and II D. Neither I nor II

20. A description of property by a description of its boundary lines, terminal points, and angles is a
       I. metes and bounds description.
      II. government survey description.
  A. I only B. II only C. Both I and II D. Neither I nor II

21. An outstanding claim or encumbrance which, if valid, would affect or impair an owner's title to real property is a
>   I. color of title.
>   II. cloud on the title.
A. I only   B. II only   C. Both I and II   D. Neither I nor II

22. A claim of title which appears to be valid, but which may or may not be valid is
>   I. color of title.
>   II. prescribed title.
A. I only   B. II only   C. Both I and II   D. Neither I nor II

23. To remove a cloud on the title by court action is to
>   I. quitclaim.
>   II. quiet title.
A. I only   B. II only   C. Both I and II   D. Neither I nor II

24. The sum of facts by which ownership is proved is a
>   I. title.
>   II. deed.
A. I only   B. II only   C. Both I and II   D. Neither I nor II

25. Protection against a future loss by reason of a defective title can be secured by means of
>   I. a title search.
>   II. title insurance.
A. I only   B. II only   C. Both I and II   D. Neither I nor II

26. Premiums for title insurance
>   I. are paid only at the time of issuance of the policy.
>   II. are nonrecurring premiums.
A. I only   B. II only   C. Both I and II   D. Neither I nor II

27. An owner's policy of title insurance protects the owner
>   I. for so long as he lives.
>   II. for so long as he or his heirs retain an interest in the policy.
A. I only   B. II only   C. Both I and II   D. Neither I nor II

28. A mortgagee policy of title insurance
>   I. declines in liability as the mortgage is amortized.
>   II. does not afford protection to the owner.
A. I only   B. II only   C. Both I and II   D. Neither I nor II

29. A title examiner who searches a title
>   I. is held responsible for any future defect in the title.
>   II. is responsible only for defects of record.
A. I only   B. II only   C. Both I and II   D. Neither I nor II

30. If a property on which there is a mortgagee policy of title insurance is sold and the loan is assumed,
>   I. the title insurance policy is cancelled.
>   II. the title insurance policy continues as before.
A. I only   B. II only   C. Both I and II   D. Neither I nor II

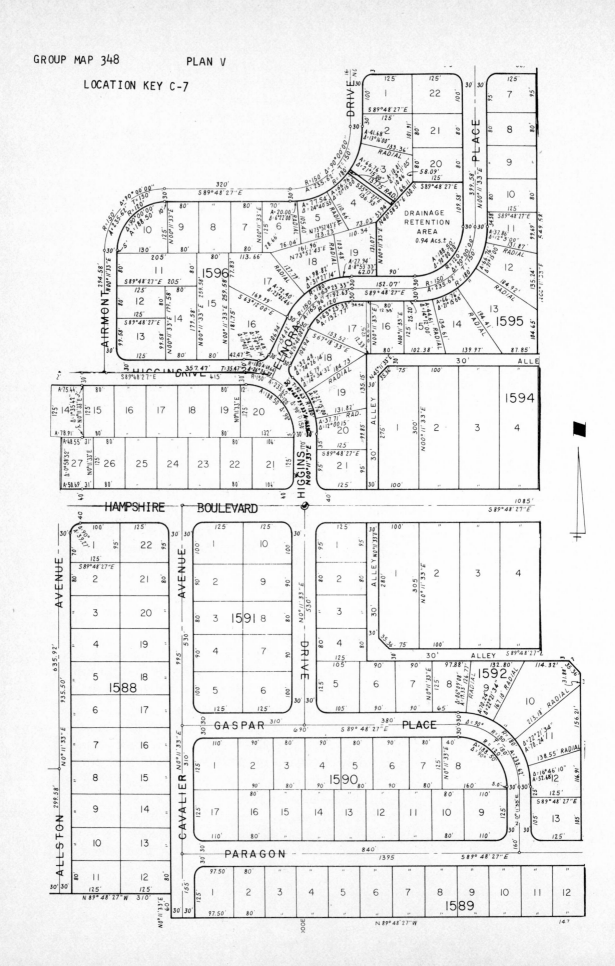

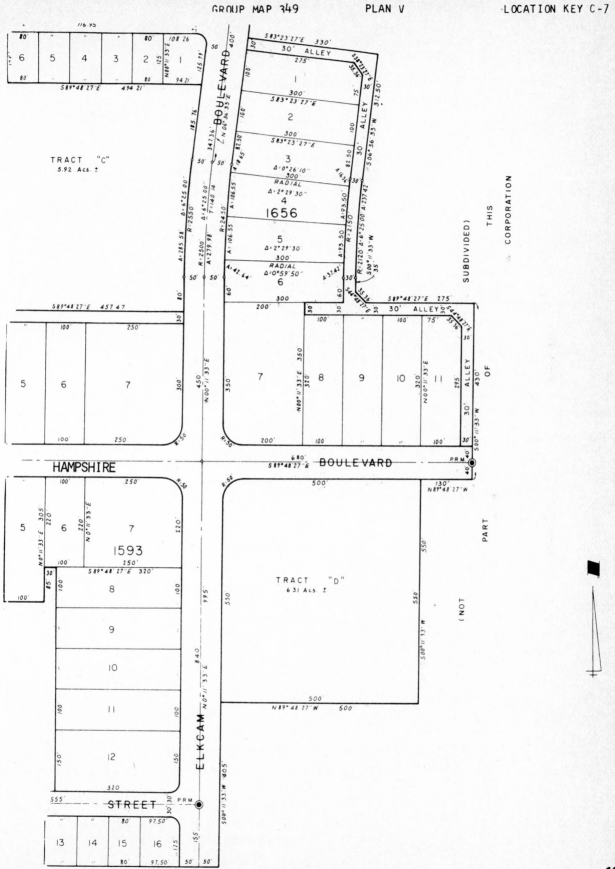

QUESTIONS ON PLATS AND LAND DESCRIPTIONS

1. On which of the following lots would a home probably face the northeast?
   - A. Lot 10, Block 1596
   - B. Lot 18, Block 1595
   - C. Lot 10, Block 1592
   - D. Lot 8, Block 1590

2. In which block do drainage easements appear between two lots?
   - A. 1594 and 1593
   - B. 1595 and 1596
   - C. 1592 and 1590
   - D. 1593 and 1591

3. Lot 7, which comprises the northwest corner of the intersection of Hampshire Boulevard and Elkcam Boulevard is a part of
   - A. Block 1593.
   - B. Tract "C".
   - C. Block 1656.
   - D. Block 1594.

4. There is an alley in the rear of all lots in Block
   - I. 1594.
   - II. 1593.

   A. I only   B. II only   C. Both I and II   D. Neither I nor II

5. Lots 1, 2, 3, and 4 of Block 1593 appear on Group Map
   - A. 349.
   - B. 350.
   - C. 348.
   - D. Not possible to tell.

6. Which of the following lots have frontage partly comprised of an arc having a radius of 120′, and a delta of 90°?
   - A. Lot 8, Block 1590
   - B. Lot 10, Block 1596
   - C. The drainage retention area in Block 1596
   - D. All of the above

7. What is the frontage of Lot 8, Block 1590?
   - A. 188.50′
   - B. 228.50′
   - C. 233.50′
   - D. 120.0′

8. Assuming most lots on Group Map 348 are residential building lots, the lots in Blocks 1593, 1594, and 1656 are most probably zoned for
   - A. heavy industry.
   - B. a shopping center.
   - C. large homesites.
   - D. farms.

9. Lots 1-6 in the northwest corner of Group Map 349 are a part of what block?
   - A. 1595
   - B. 1656
   - C. 1594
   - D. Not possible to tell

10. How many lots are shown in Block 1589?
    - A. 12
    - B. 16
    - C. Block 1589 not shown
    - D. 24

11. Identify the property described below:

    Beginning at a point 550′ East of the center line of Elkcam Blvd., and 40′ North of the center line of Hampshire Blvd., bearing N00°11′33″E for a distance of 320′; thence easterly on bearing S89°48′27″E for 75′; thence southeasterly on bearing S44°48′27″E for 35.36′; thence southerly on bearing S00° 11′ 33″ W for distance of

295'; thence West along course N89° 48'27"W for 100'. This describes

   A. Lot 10, Block 1656.   C. Lot 1, Block 1593.
   B. Lot 1, Block 1594.   D. Lot 11, Block 1656.

12. What lot does the following description fit?

   Northern boundary 560' South of the center line of Hampshire Blvd. Western boundary 310' East of center line of Cavalier Avenue. Southern boundary 155' South of center line of Gaspar Place. Eastern boundary 90' East of the parallel to western boundary.

   A. Lot 4, Block 1590   C. Lot 14, Block 1590
   B. Lot 3, Block 1590   D. No lot in Block 1590

QUESTIONS ON FAIR HOUSING LAWS

1. The Civil Rights Act of 1866 provides against discrimination in housing
   I. on the basis of race.
   II. on the basis of race or religion.
   A. I only   B. II only   C. Both I and II   D. Neither I nor II

2. The 1968 Fair Housing Act provides against discrimination based on
   I. race only.
   II. race, color, or religion.
   III. race, color, religion, or national origin.
   A. I only   B. II only   C. III only   D. Neither

3. Under the 1968 Fair Housing Act, if such acts are based on race, color, religion, sex or national origin, it is illegal to
   I. refuse to sell, rent, negotiate, or deal with any person.
   II. differentiate terms or conditions for buying or renting housing.
   A. I only   B. II only   C. Both I and II   D. Neither I nor II

4. Under the 1968 Fair Housing Act, if such acts are based on race, color, religion, sex or national origin, it is illegal to
   I. advertise housing as available only to persons of certain race, color, religion, or national origin.
   II. falsify availability of housing for inspection, sale, or rent.
   A. I only   B. II only   C. Both I and II   D. Neither I nor II

5. Under the 1968 Fair Housing Act, if such acts are based on race, color, religion, sex or national origin, it is illegal to
   I. use, for profit, threats of minority groups moving into a neighborhood to persuade owners to sell or rent housing.
   II. present different terms or conditions for home loans or deny such loans by commercial lenders.
   A. I only   B. II only   C. Both I and II   D. Neither I nor II

6. The prohibitions of the 1968 Fair Housing Act apply to privately-owned housing when
   I. a broker or other person engaged in selling or renting dwellings is used.
   II. discriminatory advertising is used.
   A. I only   B. II only   C. Both I and II   D. Neither I nor II

7. The prohibitions of the 1968 Fair Housing Act apply to single family housing when
      I. it is single family housing not privately owned.
      II. it is single family housing privately owned by an individual who owns three or more such houses, or who sells, in any two-year period, more than one house of which he was not the most recent occupant.
  A. I only B. II only C. Both I and II D. Neither I nor II

8. These prohibitions of the 1968 Fair Housing Act apply to multi-family housing in cases of
      I. multi-family dwellings of five or more units.
      II. multi-family dwellings of four or less units if owner does not occupy one of said units.
  A. I only B. II only C. Both I and II D. Neither I nor II

9. Single family houses privately owned by an individual owning less than three such houses may be sold or rented without being subject to the provisions of the Fair Housing Act if
      I. a broker is not used.
      II. discriminatory advertising is not used.
  A. I only B. II only C. Both I and II D. Neither I nor II

10. Single family houses privately owned by an individual owning less than three such houses may be sold or rented without being subject to the provisions of the Fair Housing Act if
      I. no more than two houses in which the owner was not the most recent occupant are sold in any two-year period.
      II. no more than one such house is sold in any two-year period.
  A. I only B. II only C. Both I and II D. Neither I nor II

11. The limiting of sale, rental, or occupancy of dwellings owned or operated by a religious organization for other than commercial purposes, provided that membership in said religion is not based on race, color, or national origin
      I. is prohibited by the Fair Housing Act.
      II. is not prohibited by the Fair Housing Act.
  A. I only B. II only C. Both I and II D. Neither I nor II

12. The limiting of rental or occupancy of lodgings owned by a private club to its own members when said club is operated for other than commercial purposes
      I. is prohibited by the Fair Housing Act.
      II. is not prohibited by the Fair Housing Act.
  A. I only B. II only C. Both I and II D. Neither I nor II

13. The 1866 law regarding fair housing
      I. is much more complicated than the 1968 law in its enforcement provisions.
      II. provides the fastest and most direct method of obtaining a remedy in cases of racial discrimination.
  A. I only B. II only C. Both I and II D. Neither I nor II

14. Under the provisions of the fair housing laws, federal courts could
    I. make it possible for the complainant to buy or rent the housing he wants.
    II. award damages and court costs and take other appropriate action to benefit the complainant.
    A. I only   B. II only   C. Both I and II   D. Neither I nor II

15. Complaints regarding the 1968 Fair Housing Act may be sent to H.U.D. on regular complaint forms or by letter.
    I. The complaint must be written within 180 days of the alleged discrimination.
    II. The complaint must be written within 30 days of the alleged discrimination.
    A. I only   B. II only   C. Both I and II   D. Neither I nor II

16. H.U.D. may do the following in the enforcement of the Fair Housing Laws:
    I. attempt to obtain informal confidential conciliation.
    II. inform the complainant of his right to immediate court action.
    A. I only   B. II only   C. Both I and II   D. Neither I nor II

17. H.U.D. may do the following in the enforcement of the Fair Housing Laws:
    I. refer the complainant to the Attorney General.
    II. refer the complainant to state or local agency.
    A. I only   B. II only   C. Both I and II   D. Neither I nor II

18. Court action may be taken by an individual under the Fair Housing Act
    I. only if no complaint is filed with H.U.D.
    II. if action is taken within sixty days of the alleged discriminatory act.
    A. I only   B. II only   C. Both I and II   D. Neither I nor II

19. Court action may be taken by the Attorney General under the Fair Housing Act
    I. if discrimination in housing is judged to deny full enjoyment of rights granted under Title VIII.
    II. if no complaint is filed with H.U.D.
    A. I only   B. II only   C. Both I and II   D. Neither I nor II

20. The Civil Rights Act of 1968
    I. makes it illegal to coerce, intimidate, threaten, or interfere with a person buying, renting, or selling housing.
    II. provides criminal penalties and criminal prosecution if violence is threatened or used.
    A. I only   B. II only   C. Both I and II   D. Neither I nor II

QUESTIONS ON TRUTH IN LENDING ACT

B

1. The Truth In Lending Act is enforced by the
    I. Department of Housing and Urban Development.
    II. Federal Trade Commission.
    A. I only   B. II only   C. Both I and II   D. Neither I nor II

C

2. A lender who violates the TIL Act may be punished by
    I. A fine of up to $5000 or one year in jail.
    II. Civil award to the borrower for twice the finance charge up to $1000.
    A. I only   B. II only   C. Both I and II   D. Neither I nor II

D

3. Which of the following are not subject to the TIL Act?
    A. Business loans.
    B. Commercial loans.
    C. Installment loans of four or less installments.
    D. All of the above.

D

4. The total of all payments and composition of finance charges need not be given on
    I. first mortgage loans.
    II. land sales contracts.
    A. I only   B. II only   C. Both I and II   D. Neither I nor II

C

5. If no disclosure statement is given to the borrower, under the TIL laws,
    I. the borrower's right to rescind continues indefinitely.
    II. there is no statute of limitations on the borrower's right to rescind.
    A. I only   B. II only   C. Both I and II   D. Neither I nor II

C

6. The total of all payments and composition of finance charges must be given on
    I. second mortgages and deeds of trust.
    II. first mortgages or deeds of trust used to finance the acquisition of a dwelling.
    A. I only   B. II only   C. Both I and II   D. Neither I nor II

C

7. Real estate agents may advertise in general terms, such as
    I. "excellent Loan Assumption."
    II. "FHA Financing Available."
    A. I only   B. II only   C. Both I and II   D. Neither I nor II

B

8. The federal truth in lending act is also referred to as
    I. Regulation Z.
    II. the Consumer Credit Protection Act.
    A. I only   B. II only   C. Both I and II   D. Neither I nor II

B

9. The TIL laws apply to
    A. commercial loan transactions involving real property.
    B. residential real estate mortgages.
    C. all personal property transactions.
    D. all of the above.

10. Regulation Z provides a right of recission
      I. to first mortgages for the purpose of financing a dwelling.
      II. which right expires after 3 business days following completion of the transaction or the date on which the lender disclosed the amount of finance charges, whichever is later.
A. I only B. II only C. Both I and II D. Neither I nor II

11. Under the advertising regulations of Regulation Z
      I. interest rates cannot be stated alone.
      II. annual percentage rates must be stated.
A. I only B. II only C. Both I and II D. Neither I nor II

12. Non-compliance with Regulation Z
      I. is punishable by a fine not to exceed $5,000 and one year in jail.
      II. may result in civil penalties up to $5,000 if the borrower has been damaged.
A. I only B. II only C. Both I and II D. Neither I nor II

13. Regulation Z requires lenders to inform prospective home mortgage borrowers of all charges, fees and interest before making a home mortgage loan.
      I. The above statement is true.
      II. Home mortgages are exempted from this requirement.
A. I only B. II only C. Both I and II D. Neither I nor II

QUESTIONS ON REAL ESTATE LICENSE LAW

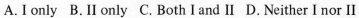

    NOTE: The questions on real estate license law which follow are selected to cover the broad spectrum of real estate license law in most states. Differences in the laws of various states may result in some of these questions not being applicable in your state. The answers given in the answer section may also not apply in all states.

1. A person who receives no compensation for selling real estate for others
      I. must be licensed.
      II. violates the License Law.
A. I only B. II only C. Both I and II D. Neither I nor II

2. King rents his neighbor's house to a prospect. The neighbor buys King a lobster dinner as promised.
      I. King does not need to be licensed.
      II. King comes under the statutory definition of a "real estate broker."
A. I only B. II only C. Both I and II D. Neither I nor II

3. An unlicensed secretary paid a salary by a broker can
      I. take listings over the phone.
      II. tell callers what listings are available.
A. I only B. II only C. Both I and II D. Neither I nor II

4. A person who appraises property for others for a fee
      I. must be licensed.
      II. may be employed by a real estate broker without being licensed.
A. I only   B. II only   C. Both I and II   D. Neither I nor II

5. An unlicensed employee of a broker could
      I. be employed only to take listings.
      II. collect a commission if one of his listings sold.
A. I only   B. II only   C. Both I and II   D. Neither I nor II

6. A motel clerk who regularly furnishes a real estate broker with leads to prospective buyers in exchange for 10% of the commission collected
      I. need not be licensed since he does no selling himself.
      II. would be in violation of the License Law if he is unlicensed.
A. I only   B. II only   C. Both I and II   D. Neither I nor II

7. Which of the following may sell real estate without the necessity of being licensed?
      I. receiver in bankruptcy.
      II. guardian acting under court order.
A. I only   B. II only   C. Both I and II   D. Neither I nor II

8. A person must be licensed as a real estate broker or salesman to
      I. appraise real property.
      II. negotiate a mortgage loan.
A. I only   B. II only   C. Both I and II   D. Neither I nor II

9. Violations of the Real Estate License Law are
      I. felonies.
      II. misdemeanors.
A. I only   B. II only   C. Both I and II   D. Neither I nor II

10. A real estate broker violating a provision of the License Law
      I. is subject to fine or imprisonment.
      II. could have his license revoked.
A. I only   B. II only   C. Both I and II   D. Neither I nor II

11. The governor of this state
      I. appoints members to the Real Estate Commission.
      II. selects the chairman of the Real Estate Commission.
A. I only   B. II only   C. Both I and II   D. Neither I nor II

12. A member of the Real Estate Commission
      I. must be a real estate broker.
      II. cannot be reappointed to succeed himself on the Commission.
A. I only   B. II only   C. Both I and II   D. Neither I nor II

13. The Real Estate Commission adjudicates disputes between
      I. licensees.
      II. licensees and their clients.
A. I only   B. II only   C. Both I and II   D. Neither I nor II

14. The Real Estate Commission is given statutory authority to
    I. enforce the provisions of the Real Estate License Law.
    II. establish rules and regulations for brokers and salesmen.
    A. I only   B. II only   C. Both I and II   D. Neither I nor II

15. A dispute between two brokers involving commissions that has been sent to the Real Estate Commission for action will be
    I. referred to the Attorney General.
    II. returned to the brokers for settlement.
    A. I only   B. II only   C. Both I and II   D. Neither I nor II

16. The Real Estate Commission is given the authority to
    I. impose fines on persons found to be violating the License Law.
    II. impose jail sentences on violations of the License Law.
    A. I only   B. II only   C. Both I and II   D. Neither I nor II

17. The Real Estate Commission is empowered to take legal action for violations of the License Law against
    I. unlicensed persons.
    II. brokers and salesmen.
    A. I only   B. II only   C. Both I and II   D. Neither I nor II

18. An original applicant for a broker's license must have
    I. been actively engaged and licensed as a salesman for at least one year.
    II. reached majority.
    A. I only   B. II only   C. Both I and II   D. Neither I nor II

19. A salesman working for a real estate broker who has had his license revoked
    I. could continue to sell real estate for the broker.
    II. would have his salesman's license automatically revoked.
    A. I only   B. II only   C. Both I and II   D. Neither I nor II

20. A broker who changes his principal business location without notifying the Real Estate Commission would
    I. have his license automatically cancelled.
    II. be automatically scheduled for a hearing before the Commission.
    A. I only   B. II only   C. Both I and II   D. Neither I nor II

21. A real estate salesman discharged by his employing broker must
    I. turn in his license to the Real Estate Commission.
    II. be notified by his broker of the termination of employment.
    A. I only   B. II only   C. Both I and II   D. Neither I nor II

22. A personnel officer of a corporation who is paid for leads to prospective buyers and seller of real estate
    I. need not be licensed.
    II. can be paid on a commission basis.
    A. I only   B. II only   C. Both I and II   D. Neither I nor II

23. A license applicant must
    - I. have a good reputation for honesty, truthfulness, and fair dealing.
    - II. demonstrate his competence to act in such a manner as to protect the interests of the public.

    A. I only   B. II only   C. Both I and II   D. Neither I nor II

24. A real estate broker may not renew his expired license unless
    - I. he proves financial responsibility or posts an appropriate bond.
    - II. he has filed an affidavit that his State Revenue License tax has been paid for the current and/or previous year.

    A. I only   B. II only   C. Both I and II   D. Neither I nor II

25. When a salesman transfers from one broker to another the old broker must
    - I. return the salesman's license by hand delivery or registered mail to the Real Estate Commission.
    - II. send notice to the salesman's last known residence address.

    A. I only   B. II only   C. Both I and II   D. Neither I nor II

26. The Real Estate Commission may take action upon a verified complaint from
    - I. any person who feels he has been aggrieved by the action of a licensee.
    - II. brokers or salesmen.

    A. I only   B. II only   C. Both I and II   D. Neither I nor II

27. A licensee could have his license revoked for
    - I. failure to devote full time to real estate business.
    - II. listing a property at less than 6% commission.

    A. I only   B. II only   C. Both I and II   D. Neither I nor II

28. The Real Estate Commission may suspend a licensee's license if he
    - I. makes promises of a nature likely to persuade or induce a prospective seller.
    - II. fails to include a specific termination date in an exclusive listing.

    A. I only   B. II only   C. Both I and II   D. Neither I nor II

29. A licensee can have his license revoked for
    - I. representing more than one party in a transaction without the knowledge and consent of all parties.
    - II. accepting a commission for an appraisal.

    A. I only   B. II only   C. Both I and II   D. Neither I nor II

30. A licensee can have his license revoked if he
    - I. receives a commission from more than one broker.
    - II. has pleaded nolo contendere to a felony within the last 10 years.

    A. I only   B. II only   C. Both I and II   D. Neither I nor II

31. A licensed real estate salesman can
    - I. obtain listings for more than one broker as long as separate properties are involved.
    - II. appraise property for a fee.

    A. I only   B. II only   C. Both I and II   D. Neither I nor II

32. Should a salesman fail to remit an earnest money deposit
    I. this would be a violation of the License Law.
    II. legal action could be taken against his broker.
    A. I only   B. II only   C. Both I and II   D. Neither I nor II

33. A licensee must account for all monies received on real estate transactions according to the
    I. License Law.
    II. Rules and Regulations.
    A. I only   B. II only   C. Both I and II   D. Neither I nor II

34. A licensee can have his license revoked for
    I. failing to account for funds which belong to others.
    II. being unworthy or incompetent to act as a broker or salesman.
    A. I only   B. II only   C. Both I and II   D. Neither I nor II

35. A licensee paying a personnel officer of a corporation for leads to prospective home purchasers would be in violation of the
    I. License Law.
    II. Rules and Regulations.
    A. I only   B. II only   C. Both I and II   D. Neither I nor II

36. Undue influence on the part of a salesman in obtaining a contract may result in
    I. the contract being voidable.
    II. revocation of the salesman's license.
    A. I only   B. II only   C. Both I and II   D. Neither I nor II

37. A broker who obtains an exclusive listing must
    I. include a definite termination date in the listing.
    II. notify all other brokers in his locality that he has the listing.
    A. I only   B. II only   C. Both I and II   D. Neither I nor II

38. A "For Sale" sign placed on property by a real estate broker
    I. can only be used in an exclusive listing.
    II. must conform to the requirements of the county real estate board.
    A. I only   B. II only   C. Both I and II   D. Neither I nor II

39. The License Laws provide that a licensee's license may be revoked for
    I. placing a "For Sale" sign on a property without the owner's permission.
    II. failing to include all the terms and conditions of the mortgage in a sales contract.
    A. I only   B. II only   C. Both I and II   D. Neither I nor II

40. In accordance with the License Laws a licensee's license may be revoked if a
    I. copy of a written listing agreement is not provided the principal.
    II. listing agreement is not in writing.
    A. I only   B. II only   C. Both I and II   D. Neither I nor II

41. A licensee must never offer property for sale
   I. without a signed listing from the owner.
   II. on terms other than those authorized by the owner.
   A. I only   B. II only   C. Both I and II   D. Neither I nor II

42. A salesman may handle the closing of a real estate transaction
   I. under the direct supervision of his real estate broker.
   II. with the consent of the property owner.
   A. I only   B. II only   C. Both I and II   D. Neither I nor II

43. A salesman selling real property which he owns
   I. may handle the closing.
   II. must not advertise the property except in the name of his employing broker.
   A. I only   B. II only   C. Both I and II   D. Neither I nor II

44. Records of deposits received by a real estate broker must show
   I. from who received.
   II. date of receipt.
   A. I only   B. II only   C. Both I and II   D. Neither I nor II

45. When handling a closing, a broker must
   I. sign the closing statements.
   II. keep copies of the closing statements in his files.
   A. I only   B. II only   C. Both I and II   D. Neither I nor II

46. A complete record of all monies received in real estate transactions must be kept
   I. in an insured depository.
   II. by a broker for the statutory period of time.
   A. I only   B. II only   C. Both I and II   D. Neither I nor II

47. A broker would be guilty of commingling funds if he keeps escrow money with
   I. general company funds.
   II. his personal account.
   A. I only   B. II only   C. Both I and II   D. Neither I nor II

48. Upon selling a $50,000 house a broker received a $2,000 earnest money deposit
   I. the money must be placed in an insured depository.
   II. the $2,000 must be paid to the principal by certified check at the close of the sale.
   A. I only   B. II only   C. Both I and II   D. Neither I nor II

49. As agent for an owner, a licensee may not
   I. charge a commission on expenditures made for the owner.
   II. accept an undisclosed commission on expenditures made for the owner.
   A. I only   B. II only   C. Both I and II   D. Neither I nor II

50. A promissory note as an earnest money deposit with a sales contract is acceptable with the permission of the
   I. broker.
   II. buyer.
   A. I only   B. II only   C. Both I and II   D. Neither I nor II

51. All advertisements listing property for sale must contain the
    I. selling price of the property.
    II. location of the property.
A. I only   B. II only   C. Both I and II   D. Neither I nor II

52. A licensee wishing to appeal the suspension of his license must submit an appeal bond to the
    I. Real Estate Commission.
    II. county in which the licensee's place of business is located.
A. I only   B. II only   C. Both I and II   D. Neither I nor II

53. Before a licensee's license can be suspended or revoked by the Real Estate Commission, the
    I. licensee must be given a hearing before the Commission.
    II. Commission must prefer a complaint in court against the licensee.
A. I only   B. II only   C. Both I and II   D. Neither I nor II

54. The Real Estate Commission may take disciplinary action against
    I. unlicensed persons.
    II. brokers and salesmen.
A. I only   B. II only   C. Both I and II   D. Neither I nor II

55. An applicant who has failed the licensing examination
    I. is entitled to a hearing before the Real Estate Commission.
    II. must file as an original applicant before he may sit for another examination.
A. I only   B. II only   C. Both I and II   D. Neither I nor II

56. The powers of the Real Estate Commission are restricted to
    I. revocation and suspension of licenses.
    II. enforcement of rules and regulations.
A. I only   B. II only   C. Both I and II   D. Neither I nor II

57. No original applicant for a broker's license will be issued a license if he is not a
    I. citizen of the United States.
    II. resident of this state.
A. I only   B. II only   C. Both I and II   D. Neither I nor II

58. Real estate salesmen's licenses are required to be displayed according to the
    I. License Law.
    II. Rules and Regulations.
A. I only   B. II only   C. Both I and II   D. Neither I nor II

59. Which of the following may file a complaint with the Real Estate Commission?
    I. Any person aggrieved by the action or inaction of a licensee.
    II. Any person aggrieved by a person acting as a licensee.
A. I only   B. II only   C. Both I and II   D. Neither I nor II

60. A licensee whose license has been suspended or revoked by the Commission

      I. may petition the Commission for a rehearing of his case.

      II. must automatically discontinue all operations as a broker or salesman.

A. I only B. II only C. Both I and II D. Neither I nor II

61. A licensee who violates the License Law while selling his own property

      I. would have committed improper dealings.

      II. could have his license revoked.

A. I only B. II only C. Both I and II D. Neither I nor II

62. A salesman who fails to account for an earnest money deposit can

      I. have his license revoked.

      II. cause his broker's license to be cancelled.

A. I only B. II only C. Both I and II D. Neither I nor II

63. A real estate salesman can have his license revoked for

      I. receiving a salary from a builder for selling homes that he is constructing while earning commissions from a licensed real estate broker.

      II. appraising.

A. I only B. II only C. Both I and II D. Neither I nor II

64. A real estate broker can have his license revoked whenever

      I. the license of a salesman which he supervises is revoked.

      II. he charges a fee in excess of that set by the Real Estate Commission.

A. I only B. II only C. Both I and II D. Neither I nor II

65. A licensee who changes his principal business location without notifying the Real Estate Commission will have his license automatically

      I. cancelled.

      II. revoked.

A. I only B. II only C. Both I and II D. Neither I nor II

66. When a salesman transfers from one broker to another, the new broker must

      I. return the salesman's license to the Real Estate Commission.

      II. pay the transfer fee.

A. I only B. II only C. Both I and II D. Neither I nor II

67. The Real Estate Commission is empowered to

      I. fine any licensee violating the License Law.

      II. prefer a complaint in court against unlicensed persons acting as licensees.

A. I only B. II only C. Both I and II D. Neither I nor II

68. A licensee would be subject to disciplinary action by the Real Estate Commission should he

      I. not give a copy of a written listing agreement to the principal.

      II. fail to include all of the terms of the sale in a sales contract.

A. I only B. II only C. Both I and II D. Neither I nor II

69. Grounds for suspension or revocation of a licensee's license include
    I. placing a "For Sale" sign on a property without the written consent of the owner.
    II. advertising a listing without the written consent of the owner.
    A. I only   B. II only   C. Both I and II   D. Neither I nor II

70. All exclusive listing contracts must
    I. be in writing.
    II. have a definite termination date.
    A. I only   B. II only   C. Both I and II   D. Neither I nor II

71. A licensee may have his license revoked for
    I. charging a lower commission than is charged by other brokers in his locality.
    II. improper, fraudulent, or dishonest dealings.
    A. I only   B. II only   C. Both I and II   D. Neither I nor II

72. A licensee can have his license revoked for
    I. accepting a commission from more than one party in a transaction.
    II. having pled nolo contendere to a felony within the past ten years.
    A. I only   B. II only   C. Both I and II   D. Neither I nor II

73. A broker would be guilty of escheat should he place deposit money with
    I. his personal accounts.
    II. general company funds.
    A. I only   B. II only   C. Both I and II   D. Neither I nor II

74. A broker's records of deposit money which he has received must
    I. be available for inspection by agents of the Real Estate Commission.
    II. contain a complete and accurate record of receipts and disbursements.
    A. I only   B. II only   C. Both I and II   D. Neither I nor II

75. For a broker to act for more than one party in a real estate transaction with the knowledge and consent of all parties is
    I. contrary to the Administrative Code.
    II. grounds for disciplinary action.
    A. I only   B. II only   C. Both I and II   D. Neither I nor II

Chapter 18

Listing and
Contract Problems

LISTING PROBLEM NO. 1

On June 1, 1973, you list the house belonging to Phil O. Dendron and his wife, Rhoda, located at 22 Sycamore Street, Forest City, Granite County, (your state), k/a Lot 2, Section 3, Happy Valley Subdivision. Two-story colonial style home, in good condition, brick and frame construction. Three bedrooms, $12' \times 15'$ living room, $10' \times 12'$ dining room, and eat-in kitchen. Full basement, side screened porch. Paneled recreation room, $12' \times 24'$, in basement. Kitchen is equipped with built-in range and oven, refrigerator, dishwasher, and disposal. Electric 50 gallon hot water heater, heated by oil fired forced air. Roof is of composition shingle. Attic is accessible by means of a trap door. Paved side driveway, one-car garage. Twelve years old, well water and septic tank. No curbs, gutters, or sidewalks. Conventional first deed of trust having a balance of $17,546.19 as of July 1, 1973, with interest at $6\frac{1}{2}$ percent p/a, held by the Blue Sky Savings and Loan Association. Monthly payment is $179.70 PITI. Owner would take back small deferred purchase money trust. Appraised by a local savings and loan association at $33,500. Tax assessment is $18,464, and tax rate is $3.80. You are instructed to call for an appointment to show, as the property is occupied by tenants, Ann Houser Bush and her mother Rose, under a lease that runs until October 31, 1973. Tenant's rent is $250 per month. Owner is selling to dispose of investments. Lot size is $100' \times 150'$. The listing is to be for a 90-day period. Two window air conditioners not included. Front storm door, and storm windows. List the house at the appraised value, at a 6 percent commission to your firm, the Cheatham and Steel Realty Company. You estimate fuel cost at $250 per year. Two baths on second floor. To reach property, go west on Main Street to Sycamore Street, right 1½ blocks to property. Valley View Shopping Center, 6 blocks. Schools: Glass High, Byrd Junior High, Wilson Elementary, and St. Agnes Parochial.

CONTRACT PROBLEM NO. 1

On June 9, 1973, you show the Dendron property to Miss Myrtle Beach, unmarried, and her mother, Virginia Beach, a widow. They like the home and make the following offer to purchase: A price of $33,000 with a down payment of 10 percent of the purchase price. Purchaser to secure a first D/T loan on a conventional basis of 80 percent of the purchase price, and seller to hold a second D/T for the remainder, at 8 percent p/a interest, payable at $45 per month, entire balance due and payable in 7 years. Purchasers are to buy the two window air conditioners under a separate bill of sale for $200, to be paid at closing. They are in no hurry for possession but desire closing to be held by their attorney, O. Howie Gypsum, on July 1, 1973. They give you a check for $1,000 as a deposit, and you write a contract on these terms, using all pertinent data from the listing. You present this offer to the seller, who accepts on June 10, 1973.

LISTING PROBLEM NO. 2

You are agent for the Earl E. Byrd Realty, Inc. On June 1, 1973, you list the property of Al E. Katz and his wife, Kitty Katz, which is a two bedroom cape cod house, on a 60′ × 120′ city lot. Recently painted, new roof of composition shingle. This work has not yet been paid for, and the Shylock Finance Company holds a second D/T note for $900 plus interest at 8 percent p/a since April 15, 1973. Full basement, half bath, paneled recreation room. On the first floor there is a 12′ × 24′ living room with fireplace, 10′ × 12′ dining room, center hall, eat-in kitchen, and small pantry. Sixteen years old, taxes $288.00/year, land assessment $2,200, building assessment $7,400. Electric range, refrigerator and washing machine are included in the listing. There is a conventional first D/T of $8,440 on the property, balance as of July 15, 1973, which has 14 years to run, at $5\frac{1}{2}$ percent p/a interest, held by the Blue Sky Insurance Company at monthly payments of $87.50. Owners will hold a small deferred purchase money trust. The address is 114 Sunset Lane, Back Royal, (your state), Queen Charlotte County. Schools are Byrd Elementary, Smith Junior High, and Queen Charlotte County High. Heat is oil forced hot air, hot water is electric. No garage, rear yard is fenced. You agree on a listed price of $26,500 at a 6 percent commission. No storm windows or doors, attic access by trap door. You secure a 90-day exclusive right to sell, possession at settlement. Nearest shopping is $\frac{3}{4}$ mile distance. Property is reached by going west on Main Street to Sunset Lane, right to house. There are two bedrooms and one bath on the second floor.

EXCLUSIVE AUTHORIZATION TO SELL

SALES PRICE: _____ TYPE HOME _____ TOTAL BEDROOMS _____ TOTAL BATHS _____

ADDRESS: _____ JURISDICTION OF: _____

AMT. OF LOAN TO BE ASSUMED $ _____ AS OF WHAT DATE: _____ TAXES & INS. INCLUDED: _____ YEARS TO GO: _____ AMOUNT PAYABLE MONTHLY $ _____ @ ___ % TYPE LOAN _____

MORTGAGE COMPANY _____ 2nd TRUST $ _____

ESTIMATED EXPECTED RENT MONTHLY $ _____ TYPE OF APPRAISAL REQUESTED: _____

OWNER'S NAME _____ PHONES: (HOME) _____ (BUSINESS) _____

TENANTS NAME _____ PHONES: (HOME) _____ (BUSINESS) _____

POSSESSION _____ DATE LISTED: _____ EXCLUSIVE FOR _____ DATE OF EXPIRATION _____

LISTING BROKER _____ PHONE _____ KEY AVAILABLE AT _____

LISTING SALESMAN _____ HOME PHONE: _____ HOW TO BE SHOWN: _____

(1) ENTRANCE FOYER ☐ CENTER HALL ☐	(18) AGE	AIR CONDITIONING ☐	(32) TYPE KITCHEN CABINETS
(2) LIVING ROOM SIZE FIREPLACE ☐	(19) ROOFING	TOOL HOUSE ☐	(33) TYPE COUNTER TOPS
(3) DINING ROOM SIZE	(20) GARAGE SIZE	PATIO ☐	(34) EAT-IN SIZE KITCHEN ☐
(4) BEDROOM TOTAL: DOWN UP	(21) SIDE DRIVE ☐	CIRCULAR DRIVE ☐	(35) BREAKFAST ROOM ☐
(5) BATHS TOTAL: DOWN UP	(22) PORCH ☐ SIDE ☐ REAR ☐	SCREENED ☐	(36) BUILT-IN OVEN & RANGE ☐
(6) DEN SIZE FIREPLACE ☐	(23) FENCED YARD	OUTDOOR GRILL ☐	(37) SEPARATE STOVE INCLUDED ☐
(7) FAMILY ROOM SIZE FIREPLACE ☐	(24) STORM WINDOWS ☐	STORM DOORS ☐	(38) REFRIGERATOR INCLUDED ☐
(8) RECREATION ROOM SIZE FIREPLACE ☐	(25) CURBS & GUTTERS ☐	SIDEWALKS ☐	(39) DISHWASHER INCLUDED
(9) BASEMENT SIZE	(26) STORM SEWERS ☐	ALLEY ☐	(40) DISPOSAL INCLUDED ☐
NONE ☐ 1/4 ☐ 1/3 ☐ 1/2 ☐ 3/4 ☐ FULL ☐	(27) WATER SUPPLY		(41) DOUBLE SINK ☐ SINGLE SINK ☐
(10) UTILITY ROOM SIZE	(28) SEWER ☐	SEPTIC ☐	STAINLESS STEEL ☐ PORCELAIN ☐
TYPE HOT WATER SYSTEM:	(29) TYPE GAS: NATURAL ☐	BOTTLED ☐	(42) WASHER INCLUDED ☐ DRYER INCLUDED ☐
(11) TYPE HEAT	(30) WHY SELLING		(43) PANTRY ☐ EXHAUST FAN ☐
(12) EST. FUEL COST			(44) LAND ASSESSMENT $
(13) ATTIC ☐	(31) DIRECTIONS TO PROPERTY		(45) IMPROVEMENTS $
PULL DOWN STAIRWAY ☐ REGULAR STAIRWAY ☐ TRAP DOOR ☐			(46) TOTAL ASSESSMENT $
(14) MAIDS ROOM ☐ TYPE BATH			(47) TAX RATE
LOCATION			(48) TOTAL ANNUAL TAXES $
(15) NAME OF BUILDER			(49) LOT SIZE
(16) SQUARE FOOTAGE			(50) LOT NO. BLOCK SECTION
(17) EXTERIOR OF HOUSE			

NAME OF SCHOOLS: ELEMENTARY: _____ JR. HIGH: _____

HIGH _____ PAROCHIAL: _____

PUBLIC TRANSPORTATION: _____

NEAREST SHOPPING AREA: _____

REMARKS: _____

Date: _____

    In consideration of the services of _____ (herein called "Broker") to be rendered to the undersigned (herein called "Owner"), and of the promise of Broker to make reasonable efforts to obtain a Purchaser therefor, Owner hereby lists with Broker the real estate and all improvements thereon which are described above (all herein called "the property"), and Owner hereby grants to Broker the exclusive and irrevocable right to sell such property from 12:00 Noon on _____, 19_____ until 12:00 Midnight on _____, 19_____ (herein called "period of time"), for the price of _____ Dollars ($ _____) or for such other price and upon such other terms (including exchange) as Owner may subsequently authorize during the period of time.

    It is understood by Owner that the above sum or any other price subsequently authorized by Owner shall include a cash fee of _____ per cent of such price or other price which shall be payable by Owner to Broker upon consummation by any Purchaser or Purchasers of a valid contract of sale of the property during the period of time and whether or not Broker was a procuring cause of any such contract of sale.

    If the property is sold or exchanged by Owner, or by Broker or by any other person to any Purchaser to whom the property was shown by Broker or any representative of Broker within sixty (60) days after the expiration of the period of time mentioned above, Owner agrees to pay to Broker a cash fee which shall be the same percentage of the purchase price as the percentage mentioned above.

    Broker is hereby authorized by Owner to place a "For Sale" sign on the property and to remove all signs of other brokers or salesmen during the period of time, and Owner hereby agrees to make the property available to Broker at all reasonable hours for the purpose of showing it to prospective Purchasers.

    Owner agrees to convey the property to the Purchaser by warranty deed with the usual covenants of title and free and clear from all encumbrances, tenancies, liens (for taxes or otherwise), but subject to applicable restrictive covenants of record. Owner acknowledges receipt of a copy of this agreement.

    WITNESS the following signature(s) and seal(s):

Date Signed: _____ _____ (SEAL)
(Owner)

Listing Broker _____

_____ _____ (SEAL)
(Owner)

Address _____ Telephone _____

OFFER TO PURCHASE AGREEMENT

This AGREEMENT made as of_____, 19_____,

among_____(herein called "Purchaser"),

and_____(herein called "Seller"),

and_____(herein called "Broker"),
provides that Purchaser agrees to buy through Broker as agent for Seller, and Seller agrees to sell the following described real estate, and all improvements

thereon, located in the jurisdiction of_____,

(all herein called "the property"):_____

_____

_____

_____

_____

_____, and more commonly known as_____

_____(street address).

   1. The purchase price of the property is_____

Dollars ($_____), and such purchase price shall be paid as follows:

_____

_____

_____

_____

_____

   2. Purchaser has made a deposit of_____ Dollars ($_____)
with Broker, receipt of which is hereby acknowledged, and such deposit shall be held by Broker in escrow until the date of settlement and then applied
to the purchase price, or returned to Purchaser if the title to the property is not marketable.

   3. Seller agrees to convey the property to Purchaser by Warranty Deed with the usual covenants of title and free and clear from all encumbrances,
tenancies, liens (for taxes or otherwise), except as may be otherwise provided above, but subject to applicable restrictive covenants of record. Seller further
agrees to deliver possession of the property to Purchaser on the date of settlement and to pay the expense of preparing the deed of conveyance.

   4. Settlement shall be made at the offices of Broker or at_____on or before

_____, 19_____, or as soon thereafter as title can be examined and necessary documents prepared, with allowance of
a reasonable time for Seller to correct any defects reported by the title examiner.

   5. All taxes, interest, rent, and F.H.A. or similar escrow deposits, if any, shall be prorated as of the date of settlement.

   6. All risk of loss or damage to the property by fire, windstorm, casualty, or other cause is assumed by Seller until the date of settlement.

   7. Purchaser and Seller agree that Broker was the sole procuring cause of this Contract of Purchase, and Seller agrees to pay Broker for services

rendered a cash fee of_____per cent of the purchase price. If either Purchaser or Seller defaults under such Contract, such defaulting party shall
be liable for the cash fee of Broker and any expenses incurred by the non-defaulting party in connection with this transaction.

Subject to:_____

_____

_____

_____

   8. Purchaser represents that an inspection satisfactory to Purchaser has been made of the property, and Purchaser agrees to accept the property in
its present condition except as may be otherwise provided in the description of the property above.

   9. This Contract of Purchase constitutes the entire agreement among the parties and may not be modified or changed except by written instrument
executed by all of the parties, including Broker.

   10. This Contract of Purchase shall be construed, interpreted, and applied according to the law of the jurisdiction of_____ and shall
be binding upon and shall inure to the benefit of the heirs, personal representatives, successors, and assigns of the parties.

All parties to this agreement acknowledge receipt of a certified copy.

WITNESS the following signatures and seals:

_____(SEAL)   _____(SEAL)
           Seller   Purchaser

_____(SEAL)   _____(SEAL)
           Seller   Purchaser

_____(SEAL)
           Broker

Deposit Rec'd $_____

Check   Cash

Sales Agent:

CONTRACT PROBLEM NO. 2

On June 15, 1973, you show the Katz property to Ernest Money and his wife, Vera Little Money, who make the following offer to purchase. They will pay a price that will net the sellers $15,335 after paying your commission, the first D/T, and the second D/T note. Purchasers are to secure an 80 percent loan at an interest rate not to exceed 8 percent p/a, and purchasers are to pay the remainder in cash at closing. All chattels included in the listing are to be included. Settlement is to be held on July 15, 1973. Purchaser gives you a deposit of $500 by check, and seller accepts these terms. Prepare a contract accordingly.

LISTING PROBLEM NO. 3

As an agent for the Tryde and Trew Real Estate Company, you list the property of Justin Case and his wife, Sudie Case. It is a three bedroom brick rambler, on a 100′ × 240′ lot. Screened side porch and built-in one car garage. Eat-in kitchen with built-in oven and range, dishwasher, and refrigerator. The house is eight years old and is in good condition. Three bedrooms, 12′ × 17′ living room, 10′ × 12′ dining room, 2 full baths, and combination storm doors and screens at all windows and doors. Paneled den, 10′ × 11′, and a 15′ × 25′ recreation room in the basement. Roof is of composition shingle. Paved side drive to the garage. Taxes are $486.40 per year, based on an assessment of $2,400 for the land and $10,400 on the improvements. (You compute the tax rate.) Taxes and insurance are included in the monthly payment of $134.80 on the conventional first D/T loan having a balance of $14,652 as of July 1, 1973. Interest on the loan is at $6\frac{1}{2}$ percent p/a, and the loan has 17 years to run. The loan is held by the Valley Trust Company. The home is heated by oil fired hot water, and there is a summer-winter hook-up for hot water. Estimated fuel cost is $250 per year. The legal description is Lot 3, Block 2, Section 1, of the Green Valley Subdivision. Mail address is 14 Wisteria Drive, East Staunton, (your state). The property is located in Augusta County, (your state), and water is supplied by well. There is a septic tank and bottled gas for cooking. Owner is selling because of transfer of employment. The owners want to list at a price that will net them $13,400 after paying your commission of 6 percent, paying off the first D/T, and also a second D/T having a balance of $2,028 at 6 percent interest, which cannot be assumed. (You compute the listing price.) This is to be a 90-day listing, to commence on May 25, 1973. Your commission is to be 6 percent of the purchase price.

CONTRACT PROBLEM NO. 3

On June 5, 1973, you find a buyer, Miss Minnie Skirt, a single woman, who makes an offer at the listed price on the following terms: She will secure

EXCLUSIVE AUTHORIZATION TO SELL

SALES PRICE: _____ TYPE HOME _____ TOTAL BEDROOMS _____ TOTAL BATHS _____

ADDRESS: _____

JURISDICTION OF: _____

| AMT. OF LOAN TO BE ASSUMED $ | AS OF WHAT DATE: | TAXES & INS. INCLUDED: | YEARS TO GO | AMOUNT PAYABLE MONTHLY $ | @ | TYPE % LOAN |

MORTGAGE COMPANY _____ 2nd TRUST $ _____

ESTIMATED EXPECTED RENT MONTHLY $ _____ TYPE OF APPRAISAL REQUESTED: _____

OWNER'S NAME _____ PHONES: (HOME) _____ (BUSINESS) _____

TENANTS NAME _____ PHONES: (HOME) _____ (BUSINESS) _____

POSSESSION _____ DATE LISTED: _____ EXCLUSIVE FOR _____ DATE OF EXPIRATION _____

LISTING BROKER _____ PHONE _____ KEY AVAILABLE AT _____

LISTING SALESMAN _____ HOME PHONE: _____ HOW TO BE SHOWN: _____

(1) ENTRANCE FOYER □ CENTER HALL □	(18) AGE	AIR CONDITIONING □	(32) TYPE KITCHEN CABINETS
(2) LIVING ROOM SIZE FIREPLACE □	(19) ROOFING	TOOL HOUSE □	(33) TYPE COUNTER TOPS
(3) DINING ROOM SIZE	(20) GARAGE SIZE	PATIO □	(34) EAT-IN SIZE KITCHEN □
(4) BEDROOM TOTAL: DOWN UP	(21) SIDE DRIVE □ CIRCULAR DRIVE □		(35) BREAKFAST ROOM □
(5) BATHS TOTAL: DOWN UP	(22) PORCH □ SIDE □ REAR □ SCREENED □		(36) BUILT-IN OVEN & RANGE □
(6) DEN SIZE FIREPLACE □	(23) FENCED YARD	OUTDOOR GRILL □	(37) SEPARATE STOVE INCLUDED □
(7) FAMILY ROOM SIZE FIREPLACE □	(24) STORM WINDOWS □ STORM DOORS □		(38) REFRIGERATOR INCLUDED □
(8) RECREATION ROOM SIZE FIREPLACE □	(25) CURBS & GUTTERS □ SIDEWALKS □		(39) DISHWASHER INCLUDED
(9) BASEMENT SIZE	(26) STORM SEWERS □	ALLEY □	(40) DISPOSAL INCLUDED □
NONE □ 1/4 □ 1/3 □ 1/2 □ 3/4 □ FULL □	(27) WATER SUPPLY		(41) DOUBLE SINK □ SINGLE SINK □
(10) UTILITY ROOM SIZE	(28) SEWER □ SEPTIC □		STAINLESS STEEL □ PORCELAIN □
TYPE HOT WATER SYSTEM:	(29) TYPE GAS: NATURAL □ BOTTLED □		(42) WASHER INCLUDED □ DRYER INCLUDED □
(11) TYPE HEAT	(30) WHY SELLING		(43) PANTRY □ EXHAUST FAN □
(12) EST. FUEL COST			(44) LAND ASSESSMENT $
(13) ATTIC □	(31) DIRECTIONS TO PROPERTY		(45) IMPROVEMENTS $
PULL DOWN STAIRWAY □ REGULAR STAIRWAY □ TRAP DOOR □			(46) TOTAL ASSESSMENT $
(14) MAIDS ROOM □ TYPE BATH			(47) TAX RATE
LOCATION			(48) TOTAL ANNUAL TAXES $
(15) NAME OF BUILDER			(49) LOT SIZE
(16) SQUARE FOOTAGE			(50) LOT NO. BLOCK SECTION
(17) EXTERIOR OF HOUSE			

NAME OF SCHOOLS: ELEMENTARY: _____ JR. HIGH: _____

HIGH _____ PAROCHIAL: _____

PUBLIC TRANSPORTATION: _____

NEAREST SHOPPING AREA: _____

REMARKS: _____

Date: _____

In consideration of the services of _____ (herein called "Broker") to be rendered to the undersigned (herein called "Owner"), and of the promise of Broker to make reasonable efforts to obtain a Purchaser therefor, Owner hereby lists with Broker the real estate and all improvements thereon which are described above (all herein called "the property"), and Owner hereby grants to Broker the exclusive and irrevocable right to sell such property from 12:00 Noon on _____, 19____ until 12:00 Midnight on _____, 19____ (herein called "period of time"), for the price of _____ Dollars ($ _____) or for such other price and upon such other terms (including exchange) as Owner may subsequently authorize during the period of time.

It is understood by Owner that the above sum or any other price subsequently authorized by Owner shall include a cash fee of _____ per cent of such price or other price which shall be payable by Owner to Broker upon consummation by any Purchaser or Purchasers of a valid contract of sale of the property during the period of time and whether or not Broker was a procuring cause of any such contract of sale.

If the property is sold or exchanged by Owner, or by Broker or by any other person to any Purchaser to whom the property was shown by Broker or any representative of Broker within sixty (60) days after the expiration of the period of time mentioned above, Owner agrees to pay to Broker a cash fee which shall be the same percentage of the purchase price as the percentage mentioned above.

Broker is hereby authorized by Owner to place a "For Sale" sign on the property and to remove all signs of other brokers or salesmen during the period of time, and Owner hereby agrees to make the property available to Broker at all reasonable hours for the purpose of showing it to prospective Purchasers.

Owner agrees to convey the property to the Purchaser by warranty deed with the usual covenants of title and free and clear from all encumbrances, tenancies, liens (for taxes or otherwise), but subject to applicable restrictive covenants of record. Owner acknowledges receipt of a copy of this agreement.

WITNESS the following signature(s) and seal(s):

Date Signed: _____ _____ (SEAL) (Owner)

Listing Broker _____

_____ (SEAL) (Owner)

Address _____ Telephone _____

214

OFFER TO PURCHASE AGREEMENT

This AGREEMENT made as of_____, 19_____,

among_____(herein called "Purchaser"),

and_____(herein called "Seller"),

and_____(herein called "Broker"),
provides that Purchaser agrees to buy through Broker as agent for Seller, and Seller agrees to sell the following described real estate, and all improvements

thereon, located in the jurisdiction of_____,

(all herein called "the property"):_____

_____

_____

_____

_____

_____, and more commonly known as_____

_____(street address).

    1. The purchase price of the property is_____

Dollars ($_____), and such purchase price shall be paid as follows:

_____

_____

_____

_____

_____

    2. Purchaser has made a deposit of_____Dollars ($_____)
with Broker, receipt of which is hereby acknowledged, and such deposit shall be held by Broker in escrow until the date of settlement and then applied
to the purchase price, or returned to Purchaser if the title to the property is not marketable.

    3. Seller agrees to convey the property to Purchaser by Warranty Deed with the usual covenants of title and free and clear from all encumbrances,
tenancies, liens (for taxes or otherwise), except as may be otherwise provided above, but subject to applicable restrictive covenants of record. Seller further
agrees to deliver possession of the property to Purchaser on the date of settlement and to pay the expense of preparing the deed of conveyance.

    4. Settlement shall be made at the offices of Broker or at_____on or before

_____, 19_____, or as soon thereafter as title can be examined and necessary documents prepared, with allowance of
a reasonable time for Seller to correct any defects reported by the title examiner.

    5. All taxes, interest, rent, and F.H.A. or similar escrow deposits, if any, shall be prorated as of the date of settlement.

    6. All risk of loss or damage to the property by fire, windstorm, casualty, or other cause is assumed by Seller until the date of settlement.

    7. Purchaser and Seller agree that Broker was the sole procuring cause of this Contract of Purchase, and Seller agrees to pay Broker for services

rendered a cash fee of_____per cent of the purchase price. If either Purchaser or Seller defaults under such Contract, such defaulting party shall
be liable for the cash fee of Broker and any expenses incurred by the non-defaulting party in connection with this transaction.

Subject to:_____

_____

_____

_____

    8. Purchaser represents that an inspection satisfactory to Purchaser has been made of the property, and Purchaser agrees to accept the property in
its present condition except as may be otherwise provided in the description of the property above.

    9. This Contract of Purchase constitutes the entire agreement among the parties and may not be modified or changed except by written instrument
executed by all of the parties, including Broker.

    10. This Contract of Purchase shall be construed, interpreted, and applied according to the law of the jurisdiction of_____and shall
be binding upon and shall inure to the benefit of the heirs, personal representatives, successors, and assigns of the parties.

All parties to this agreement acknowledge receipt of a certified copy.

WITNESS the following signatures and seals:

_____(SEAL)   _____(SEAL)
                  Seller   Purchaser

_____(SEAL)   _____(SEAL)
                  Seller   Purchaser

_____(SEAL)
                  Broker

Deposit Rec'd $_____

Check   Cash

Sales Agent:

a 75 percent loan to be amortized at 8.0 percent p/a interest and repaid in equal monthly installments for a 25-year term. She will pay 60 percent of the remainder as a down payment, and owner must take back a deferred purchase money trust for 40 percent of the remainder, at 8.0 percent p/a interest, to be repaid at the rate of $35/month, with the entire balance due and payable in seven years. She desires occupancy of the premises on July 1, 1973, and offers to pay a rent of $8 per day from that date until settlement is accomplished. Purchaser gives you a check for $1,000 as a deposit and signs an offer on these terms. Seller accepts this offer. Prepare a contract on these terms, converting loan percentages to dollar amounts. Settlement is to take place on or before July 15, 1973.

LISTING PROBLEM NO. 4

As agent for the Hiram N. Fyram Realtors, on May 5, 1973, you secure a 120 day exclusive right to sell listing on the property owned by Miss Hedda Akers and her sister, Belle E. Akers, located at 44 Swampview Terrace, Portsmouth, (your state), Nansemond County. Legal description is Lot 4, Block 2, Underwater Acres Subdivision. The lot is 74 × 150 feet in size. Heat is gas fired, hot water baseboard, with summer-winter hookup. No basement, roof of composition shingle. The house is in good condition, 5 years old. Concrete driveways and sidewalks. Combination storm windows and doors at all openings. There are to be two window air conditioners, electric refrigerator, dryer, and automatic washer included. There is an F.H.A. first D/T of $20,771.34, as of July 1, 1973, with 16 years to go on its amortization. Interest rate is $5\frac{1}{2}$ percent, and payments of $147.45 PITI, held by the Virginia Savings and Loan. Seller will take back a second D/T of $3,500, with interest at 8 percent for 5 years. You list the house at a net price of $32,900 after paying your commission of 6 percent. The house is a colonial, 4 bedroom and 2 baths on second floor, living room 22′ × 15′, dining room 10′ × 12′, family room 12′ × 16′, with half bath and kitchen with eating space on the first floor. There is a two car garage, PDS to attic, fireplace in living room. Brick construction, fenced rear yard, connected to all city utilities. Land is assessed at $8,400, home at $14,000, tax rate is $3.95. Owner advises that there is an unpaid sewer assessment of $250 which will be paid at settlement. Heat last year was $245. The house contains 2,456 square feet. To reach, go west on Braddock Road, left on Swampview Terrace to house.

CONTRACT PROBLEM NO. 4

On May 20, 1973, you show the Akers home to Rays D. Kidds and Minnie Moore Kidds, his wife, who make the following offer: They agree to pay the asking price but ask that the sellers include their membership in the community swimming pool at the contract price. Purchasers are to pay 5 percent down payment and secure a 95 percent insured loan from a local savings and loan association. You present the offer to the sellers, who accept on these terms. Complete a contract, including all pertinent information from the listing. Purchaser makes a $1,000 deposit by check.

EXCLUSIVE AUTHORIZATION TO SELL

SALES PRICE: _____ TYPE HOME _____ TOTAL BEDROOMS _____ TOTAL BATHS _____

ADDRESS: _____ JURISDICTION OF: _____
AMT. OF LOAN   AS OF   TAXES & INS.   YEARS   AMOUNT PAYABLE   TYPE
TO BE ASSUMED $ _____ WHAT DATE: _____ INCLUDED: _____ TO GO: ___ MONTHLY $ _____ @ ___ % LOAN ___

MORTGAGE COMPANY _____ 2nd TRUST $ _____
ESTIMATED   TYPE OF APPRAISAL
EXPECTED RENT MONTHLY $ _____ REQUESTED: _____

OWNER'S NAME _____ PHONES: (HOME) _____ (BUSINESS) _____

TENANTS NAME _____ PHONES: (HOME) _____ (BUSINESS) _____

POSSESSION _____ DATE LISTED: _____ EXCLUSIVE FOR _____ DATE OF EXPIRATION _____

LISTING BROKER _____ PHONE _____ KEY AVAILABLE AT _____

LISTING SALESMAN _____ HOME PHONE: _____ HOW TO BE SHOWN: _____

(1) ENTRANCE FOYER ☐ CENTER HALL ☐	(18) AGE AIR CONDITIONING ☐	(32) TYPE KITCHEN CABINETS
(2) LIVING ROOM SIZE FIREPLACE ☐	(19) ROOFING TOOL HOUSE ☐	(33) TYPE COUNTER TOPS
(3) DINING ROOM SIZE	(20) GARAGE SIZE PATIO ☐	(34) EAT-IN SIZE KITCHEN ☐
(4) BEDROOM TOTAL: DOWN UP	(21) SIDE DRIVE ☐ CIRCULAR DRIVE ☐	(35) BREAKFAST ROOM ☐
(5) BATHS TOTAL: DOWN UP	(22) PORCH ☐ SIDE ☐ REAR ☐ SCREENED ☐	(36) BUILT-IN OVEN & RANGE ☐
(6) DEN SIZE FIREPLACE ☐	(23) FENCED YARD OUTDOOR GRILL ☐	(37) SEPARATE STOVE INCLUDED ☐
(7) FAMILY ROOM SIZE FIREPLACE ☐	(24) STORM WINDOWS ☐ STORM DOORS ☐	(38) REFRIGERATOR INCLUDED ☐
(8) RECREATION ROOM SIZE FIREPLACE ☐	(25) CURBS & GUTTERS ☐ SIDEWALKS ☐	(39) DISHWASHER INCLUDED
(9) BASEMENT SIZE	(26) STORM SEWERS ☐ ALLEY ☐	(40) DISPOSAL INCLUDED ☐
NONE ☐ 1/4 ☐ 1/3 ☐ 1/2 ☐ 3/4 ☐ FULL ☐	(27) WATER SUPPLY	(41) DOUBLE SINK ☐ SINGLE SINK ☐
(10) UTILITY ROOM SIZE	(28) SEWER ☐	STAINLESS STEEL ☐ PORCELAIN ☐
TYPE HOT WATER SYSTEM:	(29) TYPE GAS: NATURAL ☐ BOTTLED ☐	(42) WASHER INCLUDED ☐ DRYER INCLUDED ☐
(11) TYPE HEAT	(30) WHY SELLING	(43) PANTRY ☐ EXHAUST FAN ☐
(12) EST. FUEL COST		(44) LAND ASSESSMENT $
(13) ATTIC ☐	(31) DIRECTIONS TO PROPERTY	(45) IMPROVEMENTS $
PULL DOWN STAIRWAY ☐ REGULAR STAIRWAY ☐ TRAP DOOR ☐		(46) TOTAL ASSESSMENT $
(14) MAIDS ROOM ☐ TYPE BATH		(47) TAX RATE
LOCATION		(48) TOTAL ANNUAL TAXES $
(15) NAME OF BUILDER		(49) LOT SIZE
(16) SQUARE FOOTAGE		(50) LOT NO. BLOCK SECTION
(17) EXTERIOR OF HOUSE		

NAME OF SCHOOLS: ELEMENTARY: _____ _____ JR. HIGH: _____

                  HIGH _____ PAROCHIAL: _____

PUBLIC TRANSPORTATION: _____

NEAREST SHOPPING AREA: _____

REMARKS: _____
_____
_____
_____

Date: _____

In consideration of the services of_____(herein called "Broker") to be rendered to the undersigned (herein called "Owner"), and of the promise of Broker to make reasonable efforts to obtain a Purchaser therefor, Owner hereby lists with Broker the real estate and all improvements thereon which are described above (all herein called "the property"), and Owner hereby grants to Broker the exclusive and irrevocable right to sell such property from 12:00 Noon on_____, 19_____until 12:00 Midnight on_____, 19_____ (herein called "period of time"), for the price of_____Dollars ($_____) or for such other price and upon such other terms (including exchange) as Owner may subsequently authorize during the period of time.

It is understood by Owner that the above sum or any other price subsequently authorized by Owner shall include a cash fee of_____ per cent of such price or other price which shall be payable by Owner to Broker upon consummation by any Purchaser or Purchasers of a valid contract of sale of the property during the period of time and whether or not Broker was a procuring cause of any such contract of sale.

If the property is sold or exchanged by Owner, or by Broker or by any other person to any Purchaser to whom the property was shown by Broker or any representative of Broker within sixty (60) days after the expiration of the period of time mentioned above, Owner agrees to pay to Broker a cash fee which shall be the same percentage of the purchase price as the percentage mentioned above.

Broker is hereby authorized by Owner to place a "For Sale" sign on the property and to remove all signs of other brokers or salesmen during the period of time, and Owner hereby agrees to make the property available to Broker at all reasonable hours for the purpose of showing it to prospective Purchasers.

Owner agrees to convey the property to the Purchaser by warranty deed with the usual covenants of title and free and clear from all encumbrances, tenancies, liens (for taxes or otherwise), but subject to applicable restrictive covenants of record. Owner acknowledges receipt of a copy of this agreement.

WITNESS the following signature(s) and seal(s):

Date Signed:_____   _____ (SEAL)
                                                                              (Owner)

Listing Broker_____

                                                _____ (SEAL)
                                                                              (Owner)

Address_____ Telephone_____

_____

217

OFFER TO PURCHASE AGREEMENT

This AGREEMENT made as of_____, 19_____,

among_____(herein called "Purchaser"),

and_____(herein called "Seller"),

and_____(herein called "Broker"),
provides that Purchaser agrees to buy through Broker as agent for Seller, and Seller agrees to sell the following described real estate, and all improvements

thereon, located in the jurisdiction of_____,

(all herein called "the property"):_____

_____

_____

_____

_____

_____, and more commonly known as_____

_____ (street address).

1. The purchase price of the property is_____

Dollars ($_____), and such purchase price shall be paid as follows:

_____

_____

_____

_____

_____

_____

2. Purchaser has made a deposit of_____Dollars ($_____)
with Broker, receipt of which is hereby acknowledged, and such deposit shall be held by Broker in escrow until the date of settlement and then applied
to the purchase price, or returned to Purchaser if the title to the property is not marketable.

3. Seller agrees to convey the property to Purchaser by Warranty Deed with the usual covenants of title and free and clear from all encumbrances,
tenancies, liens (for taxes or otherwise), except as may be otherwise provided above, but subject to applicable restrictive covenants of record. Seller further
agrees to deliver possession of the property to Purchaser on the date of settlement and to pay the expense of preparing the deed of conveyance.

4. Settlement shall be made at the offices of Broker or at_____on or before

_____, 19_____, or as soon thereafter as title can be examined and necessary documents prepared, with allowance of
a reasonable time for Seller to correct any defects reported by the title examiner.

5. All taxes, interest, rent, and F.H.A. or similar escrow deposits, if any, shall be prorated as of the date of settlement.

6. All risk of loss or damage to the property by fire, windstorm, casualty, or other cause is assumed by Seller until the date of settlement.

7. Purchaser and Seller agree that Broker was the sole procuring cause of this Contract of Purchase, and Seller agrees to pay Broker for services

rendered a cash fee of_____per cent of the purchase price. If either Purchaser or Seller defaults under such Contract, such defaulting party shall
be liable for the cash fee of Broker and any expenses incurred by the non-defaulting party in connection with this transaction.

Subject to:_____

_____

_____

_____

8. Purchaser represents that an inspection satisfactory to Purchaser has been made of the property, and Purchaser agrees to accept the property in
its present condition except as may be otherwise provided in the description of the property above.

9. This Contract of Purchase constitutes the entire agreement among the parties and may not be modified or changed except by written instrument
executed by all of the parties, including Broker.

10. This Contract of Purchase shall be construed, interpreted, and applied according to the law of the jurisdiction of_____ and shall
be binding upon and shall inure to the benefit of the heirs, personal representatives, successors, and assigns of the parties.

All parties to this agreement acknowledge receipt of a certified copy.

WITNESS the following signatures and seals:

_____(SEAL)   _____(SEAL)
Seller   Purchaser

_____(SEAL)   _____(SEAL)
Seller   Purchaser

_____(SEAL)
Broker

Deposit Rec'd $_____

Check   Cash

Sales Agent:

218

EXCLUSIVE AUTHORIZATION TO SELL

SALES PRICE: _____ TYPE HOME _____ TOTAL BEDROOMS _____ TOTAL BATHS _____

ADDRESS: _____ JURISDICTION OF: _____

AMT. OF LOAN _____ AS OF _____ TAXES & INS. YEARS AMOUNT PAYABLE TYPE
TO BE ASSUMED $ _____ WHAT DATE: _____ INCLUDED: _____ TO GO: MONTHLY $ _____ @ ___ % LOAN

MORTGAGE COMPANY _____ 2nd TRUST $ _____

ESTIMATED TYPE OF APPRAISAL
EXPECTED RENT MONTHLY $ _____ REQUESTED: _____

OWNER'S NAME _____ PHONES: (HOME) _____ (BUSINESS) _____

TENANTS NAME _____ PHONES: (HOME) _____ (BUSINESS) _____

POSSESSION _____ DATE LISTED: _____ EXCLUSIVE FOR _____ DATE OF EXPIRATION _____

LISTING BROKER _____ PHONE _____ KEY AVAILABLE AT _____

LISTING SALESMAN _____ HOME PHONE: _____ HOW TO BE SHOWN: _____

(1) ENTRANCE FOYER ☐ CENTER HALL ☐	(18) AGE	AIR CONDITIONING ☐	(32) TYPE KITCHEN CABINETS
(2) LIVING ROOM SIZE FIREPLACE ☐	(19) ROOFING	TOOL HOUSE ☐	(33) TYPE COUNTER TOPS
(3) DINING ROOM SIZE	(20) GARAGE SIZE	PATIO ☐	(34) EAT-IN SIZE KITCHEN ☐
(4) BEDROOM TOTAL: DOWN UP	(21) SIDE DRIVE ☐	CIRCULAR DRIVE ☐	(35) BREAKFAST ROOM ☐
(5) BATHS TOTAL: DOWN UP	(22) PORCH ☐ SIDE ☐ REAR ☐	SCREENED ☐	(36) BUILT-IN OVEN & RANGE ☐
(6) DEN SIZE FIREPLACE ☐	(23) FENCED YARD	OUTDOOR GRILL ☐	(37) SEPARATE STOVE INCLUDED ☐
(7) FAMILY ROOM SIZE FIREPLACE ☐	(24) STORM WINDOWS ☐	STORM DOORS ☐	(38) REFRIGERATOR INCLUDED ☐
(8) RECREATION ROOM SIZE FIREPLACE ☐	(25) CURBS & GUTTERS ☐	SIDEWALKS ☐	(39) DISHWASHER INCLUDED ☐
(9) BASEMENT SIZE	(26) STORM SEWERS ☐	ALLEY ☐	(40) DISPOSAL INCLUDED ☐
NONE ☐ 1/4 ☐ 1/3 ☐ 1/2 ☐ 3/4 ☐ FULL ☐	(27) WATER SUPPLY		(41) DOUBLE SINK ☐ SINGLE SINK ☐
(10) UTILITY ROOM SIZE	(28) SEWER ☐	SEPTIC ☐	STAINLESS STEEL ☐ PORCELAIN ☐
TYPE HOT WATER SYSTEM:	(29) TYPE GAS: NATURAL ☐	BOTTLED ☐	(42) WASHER INCLUDED ☐ DRYER INCLUDED ☐
(11) TYPE HEAT	(30) WHY SELLING		(43) PANTRY ☐ EXHAUST FAN ☐
(12) EST. FUEL COST			(44) LAND ASSESSMENT $
(13) ATTIC ☐	(31) DIRECTIONS TO PROPERTY		(45) IMPROVEMENTS $
PULL DOWN STAIRWAY ☐ REGULAR STAIRWAY ☐ TRAP DOOR ☐			(46) TOTAL ASSESSMENT $
(14) MAIDS ROOM ☐ TYPE BATH			(47) TAX RATE
LOCATION			(48) TOTAL ANNUAL TAXES $
(15) NAME OF BUILDER			(49) LOT SIZE
(16) SQUARE FOOTAGE			(50) LOT NO. BLOCK SECTION
(17) EXTERIOR OF HOUSE			

NAME OF SCHOOLS: ELEMENTARY: _____ JR. HIGH: _____

HIGH _____ PAROCHIAL: _____

PUBLIC TRANSPORTATION: _____

NEAREST SHOPPING AREA: _____

REMARKS: _____

Date: _____

In consideration of the services of _____ (herein called "Broker") to be rendered to the undersigned (herein called "Owner"), and of the promise of Broker to make reasonable efforts to obtain a Purchaser therefor, Owner hereby lists with Broker the real estate and all improvements thereon which are described above (all herein called "the property"), and Owner hereby grants to Broker the exclusive and irrevocable right to sell such property from 12:00 Noon on _____, 19_____ until 12:00 Midnight on _____, 19_____ (herein called "period of time"), for the price of _____ Dollars ($_____) or for such other price and upon such other terms (including exchange) as Owner may subsequently authorize during the period of time.

It is understood by Owner that the above sum or any other price subsequently authorized by Owner shall include a cash fee of _____ per cent of such price or other price which shall be payable by Owner to Broker upon consummation by any Purchaser or Purchasers of a valid contract of sale of the property during the period of time and whether or not Broker was a procuring cause of any such contract of sale.

If the property is sold or exchanged by Owner, or by Broker or by any other person to any Purchaser to whom the property was shown by Broker or any representative of Broker within sixty (60) days after the expiration of the period of time mentioned above, Owner agrees to pay to Broker a cash fee which shall be the same percentage of the purchase price as the percentage mentioned above.

Broker is hereby authorized by Owner to place a "For Sale" sign on the property and to remove all signs of other brokers or salesmen during the period of time, and Owner hereby agrees to make the property available to Broker at all reasonable hours for the purpose of showing it to prospective Purchasers.

Owner agrees to convey the property to the Purchaser by warranty deed with the usual covenants of title and free and clear from all encumbrances, tenancies, liens (for taxes or otherwise), but subject to applicable restrictive covenants of record. Owner acknowledges receipt of a copy of this agreement.

WITNESS the following signature(s) and seal(s):

Date Signed: _____ _____ (SEAL)
(Owner)

Listing Broker _____

_____ (SEAL)
(Owner)

Address _____ Telephone _____

OFFER TO PURCHASE AGREEMENT

This AGREEMENT made as of_____, 19_____,

among_____(herein called "Purchaser"),

and_____(herein called "Seller"),

and_____(herein called "Broker"),
provides that Purchaser agrees to buy through Broker as agent for Seller, and Seller agrees to sell the following described real estate, and all improvements

thereon, located in the jurisdiction of_____,

(all herein called "the property"):_____

_____

_____

_____

_____

_____, and more commonly known as_____

_____(street address).

    1. The purchase price of the property is_____

Dollars ($_____), and such purchase price shall be paid as follows:

_____

_____

_____

_____

_____

_____

    2. Purchaser has made a deposit of_____Dollars ($_____)
with Broker, receipt of which is hereby acknowledged, and such deposit shall be held by Broker in escrow until the date of settlement and then applied
to the purchase price, or returned to Purchaser if the title to the property is not marketable.

    3. Seller agrees to convey the property to Purchaser by Warranty Deed with the usual covenants of title and free and clear from all encumbrances,
tenancies, liens (for taxes or otherwise), except as may be otherwise provided above, but subject to applicable restrictive covenants of record. Seller further
agrees to deliver possession of the property to Purchaser on the date of settlement and to pay the expense of preparing the deed of conveyance.

    4. Settlement shall be made at the offices of Broker or at_____on or before

_____, 19_____, or as soon thereafter as title can be examined and necessary documents prepared, with allowance of
a reasonable time for Seller to correct any defects reported by the title examiner.

    5. All taxes, interest, rent, and F.H.A. or similar escrow deposits, if any, shall be prorated as of the date of settlement.

    6. All risk of loss or damage to the property by fire, windstorm, casualty, or other cause is assumed by Seller until the date of settlement.

    7. Purchaser and Seller agree that Broker was the sole procuring cause of this Contract of Purchase, and Seller agrees to pay Broker for services

rendered a cash fee of_____per cent of the purchase price. If either Purchaser or Seller defaults under such Contract, such defaulting party shall
be liable for the cash fee of Broker and any expenses incurred by the non-defaulting party in connection with this transaction.

Subject to:_____

_____

_____

_____

    8. Purchaser represents that an inspection satisfactory to Purchaser has been made of the property, and Purchaser agrees to accept the property in
its present condition except as may be otherwise provided in the description of the property above.

    9. This Contract of Purchase constitutes the entire agreement among the parties and may not be modified or changed except by written instrument
executed by all of the parties, including Broker.

    10. This Contract of Purchase shall be construed, interpreted, and applied according to the law of the jurisdiction of_____and shall
be binding upon and shall inure to the benefit of the heirs, personal representatives, successors, and assigns of the parties.

All parties to this agreement acknowledge receipt of a certified copy.

WITNESS the following signatures and seals:

_____(SEAL)   _____(SEAL)
                Seller   Purchaser

_____(SEAL)   _____(SEAL)
                Seller   Purchaser

_____(SEAL)
                Broker

Deposit Rec'd $_____

Check   Cash

Sales Agent:

Chapter 19

Closing Statement
Problems

These problems are based on the previously completed listing and contract problems. Each problem corresponds numerically with the similar listing and contract. It will be necessary to refer to your solution in order to complete the closing statement problems.

CLOSING STATEMENT PROBLEM NO. 1

Myrtle Beach and Virginia Beach—Purchasers
Phil O. Dendron and Rhoda Dendron—Sellers

Using the data from the listing and contract solutions, plus the following additional information, complete the Dendron to Beach closing. As in previous problems, do not adjust loan balances, nor include clerk's fees, etc. Title examination, $163.25; title insurance, $66.00; recording tax, $.20 per $100; taxes have been paid for year. Buyer is to assume seller's hazard insurance policy, purchased 1-10-72 at a cost of $97.20 for a 3 year policy; preparation of second deed of trust, $20; preparation of deed, $25; preparation of first D/T, $20. Tenant's rent is paid to 7-15-73. Use a 30-day method of computation.

CLOSING STATEMENT PROBLEM NO. 2

Ernest Money and Vera Little Money—Purchasers
Al E. Katz and Kitty Katz—Sellers

Use the listing and contract solutions to determine taxes and other pertinent information. To save time, do not compute interest on the first D/T loan. Clerk's fees, notary fees, etc., are purposely omitted. Use 12 month, 30 day method of prorations. Sale is to be settled on 7-15-73. Total loan discount is 3 percent. Examination of title, $125; title insurance, $52.50; buyer to assume seller's hazard insurance policy, purchased 6-1-72 at a cost of $93.60 for a 3 year policy. Preparation of deed, $30; preparation of first

SETTLEMENT STATEMENT WORKSHEET

Complete the Settlement Statement Worksheet on the basis of the information given in the loose data sheet, even if that information in some respects differs from current real estate practice in your area. Use 30-day method of computation.

	BUYER'S STATEMENT		SELLER'S STATEMENT	
	DEBIT	CREDIT	DEBIT	CREDIT

D/T, $25; recording tax, $.20 per $100. Taxes for year have not been paid by seller, are due 12-31-73.

CLOSING STATEMENT PROBLEM NO. 3

Minnie Skirt—Purchaser
Justin Case and Sudie Case—Sellers

Using the listing and sale contract information, close the Case to Skirt sale. For simplicity and to save time, do not prorate interest on loans or monthly payments if involved. Clerk's fees, credit reports, etc., are purposely omitted. The following information is given to assist you. Title examination, $160; title insurance, $84.50; preparation of deed, $30; recording tax, $.20 per $100; taxes for year have not been paid; buyer to furnish new hazard insurance policy (three years) at cost of $99; 1 percent loan service fee to be paid by purchaser; preparation of deeds of trust, $25. Settlement to be held on July 15, 1973. Purchaser to be charged rent from July 1, 1973 to closing at $8 a day. Use a 30-day method of computation.

CLOSING STATEMENT PROBLEM NO. 4

Rays D. Kidds and Minnie Moore Kidds—Purchasers
Hedda Akers and Belle E. Akers—Sellers

Close the Akers to Kidds sale, using the information in the listing and sale contract, plus the additional information given below. Do not adjust loan balances or compute interest due. Clerk's fees, notary fees, etc., are not to be included. Title examination, $225; title insurance, $122.50; annual taxes have been paid to 12-31-73. Survey, $55; loan origination fee, 1 percent; preparation of deed, $30; preparation of D/T, $25; recording tax, $.20 per $100; buyer to furnish new hazard insurance policy at cost of $145 for 3 year policy. Mortgage insurance premium, $\frac{1}{2}$ percent; loan discount, 1 percent each to purchaser and seller. Date of settlement, July 20, 1973. Use a 30-day method of computation.

QUESTIONS ON PROBLEM NO. 1

1. The annual taxes on the Dendron property are
   A. $397.63.   C. $485.89.
   B. $70.16.   D. $701.63.
2. If the property is sold during the listing term,
   I. the tenants' lease is cancelled by the sale.
   II. the lease is not affected by the sale.
   A. I only   B. II only   C. Both I and II   D. Neither I nor II

SETTLEMENT STATEMENT WORKSHEET

Complete the Settlement Statement Worksheet on the basis of the information given in the loose data sheet, even if that information in some respects differs from current real estate practice in your area. Use 30-day method of computation.

	BUYER'S STATEMENT		SELLER'S STATEMENT	
	DEBIT	CREDIT	DEBIT	CREDIT

SETTLEMENT STATEMENT WORKSHEET

Complete the Settlement Statement Worksheet on the basis of the information given in the loose data sheet, even if that information in some respects differs from current real estate practice in your area. Use 30-day method of computation.

	BUYER'S STATEMENT		SELLER'S STATEMENT	
	DEBIT	CREDIT	DEBIT	CREDIT

SETTLEMENT STATEMENT WORKSHEET

Complete the Settlement Statement Worksheet on the basis of the information given in the loose data sheet, even if that information in some respects differs from current real estate practice in your area. Use 30-day method of computation.

	BUYER'S STATEMENT		SELLER'S STATEMENT	
	DEBIT	CREDIT	DEBIT	CREDIT

3. The listed price is
        A. $35,638.   C. $33,500.
        B. $35,510.   D. none of the above.

4. If the property were sold at the listed price, the total commission would be
        I. $2,130.60.
        II. $2,138.28.
A. I only   B. II only   C. Both I and II   D. Neither I nor II

5. The contract sale price of the property is
        I. $33,000.
        II. $33,500.
A. I only   B. II only   C. Both I and II   D. Neither I nor II

6. The cash due at settlement, according to the sale contract, is
        I. $3,300.
        II. $2,300.
A. I only   B. II only   C. Both I and II   D. Neither I nor II

7. The second D/T to be held by the seller is
        I. $2,300.
        II. $3,300.
A. I only   B. II only   C. Both I and II   D. Neither I nor II

8. The purchaser must secure a first D/T loan of
        I. $26,400.
        II. $26,800.
A. I only   B. II only   C. Both I and II   D. Neither I nor II

9. The taxes are prorated on the settlement statement as
        I. a debit to purchaser.
        II. a credit to seller.
A. I only   B. II only   C. Both I and II   D. Neither I nor II

10. The amount of the prorated taxes is
        I. $409.28.
        II. $292.35.
A. I only   B. II only   C. Both I and II   D. Neither I nor II

11. The charge for preparation of deed is
        I. a debit to purchaser.
        II. a debit to seller.
A. I only   B. II only   C. Both I and II   D. Neither I nor II

12. The insurance is prorated as a
        I. debit to purchaser.
        II. credit to seller.
A. I only   B. II only   C. Both I and II   D. Neither I nor II

13. The amount of the insurance proration is
        I. $49.49.
        II. $47.71.
A. I only   B. II only   C. Both I and II   D. Neither I nor II

14. The earnest money deposit is shown as a
    I. credit to seller.
    II. debit to purchaser.
    A. I only   B. II only   C. Both I and II   D. Neither I nor II

15. The new first D/T loan is shown as a
    I. debit to purchaser.
    II. credit to purchaser.
    A. I only   B. II only   C. Both I and II   D. Neither I nor II

16. The tenants rent from 7-1-73 to 7-15-73 is a
    I. credit to purchaser.
    II. debit to seller.
    A. I only   B. II only   C. Both I and II   D. Neither I nor II

17. The recording tax for the second D/T is
    I. $6.60.
    II. $66.00.
    A. I only   B. II only   C. Both I and II   D. Neither I nor II

18. The charge for preparation of deed is
    I. $26.50.
    II. $33.00.
    A. I only   B. II only   C. Both I and II   D. Neither I nor II

19. The balance due from buyer to close is
    I. $2,990.00, credit to buyer.
    II. $2,990.00, debit to buyer.
    A. I only   B. II only   C. Both I and II   D. Neither I nor II

20. The total of seller's credits is
    I. $33,541.84.
    II. $33,539.14
    A. I only   B. II only   C. Both I and II   D. Neither I nor II

QUESTIONS ON PROBLEM NO. 2

1. The tax rate on the Katz property is
   I. $3.30 per $100.
   II. $3.00 per $100.
   A. I only   B. II only   C. Both I and II   D. Neither I nor II

2. The second D/T of $900, held by the Shylock Finance Co.,
   I. is a deferred purchase money trust.
   II. is a borrowed money trust.
   A. I only   B. II only   C. Both I and II   D. Neither I nor II

3. The age of the property is
   I. 16 years.
   II. 14 years.
   A. I only   B. II only   C. Both I and II   D. Neither I nor II

4. The assessment on the land is
        A. $9,600.   C. $2,200.
        B. $7,400.   D. none of the above.

5. The interest rate on the existing first D/T is
        I. $5\frac{1}{2}$ percent p/a.
        II. 8 percent p/a.
A. I only B. II only C. Both I and II D. Neither I nor II

6. The contract price on the Katz to Money sale is
        I. $26,500.
        II. $26,250.
A. I only B. II only C. Both I and II D. Neither I nor II

7. The first D/T loan to be secured by the purchaser is in the amount of
        I. $21,200.
        II. $21,000.
A. I only B. II only C. Both I and II D. Neither I nor II

8. Cash to be paid by purchaser at settlement, according to contract, is
        I. $5,250.
        II. $4,750.
A. I only B. II only C. Both I and II D. Neither I nor II

9. Appliances included in the sale at the listed price are
        I. electric stove, refrigerator, and washer.
        II. electric stove and refrigerator only.
A. I only B. II only C. Both I and II D. Neither I nor II

10. The date of the sale of the Katz property is
        I. July 15, 1973.
        II. August 15, 1973.
A. I only B. II only C. Both I and II D. Neither I nor II

11. The amount of the prorated taxes is
        I. $132.00.
        II. $156.00.
A. I only B. II only C. Both I and II D. Neither I nor II

12. Prorated taxes are shown as
        I. a debit to seller and credit to purchaser.
        II. a credit to purchaser only.
A. I only B. II only C. Both I and II D. Neither I nor II

13. The amount of the prorated insurance is
        I. $58.50
        II. $35.10
A. I only B. II only C. Both I and II D. Neither I nor II

14. The expense of title examination is borne by the
        I. seller.
        II. purchaser.
A. I only B. II only C. Both I and II D. Neither I nor II

15. The agent's commission is in the amount of
       I. $1,575.
       II. $1,590.
A. I only   B. II only   C. Both I and II   D. Neither I nor II

16. Recording tax is for the first D/T
       I. $21.00.
       II. $42.00.
A. I only   B. II only   C. Both I and II   D. Neither I nor II

17. The charge for preparation of deed is
       I. $21.00, paid by the seller.
       II. $30.00, paid by the purchaser.
A. I only   B. II only   C. Both I and II   D. Neither I nor II

18. The balance due from purchaser to close is
       I. $4,949.60.
       II. shown as a credit to the purchaser.
A. I only   B. II only   C. Both I and II   D. Neither I nor II

19. The expense of preparation of the deed is borne by the
       I. seller.
       II. purchaser.
A. I only   B. II only   C. Both I and II   D. Neither I nor II

20. The amount due seller to close is
       I. $15,207.50.
       II. shown as a debit to seller.
A. I only   B. II only   C. Both I and II   D. Neither I nor II

QUESTIONS ON PROBLEM NO. 3

1. The annual tax rate on the Case home is
       I. $3.80 per $100.
       II. $3.92 per $100.
A. I only   B. II only   C. Both I and II   D. Neither I nor II

2. The monthly payment on the existing first D/T loan on the Case property is
       I. $154.80.
       II. $134.80.
A. I only   B. II only   C. Both I and II   D. Neither I nor II

3. The listed price of the Case home is
       I. $32,000.00.
       II. $31,884.80.
A. I only   B. II only   C. Both I and II   D. Neither I nor II

4. The listing on the Case home will expire on
       I. August 25, 1973.
       II. July 25, 1973.
A. I only   B. II only   C. Both I and II   D. Neither I nor II

5. The cash due at settlement, according to the Case to Skirt sale contract, is

        I. $4,800.

        II. $3,800.

A. I only B. II only C. Both I and II D. Neither I nor II

6. The amount of the first D/T loan to be secured by Miss Skirt is

        I. $3,200.

        II. $25,000.

A. I only B. II only C. Both I and II D. Neither I nor II

7. The settlement date of the Case to Skirt sale is to be

        I. on or before July 15, 1973.

        II. on July 1, 1973.

A. I only B. II only C. Both I and II D. Neither I nor II

8. Rent is to be paid by purchaser to seller at the rate of

        I. $8 per day from June 5, 1973 to settlement.

        II. $8 per day from July 1, 1973 to settlement.

A. I only B. II only C. Both I and II D. Neither I nor II

9. The earnest money paid by the purchaser is

        I. $1,000.

        II. $4,800.

A. I only B. II only C. Both I and II D. Neither I nor II

10. On the closing statement, the loan service fee is charged to the

        I. purchaser.

        II. seller.

A. I only B. II only C. Both I and II D. Neither I nor II

11. The second D/T held by the seller is a

        I. debit to seller.

        II. credit to purchaser.

A. I only B. II only C. Both I and II D. Neither I nor II

12. The $30 charge for preparation of deed is a

        I. debit to purchaser.

        II. debit to seller.

A. I only B. II only C. Both I and II D. Neither I nor II

13. The amount of the prorated taxes is

        I. $263.47.

        II. $222.93.

A. I only B. II only C. Both I and II D. Neither I nor II

14. The prorated taxes are a

        I. debit to purchaser.

        II. credit to seller.

A. I only B. II only C. Both I and II D. Neither I nor II

15. Recording tax for the first D/T is

        I. $48.

        II. $64.

A. I only B. II only C. Both I and II D. Neither I nor II

16. The rent to be paid by purchaser is a
    I. credit to seller.
    II. debit to purchaser.
A. I only B. II only C. Both I and II D. Neither I nor II

17. The second D/T to be given by the purchaser is a
    I. debit to purchaser.
    II. credit to seller.
A. I only B. II only C. Both I and II D. Neither I nor II

18. The amount of the loan service fee is
    I. $240.
    II. $320.
A. I only B. II only C. Both I and II D. Neither I nor II

19. The amount due seller to close is
    I. $9,994.53.
    II. a debit to the seller.
A. I only B. II only C. Both I and II D. Neither I nor II

20. The purchaser's total debits are
    I. $32,846.90.
    II. $32,776.50.
A. I only B. II only C. Both I and II D. Neither I nor II

QUESTIONS ON PROBLEM NO. 4

1. The price at which you list the Akers home is
    A. $34,874.   C. $32,900.
    B. $35,000.   D. $34,500.

2. The annual taxes on the Akers home are
    A. $889.00.   C. $884.80.
    B. $8,848.00.   D. $8,400.00.

3. The legal description of the Akers property is
    I. 44 Swampview Terrace, Portsmouth, (your state).
    II. Lot 4, Block 2, Underwater Acres Subdivision, Nansemond County, (your state).
A. I only B. II only C. Both I and II D. Neither I nor II

4. The contract of sale between the Kidds and the Akers calls for cash at settlement in the amount of
    I. $750.
    II. $1,750.
A. I only B. II only C. Both I and II D. Neither I nor II

5. The first D/T loan on the Akers to Kidds contract is to be in the amount of
    I. $33,250.
    II. $33,130.
A. I only B. II only C. Both I and II D. Neither I nor II

6. The unpaid sewer assessment mentioned in the contract of sale is to be paid by the
>   I. purchaser.
>   II. seller.
>
> A. I only   B. II only   C. Both I and II   D. Neither I nor II

7. Should the purchasers be unable to secure the first D/T loan mentioned in the contract of sale,
>   I. the earnest money deposit will be forfeited.
>   II. the earnest money deposit will be returned to the purchaser.
>
> A. I only   B. II only   C. Both I and II   D. Neither I nor II

8. Should the property suffer a casualty loss after the contract of sale is signed, but prior to settlement, the loss would fall upon the
>   I. purchaser.
>   II. seller.
>
> A. I only   B. II only   C. Both I and II   D. Neither I nor II

9. On the settlement statement, the purchase price of the property is shown as a
>   I. debit to purchaser and credit to seller.
>   II. credit to purchaser and debit to seller.
>
> A. I only   B. II only   C. Both I and II   D. Neither I nor II

10. The earnest money deposit is a
>   I. credit to seller.
>   II. debit to seller.
>
> A. I only   B. II only   C. Both I and II   D. Neither I nor II

11. The annual taxes are shown as a
>   I. debit to purchaser.
>   II. credit to seller.
>
> A. I only   B. II only   C. Both I and II   D. Neither I nor II

12. The prorated amount of the annual taxes is
>   I. $393.00.
>   II. $390.85.
>
> A. I only   B. II only   C. Both I and II   D. Neither I nor II

13. Recording tax for the D/T is charged to the
>   I. seller.
>   II. purchaser.
>
> A. I only   B. II only   C. Both I and II   D. Neither I nor II

14. The loan discount charged by the lender is
>   I. $332.50, paid by the seller.
>   II. $332.50, each to purchaser and seller.
>
> A. I only   B. II only   C. Both I and II   D. Neither I nor II

15. The loan organization fee is
>   I. $35.00, charged to the purchaser.
>   II. $33.25, charged to the seller.
>
> A. I only   B. II only   C. Both I and II   D. Neither I nor II

16. The mortgage insurance premium is
    - I. $166.25, charged to the seller.
    - II. $175.00, charged to the seller.

    A. I only   B. II only   C. Both I and II   D. Neither I nor II

17. Balance due from purchaser to close is
    - I. $2,616.75, shown as a credit to purchaser.
    - II. $2,616.75, shown as a debit to purchaser.

    A. I only   B. II only   C. Both I and II   D. Neither I nor II

18. The balance due seller to close is
    - I. $11,909.15.
    - II. shown as a debit to the seller.

    A. I only   B. II only   C. Both I and II   D. Neither I nor II

19. The charge for preparation of the deed is a debit to the
    - I. seller.
    - II. purchaser.

    A. I only   B. II only   C. Both I and II   D. Neither I nor II

20. The total of debits and credits to the seller is
    - I. $35,393.00.
    - II. $36,866.75.

    A. I only   B. II only   C. Both I and II   D. Neither I nor II

Chapter 20

Improved Property
Summary Card Problems

Read the problems which follow and answer the questions pertaining to them.

Problem No. 1

As a salesperson for the PDQ Realty, you secure a listing on a home owned by Sean O'Reilly and his wife, Kathleen. The property consists of a large two story house of brick construction on a corner lot, located at the corner of Early Street and Green Street in your city. The address of the property is 3809 Early Street. The O'Reillys also give you a listing on an adjoining vacant lot.

The house contains three large bedrooms, plus two baths on the second floor. On the first floor, there is a living room, family room, dining room, kitchen, and half bath. There are hardwood floors throughout the first floor except for the kitchen, which has vinyl floor covering. The entire second floor, including stairs and baths, is carpeted. There is central air conditioning, and the house is connected to all city utilities.

From the Owner's records, you determine that the dimensions of the lots are 90' X 180' each. The two story part of the house measures 28' X 50', and there is a one story wing which contains a two car garage plus a 6' X 8' utility area and a 6' X 12' workshop area. The taxes for this year are $1275. You know the local tax rate to be $2.25/$100 of assessed valuation. There is an automatic washer and electric dryer in the utility area.

You list the house at a price of $85,000 and the lot for $15,000. The owners tell you that there is a first mortgage of $48,000 on the house and that the extra lot is owned free and clear. You are to receive a 6 percent commission on the sale of the property.

Questions

1. You can assume that the vacant lot is situated on Early Street.
   A. True
   B. False
2. The house contains _____ than 3000 square feet.
                                 (more or less)
   A. More
   B. Less
   C. Can't tell
3. The assessed valuation of the property is approximately
   A. $19,000.
   B. $5,100.
   C. $51,000.
   D. Can't tell
4. You can assume that there are hardwood floors under the carpet on the second floor.
   A. True
   B. False
5. The washer and dryer are included in the listed price
   A. True
   B. False
   C. Can't tell

Problem No. 2

Description

One story ranch style dwelling, located on half-acre lot. House has living room, dining room, kitchen, den, three bedrooms, two baths. Attached one-car garage. Oil fired warm air furnace, electric hot water heater in full basement. City water and sewer are connected. Underground electric and telephone wires. Rear yard enclosed by split rail fence.

Owner/Financial Data

Owned by Charles and Mabel Brown. Present mortgage of $32,000 may be assumed. Tax assessment for the current year is $20,000 on improvements and $4,000 on land. Tax rate is $3.50/$100 of assessment. Property has been appraised by FHA for $42,500.

Listing/Transaction History

January 15 – Property listed for FHA appraised value at 6% brokerage fee. 120 day exclusive right to sell listing. Washer and dryer now on premises are not to be included in listed price, but owner indicates that they are "negotiable."

February 5 – Property shown to Mr. & Mrs. Samuel Green, who made offer of $41,500. Purchasers are to make a cash down payment of 10 percent and secure a conventional loan for the balance, at interest rate not to exceed $9\frac{1}{2}\%$ per annum, for 30 year term. Offer accepted by sellers, subject to purchaser being able to secure above loan.

February 25 – Purchasers secure commitment from local savings and loan association to make loan on the terms of the purchase agreement.

March 5 – Transaction closed.

Questions

1. Can you tell if all utilities are underground, from the information furnished?
   A. Yes
   B. No
2. The taxes for the current year are
   A. $700.
   B. $840.
   C. $1,487.50
   D. $571.
3. The term "negotiable" in reference to the washer and dryer means that
   I. The owner will not consider any offer which included these items.
   II. The owner would consider including these items upon receipt of an offer to purchase.
   A. I only   B. II only   C. Both I and II   D. Neither I nor II
4. The conventional loan secured by the Greens was in the amount of
   A. $32,000.
   B. $33,200.
   C. $37,350.
   D. None of the above
5. Had the Greens not been able to secure the loan,
   I. The contract would have been voidable.
   II. The Browns could have retained the earnest money deposit.
   A. I only   B. II only   C. Both I and II   D. Neither I nor II

Chapter 21

Arithmetic Problems

Problems on Percentages

1. Change the following numbers to decimal fractions:
   (a) 37.5% =_____   (b) 45% =_____
   (c) 3% =_____   (d) 105% =_____
2. Change the following decimal fractions to percent:
   (a) .47 =_____   (b) 1.25 =_____
   (c) .075 =_____   (d) .825 =_____
3. Change the following percent figures to common fractions:
   (a) 12.5% =_____   (b) 30% =_____
   (c) 75% =_____   (d) 5% =_____
4. Change the following common fractions to percent figures:
   (a) $\frac{1}{16}$ =_____   (b) $\frac{2}{5}$ =_____
   (c) $\frac{7}{10}$ =_____   (d) $\frac{3}{8}$ =_____
5. Divide the following numbers:
   (a)   (b)
   $3\overline{)3.75}$ $4\overline{)1.8}$
   (c)   (d)
   $8\overline{)10.2}$ $16\overline{)12.00}$

6. Divide the following numbers:
   (a) $37.5 \overline{)168.75}$ (b) $22.75 \overline{)182}$
   (c) $6.75 \overline{)84.375}$ (d) $5.5 \overline{)126.5}$

7. Multiply the following decimal numbers:

(a)	(b)	(c)	(d)
.4375	1.80	17.5	101.75
x 22.5	x 2.3	x .065	x .25

8. Add the following decimal numbers:
   (a) 28.225 + 101.65 (b) 18.5 + 6.75
   (c) 16.37 + 22.8 (d) 7.65 + 9.35

9. Subtract the following numbers:
   (a) 123.5 − 48.75 (c) 88 − 22.6
   (b) 17.075 − 12.5 (d) 76.20 − 43

10. $26,790 is 94 percent of what number?

11. You are the sales agent for an owner who nets $10,000 from the sale of his house after paying off his first D/T of $14,863 and your 6 percent commission. What was the selling price of the house?

12. A purchaser obtains a 75 percent loan on a new home at an annual interest rate of $7\frac{1}{2}$ percent. His first month's interest is $150. What is the purchase price of the house?

13. You make payments of $80 a month to pay off a loan of $10,000 at 6 percent per annum interest. If your monthly payment is applied first to interest then to principal, how much of the 1st month's payment will be applied to principal? How much will be applied to the principal the second month?

14. You receive a commission of $955.35 for both listing and selling a house. If your share was figured on the basis of 20 percent of the total 6 percent commission for listing the house, and 35 percent of the total for selling it, what was the selling price of the house?

15. Mr. Jones sold a house for 8 percent more than he had paid for it. If his selling price was $45,900, what had he paid for the house when he bought it?

16. An investor knows that the gross rental from an apartment house is $712.50 per month. If he buys the building for $95,000, what will be the annual rate of return on his investment?

17. An owner netted $18,050 from the sale of his house after paying the sales agent his commission. The selling price of the property was $19,000. At what rate was the commission paid?

18. A house sells for $28,000 at 6 percent commission. If the agent who listed the house receives 15 percent of the total commission and one-third of the remainder goes to the selling agent, how much would the agent who sold the house receive?

19. You borrow $800 at 6 percent per annum interest for a period of 6 months. You will repay the complete loan plus interest at the end of that period. What will your payment be?

20. Mr. Smith bought a house for $31,000, which he later offered for sale at an increase of 15 percent. When the house did not sell, he reduced his asking price by 20 percent and sold the house for the latter price. What percent was his loss?

21. You borrow $500 for a period of 6 months, agreeing to pay off the loan, plus interest, at the end of the period. If your interest amounts to $18.75, what is your annual interest rate?

22. You make payments of $90 a month to pay off a loan of $10,000 at $7\frac{1}{2}$ percent per annum. How much of the first month's payment will be applied to principal? How much will be applied to principal the second month?

23. The gross rental from an apartment building is $840 per month. If this represents a return of 14 percent annually on the investment, what did the building cost?

24. If you buy a piece of property at a given price, offer it for sale at 25 percent more than you paid for it, then reduce your asking price by 20 percent and sell at the latter price, will you gain or lose money?

25. An insurance policy purchased by the seller in the amount of $12,000 is to be assumed by the buyer. The seller purchased the policy on September 25, 1966 for a 3-year period at the annual rate of $4.75 per thousand, with a saving of 20 percent for purchasing a 3-year policy. If settlement takes place on November 10, 1968, what charge would be made to the buyer?

26. The seller has paid his annual taxes of $228 for 1969. If settlement takes place on October 15, 1969, what refund should he receive?

27. Assessment is $14,000; rate is $2.60 per hundred; determine the tax.

28. Taxes are $503.75; rate is $3.25 per hundred; determine the assessment.

29. Assessment is $19,400; taxes are $533.50; determine the rate.

Problems on Area and Volume

1. A lot measures 200 feet × 508.2 feet. How many acres does it contain?

2. A lot measuring 90 feet × 150 feet sold for $57.5 per front foot. What was the selling price?

3. In order to purchase paint for your living room, you must determine the number of square feet in the room to be painted. The room measures 18 feet by 20 feet, has an eight foot ceiling, one picture window measures 60 inches by 120 inches and 2 doors 3 feet by 7 feet each. You will paint all four walls and the ceiling. What is the total area in square feet to be painted?

4. A square lot containing 6889 square feet sold for $4,565. What was its cost per front foot?

5. A triangular lot, with a frontage of 200 feet, and measuring 217.8 feet in depth sold for $4,000 an acre. What was its selling price?

6. A sidewalk is to be constructed around the outside of a corner lot which measures 120 feet by 90 feet. If it is 6 inches deep and 6 feet wide, how many cubic yards of concrete will be required to build it?

7. A building is constructed at the cost of $.45 per cubic foot. It measures 22 feet long by 18 feet wide, and is 10 feet high. What was the cost of constructing the building?

8. A sidewalk is constructed on a corner lot which measures 120 feet by 90 feet. It is 6 feet wide and 6 inches thick. How many cubic yards of concrete are required to build it?

9. A triangular piece of land has a frontage of 660 feet and measures one-quarter mile in depth. How many acres does it contain?

10. If the excavation of a basement costs $2.50 per cubic yard, what would the cost be for a basement measuring 33 feet wide by 45 feet long by 10 feet deep?

11. Find the number of cubic feet of space in an attic which is 22.5 feet wide, 30 feet long, and the height at the peak is 8 feet.

Supplemental Arithmetic Problems

The following arithmetic problems are given for your benefit if needed. These problems may be worked for practice.

1. A note is dated April 15, 1963, the amount of the note is $1,700; the interest rate is 5 percent; no interest is paid. How much interest will be due on January 15, 1964?

2. Over a period of years you have established the average operating cost of $10 per prospect to show a house. After showing a certain house to nine prospects, you sold it to the tenth for $15,000. Your commission was 6 percent. What is your taxable income on this sale?

3. A house originally cost $20,000 to construct. Two years later it was sold for 8 percent more than it cost. Subsequently the new owner sold it for $19,440. What percent was his loss?

4. The taxes on a house were $126. The taxes were due January 1 and were paid by the owner. What refund would he get from a purchaser if he sold the house and the taxes were prorated as of September 15?

5. A lot 75 feet wide and 165 feet deep sold for $193.50 per front foot. What was the selling price?

6. A broker receives half the first month's rent for leasing an apartment

and 5 percent of each month's rent thereafter for collecting the rent of $85 per month. What would his total commission be after 18 months?

7. A seller netted from the sale of his house, after all costs, $16,710.40. Total costs as shown by settlement statement were $679.60 plus 6 percent commission of the sales price. What did the house sell for?

8. A corner lot measures 60 feet by 90 feet. The city will construct a sidewalk around the outside of the lot 6 feet wide and 6 inches thick.
   a. How many square feet in the sidewalk?
   b. How many square yards in the sidewalk?
   c. How many cubic yards of concrete will be required to construct the sidewalk?

9. A lot measures 60 feet by 120 feet. The state is going to condemn the portion south of a line running from the northeast corner to the southwest corner. How many square feet in the condemned portion?

10. A lot measures 200 feet by 726 feet. How many acres does it contain?

11. You build a house on a square lot, containing 9,216 square feet. The house is 24 feet deep by 62 feet wide with an average height of 27 feet. It cost $.25 per cubic foot to build, and the lot cost $40 per front foot. What is your total cost?

12. A property sold for $21,750. An 80 percent loan was placed upon the property, and the monthly payment for interest and principal was $6.45 per thousand. Insurance is required for the amount of the loan and is $.30 per hundred per year. One-twelfth of the annual premium is to be paid monthly. Tax assessment is 60 percent of sales price, and tax rate is $3 per hundred. What is total monthly payment?

13. You own a lot that is 180 feet deep and 100 feet wide. You have a concrete driveway installed from your front line 45 percent of the depth of the lot, 6 feet wide and 4 inches thick. How many cubic yards of concrete would be required for the job?

14. In the above problem, what would be the cost if labor was $.80 per square foot, and concrete cost $18.00 per cubic yard?

15. An insurance policy is dated May 10, 1965, and was written for a three-year period. What proration of premium would be due the seller if settlement was made on September 20, 1966, if the annual premium was $.72 per hundred, and a savings of 30 percent of a year's premium was made by writing the insurance on a three-year basis? Amount of insurance: $12,000.

16. Jones owns a farm, of which 75 acres are in timber; 37.5 percent of the farm is pasture land; $\frac{3}{16}$ of the farm is planted in corn; and $\frac{1}{16}$ is devoted to dwelling house, barns, etc. What is the total acreage of the farm?

17. Johnson bought a plot of land 45 feet square and paid 25 cents per square foot for it. He constructed a building on the land, 25 feet square and 10 feet high at a cost of 60 cents per cubic foot. What was the total property cost?

18. Your agreement with your broker calls for the following division of commission: $\frac{1}{5}$ of the total to the listing salesman; 45 percent of the remainder to the selling salesman; and the rest to the broker. Your share of the 6 percent commission on the sale of a property which you both listed and sold was $756. What was the selling price of the property?

19. Smith sells an investment property to Brown, on which the tenant's lease has several months to run. The rent of $282 per month is paid in advance on the first day of the month in which settlement is to occur. If settlement is held on the eighteenth day of the month, how much rental credit will Brown receive at settlement?

20. The gross rental from an apartment house is $750 per month. If the gross income represents a return of 12 percent annually on the investment, what did the property cost?

21. What taxes would be charged to the seller if a sale were settled on June 15 and taxes of $375 for the full calendar year beginning January 1 had not been paid by the seller at time of settlement?

22. A rectangular lot 210 feet long and 200 feet wide was subdivided into 8 lots of 50 by 90 with a road running through the middle of the lot. What percent of the lot area was reserved for the road?

23. A three-year fire insurance policy costing $144.72 is assumed by a buyer at settlement. The policy was purchased on April 15, 1964, and settlement is to be held on July 25, 1966. How much refund will the seller get at settlement?

24. A rectangular lot measures 400 feet by 490.5 feet. How many acres does it contain?

25. The taxes on a property are $150 per year due on January 1. If a seller pays the taxes in advance for a year and later sells his property, what refund would he get if settlement is to be made on August 15?

26. If building costs are $12.50 per square foot, and you were to build a house 33 feet wide and 48 feet long, plus an offset family room 10 feet by 20 feet, how much would it cost to build the house?

27. A certain property is valued at $20,000 and is to be insured at 80 percent of its value. The rate for the insurance is $3.50 per thousand dollars. The furnishings, also to be insured at 80 percent of value, are worth $6,000, and the rate is $4.25 per thousand dollars. A three-year policy will cost $2\frac{1}{2}$ times the cost of annual policies purchased separately for three years. How much can be saved by purchasing a three-year policy?

28. A property sale is to be settled on August 15. The sewer charge of $9.75 per quarter has been paid in advance for the full year. What refund would the seller get at settlement?

29. A salesman brings in a listing on a $5,000 home and is to receive 10 percent of the total 5 percent commission when the property is sold. If a second salesman sells the house and the 10 percent is deducted from his half of the commission, the second salesman would receive how much?

30. A building is insured for $24,500. The annual rate is $.16 per $100 and the owner buys a three-year policy, the rate of which is $2\frac{1}{2}$ times the annual rate. What is the monthly cost?

31. A rectangular tract of land measures $\frac{1}{2}$ mile by $\frac{1}{4}$ mile. How many acres does it contain?

32. I. M. Schrood is considering the purchase of an apartment house which is earning $1,800 per year after taxes and other expenses. He wishes to earn 6 percent on his investment. What price would he pay for the property to realize this return?

33. A property is worth $12,000, and the furniture and household goods are worth $4,000. The owner insures them for 80 percent of their value. The annual rate on the dwelling is $2.80 per $1,000, and on the furniture and household goods, $3.30 per $1,000. If the premium for a three-year policy is $2\frac{1}{2}$ times the premium for one year, what savings could be effected by taking out a three-year policy?

34. A buyer purchases a property on which he is placing a first trust of $12,000 at 6 percent interest. Settlement is to be held on September 20 and the first payment will be due on November 1. How much interest will be charged to the buyer at settlement to adjust the interest to the first of October?

35. A mortgage company agrees to lend the owner of a property a sum equal to $66\frac{2}{3}$ percent of its appraised valuation, at interest rate of 5 percent. The first year's interest is $200. What is the appraised valuation?

36. A triangular field, having a base of 88 rods and an altitude of 24 rods is purchased at $175 an acre. What is the purchase price?

37. The annual taxes on a property are $250.24. The property is assessed at $7,820. What is the annual tax rate?

38. You borrow $330 for 6 months, agreeing to pay 6 percent per annum interest on the face of the loan and to repay the loan, including interest in 6 equal monthly installments. Your monthly payment will be_____.

39. If the state recording tax on deeds and deeds of trust were 15 cents per $100, and the county tax is 5 cents per $100, what would be the total tax on a sale in the amount of $22,500?

40. What would be the cost of title search on a property which sold for $36,500 if the rate of charge was $\frac{3}{4}$ of 1 percent on the first $20,000 of consideration and $\frac{1}{2}$ of 1 percent on all above $20,000?

41. Mr. Entrepreneur sells two parcels of real estate in the same year. The sale price of each parcel of real estate was $95,000. One sale represented a 5 percent profit on his original investment, while the other sale represented a 5 percent loss on the original investment. Did Mr. Entrepreneur break even? If not, what was the amount of the loss?

42. A builder, in getting prices on building material which sells for $3,500, is offered two choices by the dealer:

A. 25 percent discount of the sale price.

B. 15 percent discount of the sale price, plus a 10 percent trade discount if he pays his bill in 90 days which he can do.

Which offer should the builder accept?

43. A farm has $\frac{1}{4}$ of its 400 acres of land not usable, $\frac{3}{5}$ under cultivation, the remainder is a grass meadow. What fraction of the land is a grass meadow? How many acres?

44. $70,000 was invested in an apartment building. If the investor netted $5,600 for the year, what was his rate of return?

45. A commission of $1,375, rate of commission 5 percent, was earned on the sale of a house. What was the selling price of the house?

46. A lender will furnish an 80 percent loan on a $12,000 house. How much cash does the buyer need? If the above loan bears an interest rate of $8\frac{1}{2}$ percent, what is the interest for 7 months?

47. If a leased building netted the owner $30,080 after paying the broker a commission of $1,920, what was the rate of commission? If the building measured 200 feet by 40 feet, what was the annual rent per square foot?

48. A broker buys property for $8,000, 20 percent less than market value. He resells the property at market value. What was the resale price? What was the profit in dollars and rate on the investment?

49. An investor sells two parcels of property for $69,000 each. One parcel was sold at a gain of 15 percent and one parcel sold at a loss of 20 percent. What was the net gain or loss on the two properties?

50. A house is insured for 80 percent of its $15,000 value. The premium paid for three years on July 1, 1965 was computed at $.72 per $100. What is the unearned premium charged to the buyer if the house is sold March 1, 1967?

51. In prorating taxes, find the amount of the apportionment of 1969 county taxes to be credited to a buyer of property at the closing on November 11, 1969. Taxes for the year are $720 which have not been paid.

52. Real value of a property is $7,000. It is assessed at 65 percent of real value. Tax rate is 65 mills on assessed value. What are the taxes?

53. What would be the cost to build a driveway 36 feet long, 9 feet wide and 4 inches thick, if concrete costs $15 per cubic yard and labor costs are 20 cents per square foot?

54. A seller receives a net amount on his property of $14,200. The broker had deducted a 5 percent commission and an allowance of $50 for advertising. The selling price was_____.

55. The loan on a property is 50 percent of its appraised value. The interest rate is 8 percent and the first semi-annual payment is $210. What is the appraised value of the property?

56. A home for sale "by owner" asked 10 percent above FHA appraisal. The asking price was later lowered to appraisal figure which was $15,500. What was the original asking price?

57. A lot 80 feet by 100 feet deep was purchased through a broker for 25 cents per square foot plus an assumption of sewer and paving bills at $5 per front foot. The purchaser relisted the lot at a 15 percent profit plus the broker's commission of $500. What is the lot's new price?

58. A lot 70 feet by 100 feet deep was sold at $60 per front foot. Your commission at 60 percent of 10 percent commission of the sale would be?

59. An investor receives rental income on an apartment of $300 per month. What was the amount of investment if the annual return is 9 percent?

60. What was the original value of a new house which after six years had an estimated value of $21,250, if depreciated at $2\frac{1}{2}$ percent per year?

61. A house with an FHA value of $18,500 has the first $15,000 insured by FHA at 97 percent and next $5,000 at 90 percent. What is the insurable loan value?

62. A lot measures 300 feet by 73 feet approximately. What fraction of an acre is the lot?

63. Wall-to-wall carpet is installed in an office 15 feet by 27 feet. Compute carpet cost at $11.50 per square yard.

64. A lot 72 feet by 122 feet sold for $5,006.88. Compute the cost per square foot.

65. $50.00 is 5 percent of what amount?

66. A salesman earned a total of $10,500 in a year receiving one-half of the broker's commission of 6 percent. Total sales for the year were _____ .

67. Five month's interest on a $20,000 loan is $625. What is the annual interest rate?

68. An investor sold 5 lots for $2,500 each and made a 25 percent profit on each. What was the original cost of the lots?

69. A farmer has a 120 acre farm that produces 160 bushels per acre of potatoes annually. He sells the potatoes at $1.40 a bushel. What would he have to sell his farm per acre and invest his proceeds at $5\frac{1}{2}\%$ to earn the same?
    A. $224.   B. $4,072.   C. $33.94   D. $57.83

70. A man has an investment of $50,000 that earns 12%. He pays $450 a month rent. He decides to sell his investment and purchase a duplex, of which he will rent one side at $175 a month and live in the other side. What is his savings or loss a year?
    A. $600 loss   B. $1,500 savings   C. $1,500 loss   D. $2,100 savings

71. How many square feet in the diagram?
    A. 1,600   B. 2,165   C. 565   D. 2,000

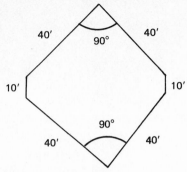

72. What is the cost of a house at $17 per square foot?
    A. $122,400   B. $124,950   C. $125,800   D. $126,650

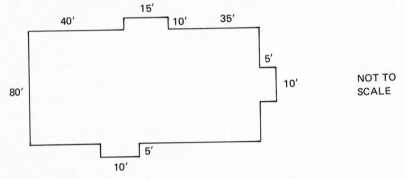

73. An 80 acre farm is subdivided into $\frac{1}{2}$ acre lots. Each house is 50 feet by 100 feet. Three acres are reserved for parks. What percent of land is used by the houses?
    A. 96.25%   B. 22%   C. 23%   D. 12.5%

74. A developer bought a tract of land measuring 600 feet × 1,300 feet for $28,000. He reserved 100 feet times the total depth of the tract for himself. Zoning laws in this area demanded that a lot contain 30,000 square feet and a depth of 300 feet. The developer then subdivided the remaining frontage into lots to meet the zoning law requirements and the remaining land was left undeveloped. The total special assessment tax was $500 and each lot sold for $3,000. In order to net 15% profit on the total project, what is the least amount he could sell the undeveloped portion for?
    A. $13,500   B. $32,200   C. $17,200   D. $17,775

75. Apartments rent as follows: 12 apartments at $250 a month; 10 apartments at $300 a month. Total expenses are $7,600 a year. There is an 80% occupancy allowance. At 10% on investment, how much should the owner ask for his property?
    A. $100,000   B. $500,000   C. $250,000   D. $50,000

76. A man has a lot that is located in a prime downtown area and has a configuration and measurements as indicated below. He can sell the property for $1 per square foot. He invested $150,000 in this land one

year ago. He is using this land for a parking lot. If his income is $100 a day and his expenses $250 per year, what is the difference between the offered purchase price of the lot and a capitalized valuation if he desires a 10% return on this investment? Use 360 days per year.

A. $157,500   B. $357,500   C. $200,000   D. $100,000

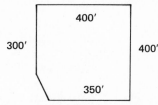

77. A perfect site for a motel was purchased by a group of investors for $464,000. It was estimated that the operation could successfully use 100 rooms. Conditions in this resort area enabled an anticipated occupancy rate of 80%. The construction cost per unit was estimated to be $15,000 with an additional 2% for over-rides. These included the conference room and restaurant. The investors insisted upon an oval swimming pool 10 feet wide and 50 feet long. This pool cost 20% more than a rectangular one having the same measurements and costing $10/sq. ft. surface area. The daily income rate was computed to be $20 per day computed on a 360 day year. The restaurant was to contribute $400 per day income. Expenses were expected to be 40% of the adjusted gross income. What is the estimated return on this venture?

A. 21.6%   B. 3.6%   C. 14.4%   D. 36%

78. An apartment produced a gross monthly return of $1,500. The annual expenses were $6,000 and the capitalization rate is $8\frac{5}{8}\%$ per annum. What is the property net worth?

A. $137,140   B. $52,100   C. $139,130   D. $57,600

79. A building and lot were purchased for $112,000 fourteen years ago. The land value is $32,000. The economic life of the building is 40 years and is depreciated using the straight line method. What is the present worth of the property?

A. $84,000   B. $39,200   C. $50,000   D. $28,000

80. A developer was anticipating the purchase of a certain parcel of land at $3,400 an acre. The parcel contained 100 acres of which $\frac{1}{4}$ was standing timber which could be sold for $1,000 an acre. Twenty percent of this land was to be dedicated to streets. Fifty percent of all the street dedication was to be for streets 40 feet wide and the remainder of the street dedication was for 30 feet wide streets. Paving for the streets would have cost $10/lineal foot. If the zoning laws were such that the developer could get only 2 lots per acre of developed land, what would be the approximate selling price of each lot to realize a 10% return on the total investment?

A. $14,025   B. $28,050   C. $1,402   D. $3,928

81. A man has a swimming pool in his yard with the measurements and general configuration as depicted below. He desires to modernize the

area and put in a 5 foot wide concrete apron around the perimeter of the pool. What is the total square feet of concrete he will need to go around the pool?

A. 1,000   B. 1,100   C. 1,050   D. 1,200

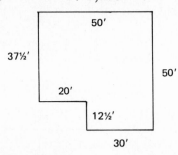

82. Two houses sold for a total of $22,500. The second house sold for $\frac{1}{4}$ more than the first. What was the selling price of the second house?

A. $12,500   B. $10,000   C. $11,250   D. $8,000

83. Mr. Smith bought a square parcel of land comprised of 10,000 square feet. He built a small warehouse containing 2,000 square feet and the height of the flat roofed building was 30 feet. His land costs were $25 per front foot and building construction costs were 35¢ per cubic foot. What was his total cost of the project if the building contractor added a profit of 10% on to the construction cost of the building?

A. $23,500   B. $23,100   C. $25,850   D. $25,600

84. A man has a corner lot and a house built on this lot as shown below. The house falls within all setback regulations. Restrictive covenants in the deed demand that the house and other structural improvements cannot cover more than 90% of the surface area of the lot after the 25 feet setback requirements on all sides of the property have been considered. According to the restrictive zonings in the deed, how many more square feet of land is available for improvement on the property?

A. 9,000   B. 2,200   C. 6,400   D. 5,800

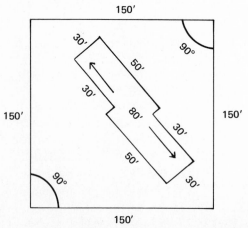

85. A lot measures 600 X 600 feet. This lot is to be the site of a two-store furniture store. The parking lot of this site will consist of 50% of the

total area and is to be finished off in rolled asphalt 6″ thick and costs $3 per square yard. Curbing is to be constructed around the entire lot at a cost of $2 per lineal yard. The price of construction for the store is estimated at $4 per square foot of total floor space. The parcel of land had an initial cost of $67,800. The developers have set the capitalization rate at 10% and the net profit is expected to be 30% of the gross income. What are the anticipated annual expenses of the store after completion?

    A. $35,000   B. $15,000   C. $59,458   D. $10,000

86. Insurance on a house costing $60,000 is at 90% of its cost. Insurance on $20,000 of personal property is also at 90% of its value. The personal property insurance costs $3 per $1,000 annually. Insurance on the house is $2 per $1,000 per year. Insurance available on a three year basis is $\frac{1}{3}$ less than that available on a yearly basis. Approximately how much could be saved by purchasing the total insurance on a three year policy?

    A. $162   B. $81   C. $54   D. $108

87. A man has a loan of $20,000 at 8%. He is in the 25% income tax bracket. How much money will he save in income tax because of his loan?

    A. $1,600   B. $800   C. $400   D. $4,000

88. You purchased a lot of commercial property which is $\frac{1}{4}$ of an acre and is 100 feet deep at a price of $1 a square foot. You later decided to sell the property after you realize a profit of 50% on the original investment and pay $3,400 in taxes, a $65 survey fee and a 10% brokerage fee on the final sale. What must the property sell for a front foot to accomplish this?

    A. $100   B. $202   C. $700   D. $2,000

89. Jones wishes to build a flat-roofed building 125 feet long, 35 feet wide and 25 feet high. Smith offers to build the building for $9 a square foot. Williams offers to build it for $.38 per cubic foot. How much will Jones save by giving the building contract to Smith?

    A. $13,437.50   B. $33,687.50   C. $2,187.50   D. $3,762.50

90. Mr. Henry has $14,800 invested in his property. What will be the return on his investment if he rents his property for $175 per month, and if yearly costs are $395 in taxes, $75 insurance, and $150 in miscellaneous expenses?

    A. 14%   B. 3%   C. 8%   D. 10%

91. An office building has a total income of $4,400 per month. The yearly expenses are: Taxes $7,364.22; Insurance $1,723.31; Heating and air-conditioning $5,237.28; and Miscellaneous expense $3,674.19. If the owner values the building at $152,800, what is the net return?

    A. $100,000   B. $187,601   C. $34,801   D. $139,201

92. Jim Jones and Sam Smith traded properties. Jones' property was valued at $21,500. Smith's property was valued at $23,750. The difference in equities was $3,207.02. Smith's equity was $4,873.02 and is less than

Jones's equity. What was the total amount of encumbrance against each property?

A. Jones $18,876.98   B. Jones $15,669.96   C. Jones $13,419.96
   Smith $13,419.96   Smith $18,876.98   Smith $21,126.98

D. Jones $13,419.96
   Smith $18,876.98

93. Mr. Williams bought a home for $30,000; built a pool costing $2,600 and spent $327 on filtering and cleaning equipment. The following month he had a job transfer and had to relocate in another state. If he listed his house for $35,000, what percent would the profit be over the investment?

A. 5.9%   B. 6.3%   C. 14.3%   D. 15.2%

94. A man can buy a house for $15,250 cash or for $6,000 and $10,200 at the end of the year. If his money can be invested at 6% compounded semi-annually, how much does he save or lose if he pays the $15,250 cash?

A. $328.82 saves B. $347.44 loses C. $328.82 loses D. $347.44 saves

95. An investor paid $38,000 for a four-unit apartment house. Each apartment rents for $95 a month. It is estimated that by good management a profit of 35% of gross sales could be made. What rate of return should this man make on his investment?

A. 35%   B. 3%   C. 1.05%   D. 4.2%

FINAL EXAMINATIONS

UNIFORM LICENSING EXAMINATION FOR REAL ESTATE SALESMEN

Name: (Print)

Place of Testing:

City:

State:

Center Code No.

Today's Date:

Signature:

Copy Examination Number Here:

1	2	3	4	5	6	7	8	9	0
1	2	3	4	5	6	7	8	9	C
1	2	3	4	5	6	7	8	9	0
1	2	3	4	5	6	7	8	9	0
1	2	3	4	5	6	7	8	9	0
1	2	3	4	5	6	7	8	9	0

Be sure each mark is *black* and *completely fills* the answer space

	A	B	C	D		A	B	C	D		A	B	C	D		A	B	C	D		A	B	C	D
1	[]	[]	[]	[]	31	[]	[]	[]	[]	51	[]	[]	[]	[]	76	[]	[]	[]	[]	101	[]	[]	[]	[]
2	[]	[]	[]	[]	32	[]	[]	[]	[]	52	[]	[]	[]	[]	77	[]	[]	[]	[]	102	[]	[]	[]	[]
3	[]	[]	[]	[]	33	[]	[]	[]	[]	53	[]	[]	[]	[]	78	[]	[]	[]	[]	103	[]	[]	[]	[]
4	[]	[]	[]	[]	34	[]	[]	[]	[]	54	[]	[]	[]	[]	79	[]	[]	[]	[]	104	[]	[]	[]	[]
5	[]	[]	[]	[]	35	[]	[]	[]	[]	55	[]	[]	[]	[]	80	[]	[]	[]	[]	105	[]	[]	[]	[]
6	[]	[]	[]	[]	36	[]	[]	[]	[]	56	[]	[]	[]	[]	81	[]	[]	[]	[]	106	[]	[]	[]	[]
7	[]	[]	[]	[]	37	[]	[]	[]	[]	57	[]	[]	[]	[]	82	[]	[]	[]	[]	107	[]	[]	[]	[]
8	[]	[]	[]	[]	38	[]	[]	[]	[]	58	[]	[]	[]	[]	83	[]	[]	[]	[]	108	[]	[]	[]	[]
9	[]	[]	[]	[]	39	[]	[]	[]	[]	59	[]	[]	[]	[]	84	[]	[]	[]	[]	109	[]	[]	[]	[]
10	[]	[]	[]	[]	40	[]	[]	[]	[]	60	[]	[]	[]	[]	85	[]	[]	[]	[]	110	[]	[]	[]	[]
11	[]	[]	[]	[]	41	[]	[]	[]	[]	61	[]	[]	[]	[]	86	[]	[]	[]	[]	111	[]	[]	[]	[]
12	[]	[]	[]	[]	42	[]	[]	[]	[]	62	[]	[]	[]	[]	87	[]	[]	[]	[]	112	[]	[]	[]	[]
13	[]	[]	[]	[]	43	[]	[]	[]	[]	63	[]	[]	[]	[]	88	[]	[]	[]	[]	113	[]	[]	[]	[]
14	[]	[]	[]	[]	44	[]	[]	[]	[]	64	[]	[]	[]	[]	89	[]	[]	[]	[]	114	[]	[]	[]	[]
15	[]	[]	[]	[]	45	[]	[]	[]	[]	65	[]	[]	[]	[]	90	[]	[]	[]	[]	115	[]	[]	[]	[]
16	[]	[]	[]	[]	46	[]	[]	[]	[]	66	[]	[]	[]	[]	91	[]	[]	[]	[]	116	[]	[]	[]	[]
17	[]	[]	[]	[]	47	[]	[]	[]	[]	67	[]	[]	[]	[]	92	[]	[]	[]	[]	117	[]	[]	[]	[]
18	[]	[]	[]	[]	48	[]	[]	[]	[]	68	[]	[]	[]	[]	93	[]	[]	[]	[]	118	[]	[]	[]	[]
19	[]	[]	[]	[]	49	[]	[]	[]	[]	69	[]	[]	[]	[]	94	[]	[]	[]	[]	119	[]	[]	[]	[]
20	[]	[]	[]	[]	50	[]	[]	[]	[]	70	[]	[]	[]	[]	95	[]	[]	[]	[]	120	[]	[]	[]	[]
21	[]	[]	[]	[]						71	[]	[]	[]	[]	96	[]	[]	[]	[]	121	[]	[]	[]	[]
22	[]	[]	[]	[]						72	[]	[]	[]	[]	97	[]	[]	[]	[]	122	[]	[]	[]	[]
23	[]	[]	[]	[]						73	[]	[]	[]	[]	98	[]	[]	[]	[]	123	[]	[]	[]	[]
24	[]	[]	[]	[]						74	[]	[]	[]	[]	99	[]	[]	[]	[]	124	[]	[]	[]	[]
25	[]	[]	[]	[]						75	[]	[]	[]	[]	100	[]	[]	[]	[]	125	[]	[]	[]	[]
26	[]	[]	[]	[]																126	[]	[]	[]	[]
27	[]	[]	[]	[]																127	[]	[]	[]	[]
28	[]	[]	[]	[]																128	[]	[]	[]	[]
29	[]	[]	[]	[]																129	[]	[]	[]	[]
30	[]	[]	[]	[]																130	[]	[]	[]	[]

REAL ESTATE TRANSACTION NARRATIVE

As salesman for the ABC Realty, you find principals Nick L. Pincher and wife, Penny Pincher. On April 11, 19__, you secure an exclusive right to sell on their one-story frame rambler, located at 700 W. Oak Street, Staunton, (your state), k/a Lot 1, Block 4, Forest Hills Subdivision. This is to be a 90-day listing, at a 6 percent commission. Inspection reveals the house to be in good condition, no basement. Attic is insulated with rock wool, access through trap door in hallway. There is an 11 x 14 foot living room, 9 x 11 foot dining room, kitchen with breakfast nook, and a 6 x 8 utility room. There is also a 10 x 14 foot den with fireplace, 1½ baths, and two bedrooms. Heat is oil fired hot water baseboard, with summer-winter hookup for hot water. House is 12 years old. Listed price is to be $45,500., with gas range, washer, dryer, venetian blinds, and carpets in bedrooms included. Owner's amortization chart shows that as of June 1, 19__, their loan balance will be $19,222.21 at interest rate of 7½ percent, monthly payments of $184.50, with 14 years to go on the G.I. loan, held by the Star Light Insurance Company. The Pinchers have bought a new home and can give possession in 30 days. There are storm windows and storm doors, and concrete side driveway. There is a one-car garage and concrete sidewalks. Land is assessed at $2,300., building at $9,000.; taxes are $282.50. Lot is 80 x 136 feet. Roof is of slag. Water is by well, and there is a septic tank. Taxes and insurance are paid monthly, as a part of regular payment. Estimated fuel cost is $200 a year. The house measures 52 x 40 feet. The property has been appraised at $45,500.

Ten days after you list the Pincher house, you are made the following offer to purchase by Cliff Dweller and his wife, Cyd E. Dweller: buyers will purchase the property at the listed price, by means of an 80 percent first D/T loan, 15 percent cash down payment, and sellers are to hold a second D/T of 5 percent of the purchase price at 9 percent per annum interest, payable at the rate of $25.00 per month, balance due and payable at the end of 5 years. The first D/T loan is to be for a 30 year term at prevailing interest rate at time of closing. The sellers accept this offer. Purchasers make a $1500. deposit by check. Complete a contract on these terms. Settlement is to occur on June 21, 19__ at the Guaranty Title Co.

EXCLUSIVE AUTHORIZATION TO SELL

SALES PRICE: _____ TYPE HOME _____ TOTAL BEDROOMS _____ TOTAL BATHS _____

ADDRESS: _____ JURISDICTION OF: _____
AMT. OF LOAN   AS OF   TAXES & INS.   YEARS   AMOUNT PAYABLE   TYPE
TO BE ASSUMED $ _____ WHAT DATE: _____ INCLUDED: ____ TO GO ____ MONTHLY $ _____ @ ___ % LOAN _____

MORTGAGE COMPANY _____   2nd TRUST $ _____
ESTIMATED   TYPE OF APPRAISAL
EXPECTED RENT MONTHLY $ _____   REQUESTED: _____

OWNER'S NAME _____   PHONES: (HOME) _____ (BUSINESS) _____

TENANTS NAME _____   PHONES: (HOME) _____ (BUSINESS) _____

POSSESSION _____ DATE LISTED: _____ EXCLUSIVE FOR _____ DATE OF EXPIRATION _____

LISTING BROKER _____   PHONE _____ KEY AVAILABLE AT _____

LISTING SALESMAN _____   HOME PHONE: _____ HOW TO BE SHOWN: _____

(1) ENTRANCE FOYER ☐ CENTER HALL ☐	(18) AGE	AIR CONDITIONING ☐	(32) TYPE KITCHEN CABINETS
(2) LIVING ROOM SIZE FIREPLACE ☐	(19) ROOFING	TOOL HOUSE ☐	(33) TYPE COUNTER TOPS
(3) DINING ROOM SIZE	(20) GARAGE SIZE	PATIO ☐	(34) EAT-IN SIZE KITCHEN ☐
(4) BEDROOM TOTAL: DOWN UP	(21) SIDE DRIVE ☐	CIRCULAR DRIVE ☐	(35) BREAKFAST ROOM ☐
(5) BATHS TOTAL: DOWN UP	(22) PORCH ☐ SIDE ☐ REAR ☐	SCREENED ☐	(36) BUILT-IN OVEN & RANGE ☐
(6) DEN SIZE FIREPLACE ☐	(23) FENCED YARD	OUTDOOR GRILL ☐	(37) SEPARATE STOVE INCLUDED ☐
(7) FAMILY ROOM SIZE FIREPLACE ☐	(24) STORM WINDOWS ☐	STORM DOORS ☐	(38) REFRIGERATOR INCLUDED ☐
(8) RECREATION ROOM SIZE FIREPLACE ☐	(25) CURBS & GUTTERS ☐	SIDEWALKS ☐	(39) DISHWASHER INCLUDED
(9) BASEMENT SIZE	(26) STORM SEWERS ☐	ALLEY ☐	(40) DISPOSAL INCLUDED ☐
NONE ☐ 1/4 ☐ 1/3 ☐ 1/2 ☐ 3/4 ☐ FULL ☐	(27) WATER SUPPLY		(41) DOUBLE SINK ☐ SINGLE SINK ☐
(10) UTILITY ROOM SIZE	(28) SEWER ☐	SEPTIC ☐	STAINLESS STEEL ☐ PORCELAIN ☐
TYPE HOT WATER SYSTEM:	(29) TYPE GAS: NATURAL ☐	BOTTLED ☐	(42) WASHER INCLUDED ☐ DRYER INCLUDED ☐
(11) TYPE HEAT	(30) WHY SELLING		(43) PANTRY ☐ EXHAUST FAN ☐
(12) EST. FUEL COST			(44) LAND ASSESSMENT $
(13) ATTIC ☐	(31) DIRECTIONS TO PROPERTY		(45) IMPROVEMENTS $
PULL DOWN ☐ REGULAR ☐ TRAP DOOR ☐ STAIRWAY STAIRWAY			(46) TOTAL ASSESSMENT $
(14) MAIDS ROOM ☐ TYPE BATH			(47) TAX RATE
LOCATION			(48) TOTAL ANNUAL TAXES $
(15) NAME OF BUILDER			(49) LOT SIZE
(16) SQUARE FOOTAGE			(50) LOT NO. BLOCK SECTION
(17) EXTERIOR OF HOUSE			

NAME OF SCHOOLS: ELEMENTARY: _____ JR. HIGH: _____

HIGH _____ PAROCHIAL: _____

PUBLIC TRANSPORTATION: _____

NEAREST SHOPPING AREA: _____

REMARKS: _____

Date: _____

In consideration of the services of _____ (herein called "Broker") to be rendered to the undersigned (herein called "Owner"), and of the promise of Broker to make reasonable efforts to obtain a Purchaser therefor, Owner hereby lists with Broker the real estate and all improvements thereon which are described above (all herein called "the property"), and Owner hereby grants to Broker the exclusive and irrevocable right to sell such property from 12:00 Noon on _____, 19____ until 12:00 Midnight on _____, 19____ (herein called "period of time"), for the price of _____ Dollars ($ _____) or for such other price and upon such other terms (including exchange) as Owner may subsequently authorize during the period of time.

It is understood by Owner that the above sum or any other price subsequently authorized by Owner shall include a cash fee of _____ per cent of such price or other price which shall be payable by Owner to Broker upon consummation by any Purchaser or Purchasers of a valid contract of sale of the property during the period of time and whether or not Broker was a procuring cause of any such contract of sale.

If the property is sold or exchanged by Owner, or by Broker or by any other person to any Purchaser to whom the property was shown by Broker or any representative of Broker within sixty (60) days after the expiration of the period of time mentioned above, Owner agrees to pay to Broker a cash fee which shall be the same percentage of the purchase price as the percentage mentioned above.

Broker is hereby authorized by Owner to place a "For Sale" sign on the property and to remove all signs of other brokers or salesmen during the period of time, and Owner hereby agrees to make the property available to Broker at all reasonable hours for the purpose of showing it to prospective Purchasers.

Owner agrees to convey the property to the Purchaser by warranty deed with the usual covenants of title and free and clear from all encumbrances, tenancies, liens (for taxes or otherwise), but subject to applicable restrictive covenants of record. Owner acknowledges receipt of a copy of this agreement.

WITNESS the following signature(s) and seal(s):

Date Signed: _____   _____ (SEAL)
                                                          (Owner)

Listing Broker _____

                                          _____ (SEAL)
                                                          (Owner)

Address _____ Telephone _____

OFFER TO PURCHASE AGREEMENT

This AGREEMENT made as of_____, 19_____,

among_____(herein called "Purchaser"),

and_____(herein called "Seller"),

and_____(herein called "Broker"),
provides that Purchaser agrees to buy through Broker as agent for Seller, and Seller agrees to sell the following described real estate, and all improvements
thereon, located in the jurisdiction of_____,
(all herein called "the property"):_____

_____

_____

_____

_____

_____, and more commonly known as_____

_____(street address).

1. The purchase price of the property is_____
Dollars ($_____), and such purchase price shall be paid as follows:

_____

_____

_____

_____

_____

_____

2. Purchaser has made a deposit of_____ Dollars ($_____)
with Broker, receipt of which is hereby acknowledged, and such deposit shall be held by Broker in escrow until the date of settlement and then applied
to the purchase price, or returned to Purchaser if the title to the property is not marketable.

3. Seller agrees to convey the property to Purchaser by Warranty Deed with the usual covenants of title and free and clear from all encumbrances,
tenancies, liens (for taxes or otherwise), except as may be otherwise provided above, but subject to applicable restrictive covenants of record. Seller further
agrees to deliver possession of the property to Purchaser on the date of settlement and to pay the expense of preparing the deed of conveyance.

4. Settlement shall be made at the offices of Broker or at_____on or before

_____, 19_____, or as soon thereafter as title can be examined and necessary documents prepared, with allowance of
a reasonable time for Seller to correct any defects reported by the title examiner.

5. All taxes, interest, rent, and F.H.A. or similar escrow deposits, if any, shall be prorated as of the date of settlement.

6. All risk of loss or damage to the property by fire, windstorm, casualty, or other cause is assumed by Seller until the date of settlement.

7. Purchaser and Seller agree that Broker was the sole procuring cause of this Contract of Purchase, and Seller agrees to pay Broker for services
rendered a cash fee of_____per cent of the purchase price. If either Purchaser or Seller defaults under such Contract, such defaulting party shall
be liable for the cash fee of Broker and any expenses incurred by the non-defaulting party in connection with this transaction.

Subject to:_____

_____

_____

_____

8. Purchaser represents that an inspection satisfactory to Purchaser has been made of the property, and Purchaser agrees to accept the property in
its present condition except as may be otherwise provided in the description of the property above.

9. This Contract of Purchase constitutes the entire agreement among the parties and may not be modified or changed except by written instrument
executed by all of the parties, including Broker.

10. This Contract of Purchase shall be construed, interpreted, and applied according to the law of the jurisdiction of_____ and shall
be binding upon and shall inure to the benefit of the heirs, personal representatives, successors, and assigns of the parties.

All parties to this agreement acknowledge receipt of a certified copy.

WITNESS the following signatures and seals:

_____(SEAL)   _____(SEAL)
                                          Seller   Purchaser

_____(SEAL)   _____(SEAL)
                                          Seller   Purchaser

_____(SEAL)
                                          Broker

Deposit Rec'd $_____

Check   Cash

Sales Agent:

UNIFORM LICENSING EXAMINATION FOR REAL ESTATE SALESPERSON

I.   REAL ESTATE CONTRACTS

1.   Your listing on the Pincher home will expire on

          I.   June 9, 19__
          II. July 11, 19__

     A. I only B. II only C. Both I and II D. Neither I nor II

2.   The monthly payment on the Pincher's existing loan includes

          I.   principal, interest, taxes and insurance
          II. principal and interest only

     A. I only B. II only C. Both I and II D. Neither I nor II

3.   The den in the Pincher home is

          I.   in the basement
          II. on the second floor

     A.I only B. II only C. Both I and II D. Neither I nor II

4.   The Pincher home contains

          I.   2,080 square feet
          II. 2 bedrooms

     A.I only B. II only C. Both I and II D. Neither I nor II

5.   The tax rate on the Pincher home is

          I. $2.00/$1000
          II. 35 mills

     A.I only B. II only C. Both I and II D. Neither I nor II

6.   In the Pincher-Dweller contract, the cash down payment is to
     be

          I. $6825.
          II. $5325.

     A.I only B. II only C. Both I and II D. Neither I nor II

7.   The amount of the first D/T loan to be secured by purchaser is

          I. $36000.
          II. $36400.

     A. I only B. II only C. Both I and II D. Neither I nor II

8.   Chattels included in the Pincher-Dweller sale are

> I. gas range, washer, dryer, venetian blinds, and dishwasher
> II. gas range, washer, dryer, venetian blinds, and carpet in bedrooms

A. I only   B. II only   C. Both I and II   D. Neither I nor II

9.   The second D/T loan in the Pincher-Dweller sale

> I. is in the amount of $1,275.
> II. carries an annual interest rate of 8 percent

A. I only   B. II only   C. Both I and II   D. Neither I nor II

10.   The contract calls for

> I. additional cash at settlement in the amount of $5325.
> II. settlement to be held on June 21, 19__

A. I only   B. II only   C. Both I and II   D. Neither I nor II

11.   The purchase price is shown on the closing statement as a

> I. debit to purchaser and credit to seller
> II. credit to purchaser and debit to seller

A. I only   B. II only   C. Both I and II   D. Neither I nor II

12.   The first D/T loan proceeds are a

> I. debit to purchaser
> II. credit to seller

A. I only   B. II only   C. Both I and II   D. Neither I nor II

13.   The earnest money deposit paid by the Dwellers is

> I. $1500.
> II. shown as a credit to purchasers

A. I only   B. II only   C. Both I and II   D. Neither I nor II

14.   The pay-off on the Pincher's first D/T loan is

> I. $9,222.21
> II. A credit to the purchaser

A. I only   B. II only   C. Both I and II   D. Neither I nor II

15.   The prorated amount of the prepaid annual taxes is

        I. $455.32
       II. $387.36

A. I only B. II only C. Both I and II D. Neither I nor II

16.   The prorated taxes are shown as a

        I. debit to purchaser and credit to seller
       II. debit to seller and credit to purchaser

A. I only B. II only C. Both I and II D. Neither I nor II

17.   The amount of the agent's commission is

        I. $2730
       II. shown as a debit to seller

A. I only B. II only C. Both I and II D. Neither I nor II

18.   Expenses for the preparation of the deed are borne by the

        I. seller
       II. purchaser

A. I only B. II only C. Both I and II D. Neither I nor II

19.   The second deed of trust given to the sellers is shown on
the closing statement as a

        I. debit to the sellers
       II. credit to the purchasers

A. I only B. II only C. Both I and II D. Neither I nor II

20.   Of the first month's payment on the second deed of trust, the
amount which will be charged to interest will be

        I. $17.06
       II. $ 7.93

A. I only B. II only C. Both I and II D. Neither I nor II

21.   The second deed of trust given to the sellers is a

        I. Balloon payment d/t
       II. purchase money deed of trust

A. I only B. II only C. Both I and II D. Neither I nor II

22.   Once the purchasers' offer to purchase is signed by the sellers, it becomes a
        I. binder
       II. contract of sale
A. I only B. II only C. Both I and II D. Neither I nor II

23. Should the purchasers not be able to secure the first deed of trust loan mentioned in the offer to purchase, the agreement would be

    I. void
    II. voidable by the purchasers

    A. I only B. II only C. Both I and II D. Neither I nor II

24. Should the property be damaged by fire after the agreement is signed by all parties, the loss will be borne by the

    I. sellers
    II. purchasers

    A. I only B. II only C. Both I and II D. Neither I nor II

25. What is the size of Lot 1, Block 4, Forest Hills Subdivision?

    I. 10880 square feet
    II. approximately 1/4 acre

    A. I only B. II only C. Both I and II D. Neither I nor II

26. Your contract with your broker calls for you to receive 20% of the total commission for listings, and 45% of the remainder for selling the property. Your share of the commission on this sale would be

    A. $1774.50   B. $1228.50
    C. $1528.80   D. None of the Above.

II. REAL ESTATE FINANCING

27. A real estate loan which is paid off in a series of install-
     ments with the payment credited first to interest and then to
     principal is

             I. an amortized loan
            II. a term loan

     A. I only   B. II only   C. Both I and II   D. Neither I nor II

28. A loan in which the final payment is greater than preceding
     payments and pays the debt off in full is a

             I. blanket loan
            II. balloon loan

     A. I only   B. II only   C. Both I and II   D. Neither I nor II

29. When a grantee takes title to a property under conditions that
     do not make him liable for payment of the mortgage loan, but
     which leave the original maker solely responsible for the debt,
     this is called

             I. assumption of mortgage
            II. subject to mortgage

     A. I only   B. II only   C. Both I and II   D. Neither I nor II

30. When a note is secured by a deed of trust, the lender is known
     as the

             I. mortgagee
            II. beneficiary

     A. I only   B. II only   C. Both I and II   D. Neither I nor II

31. The right of a mortgagee to reclaim property which was sold
     through foreclosure proceedings is the right of

             A. repossession
             B. forfeiture
             C. hypothecation
             D. redemption

32. Which of the following could accompany a deed of trust?

             A. an installment note
             B. a joint note
             C. a bond
             D. all of the above

33. A mortgage which allows the borrower to borrow additional mon-
     ey after the principal balance on the loan has been reduced is
     known as a(n)

     A. package mortgagee   C. open-end mortgage
     B. budget mortgage   D. balloon mortgage

34.   In order for a veteran purchaser to secure a VA guaranteed
      loan,

            I. the sale price must not exceed the appraised
               value of the property
           II. there must not be any junior financing

      A. I only B. II only C. Both I and II D. Neither I nor II

35.   Which of the following may be used to secure a loan on real
      estate?

            I. a mortgage note
           II. a deed of trust note

      A. I only B. II only C. Both I and II D. Neither I nor II

36.   Which of the following is a negotiable instrument?

            I. a deed of trust note
           II. a mortgage

      A. I only B. II only C. Both I and II D. Neither I nor II

37.   An acceleration clause in a mortgage

            I. calls for the entire balance to become due and
               payable if the terms of repayment are not met.
           II. makes the mortgage null and void if the debt is
               paid on time and in full

      A. I only B. II only C. Both I and II D. Neither I nor II

38.   Under the truth of lending laws a lender may not

            I. refuse a loan to a member of a minority race
           II. investigate the credit of a member of a minority
               race

      A. I only B. II only C. Both I and II D. Neither I nor II

39.   The truth in lending laws require a lender to disclose the
      total of all payments and composition of finance charges on

            I. all real estate loans
           II. loans made to finance the construction or
               acquisition of a dwelling

      A. I only B. II only C. Both I and II D. Neither I nor II

40.   Brown borrowed $30,000. at 9% interest per annum, and agreed
      to pay $241.05 per month, to be credited first to interest,
      then to principal. Of his first month's payment, how much was
      applied to interest and how much to principal?

A. $214.05 to interest, $27.00 to principal
B. $225.00 to principal, $16.05 to interest
C. $225.00 to interest, $16.05 to principal
D. Can't determine from the information given

41. A man wants to buy a property which will cost $80,000. A lender agrees to make a loan equivalent to 80% of the first $50,000. and 60% the remainder. What down payment will be required in order to buy the property on these terms?

    A. $12,000.   B. $22,000.   C. $18,000.   D. $15,000.

42. Jones borrowed $15,000. on a term loan at 8% per annum interest for five years, with interest payments due annually. What will be the total amount repaid over the term of the loan?

    A. $1,200.   B. $6,000.   C. $21,000.   D. $16,200.

43. What would be the monthly payment on a loan of $37,650. if the scheduled payment is $8.06 per thousand dollars per month?

    A. $303.46   B. $302.73   C. $296.20   D. $288.14

44. The quarterly interest on a term loan is $3200. at an annual rate of interest of 9%. How much money was invested?

    A. $35,555.   B. $71,111.   C. $142,222.   D. $12,800.

45. Smith borrowed $50,000. at .09 per annum, and agreed to make monthly payments of $8.40 per thousand dollars per month, to include principal and interest only. In addition, he agreed to deposit in escrow each month 1/12th of the annual taxes of $1260. and 1/12th of the annual homeowners' insurance premium of $186. What would be the total of his monthly payment?

    A. $420.   B. $525.   C. $540.50   D. None of the above

46. A home sold on the following terms: Down payment 15% of the purchase price; second mortgage 10% of the purchase price; first mortgage 75% of the purchase price. The first mortgage was in the amount of $69,450. What was the selling price of the property?

    A. $81,705.   B. $69,450.   C. $92,600.   D. $89,450.

III.   REAL ESTATE OWNERSHIP - 19 points

47.   Deeds are recorded for which of the following reasons?

I. Because the law requires recordation
II. To provide the constructive notice

A. I only B. II only C. Both I and II D. Neither I nor II

48.   From the grantee's point of view, the best deed to receive is a

A. Special warranty deed
B. Quitclaim deed
C. Trustee's deed
D. General warranty deed

49.   Title to real estate passes to the grantee when

A. the deed is signed by the grantor
B. the deed is signed by the grantee
C. the deed is delivered and accepted
D. the deed is recorded

50.   Covenants may be placed in deeds by the grantor in order to

I. warrant the title to the property
II. protect the view from the property

A. I only B. II only C. Both I and II D. Neither I nor II

51.   In order to be valid, a deed must

I. be signed by grantee and grantor
II. contain words of conveyance

A. I only B. II only C. Both I and II D. Neither I nor II

52.   A deed is considered to be executed when it is

A. signed by the grantor
B. accepted by the grantee
C. delivered
D. recorded

53.   The term "real property" includes rights to

A. the surface of the land
B. the air space above the surface of the land
C. things beneath the surface of the land
D. all of the above

54.   An interest in real property for less than a lifetime is classified in law as
I. real property
II. personal property

A. I only B. II only C. Both I and II   D. Neither I nor II

55. Which of the following rights in real property may not be held by a private owner?

>   I. Eminent domain or police power
>   II. taxation or escheat

A. I only   B. II only   C. Both I and II   D. Neither I nor II

56. A freehold estate is

>   A. an estate less than a lifetime in duration
>   B. an estate greater than a lifetime in duration
>   C. an estate of at least a lifetime in duration
>   D. none of the above

57. Which of the following are essential to joint tenancy?

>   I. the unities of time, interest, title, & possession
>   II. the joint tenants must be husband and wife

A. I only   B. II only   C. Both I and II   D. Neither I nor II

58. Survivorship cannot exist among

>   A. joint tenants
>   B. tenants by the entireties
>   C. tenants in common
>   D. none of the above

59. Ownership of real property by one person is considered to be

>   I. separate property
>   II. severalty ownership

A. I only   B. II only   C. Both I and II   D. Neither I nor II

60. An easement acquired through regular and constant use over a period of time is acquired by

>   A. subscription
>   B. description
>   C. conscription
>   D. prescription

61. The owner of a condominium unit

>   I. owns a share of the common elements along with the other tenants
>   II. may hold fee simple title to his unit

A. I only   B. II only   C. Both I and II   D. Neither I nor II

62. Which of the following may have a separate mortgage on his unit?

I. The owner of a condominium unit
II. A tenant in a cooperative development

A. I only   B. II only   C. Both I and II   D. Neither I nor II

63.   A commercial lending institution may not, under the fair housing laws

I. deny a loan to a member of a minority race
II. deny a loan to a person because of his/her sex or age

A. I only   B. II only   C. Both I and II   D. Neither I nor II

64.   The fair housing laws provide an exemption for

I. the owner of a four unit apartment building who lives in one of the units
II. the owner of a single family residence who does not employ the services of a real estate broker

A. I only   B. II only   C. Both I and II   D. Neither I nor II

65.   A real estate broker would be in violation of the fair housing laws if he

I. refused to take a listing on property owned by a member of a minority race
II. refused to show a listed property to a member of a minority race

A. I only   B. II only   C. Both I and II   D. Neither I nor II

IV.   REAL ESTATE BROKERAGE - 20 points

66.   The relationship of a real estate broker to his principal is that of a

      I. trustee
      II. fiduciary

      A. I only B. II only C. Both I and II D. Neither I nor II

67.   In order to be a principal under an agency agreement, one must

      I. have reached majority
      II. possess whatever authority the agency agreement conveys upon the agent

      A. I only B. II only C. Both I and II D. Neither I nor II

68.   A real estate listing signed under duress would be

      I. voidable by the person who signed under duress
      II. voidable by either party

      A. I only B. II only C. Both I and II D. Neither I nor II

69.   A general or open real estate listing

      I. permits the owner to sell of his own efforts without liability to pay a commission
      II. must always contain a definite termination date

      A. I only B. II only C. Both I and II D. Neither I nor II

70.   Under an exclusive authorization to sell listing

      I. the agent receives a commission regardless of whether the property is sold during the term of the listing
      II. the owner may sell of his own efforts without liability for a commission

      A. I only B. II only C. Both I and II D. Neither I nor II

71.   In most states, an exclusive agency listing

      I. must contain a definite terminal date
      II. must be in writing

      A. I only B. II only C. Both I and II D. Neither I nor II

72.   In accepting a listing from a principal, a real estate broker undertakes the following obligation(s) to his principal:
      A. loyalty to the principals interests
      B. due care in handling the principal's property
      C. Notice of material fact concerning the principal's
      D. All of the above

73. An agent will usually be entitled to receive a commission if he

   I. is the procuring cause of a sale
   II. produces a ready, willing, and able purchaser on the terms of the seller's offer to sell

   A. I only B. II only C. Both I and II D. Neither I nor II

74. A real estate listing may be terminated by

   I. expiration of time
   II. destruction of the property by flood

   A. I only B. II only C. Both I and II D. Neither I nor II

75. Your contract with your broker calls for you to receive 20% of the total commission for listing a property, and 30% of the remainder for selling the property. If you are both listing and selling agent on a property which sold for $55,000. at a commission of 6%, you will receive

   A. $1650.   B. $1500.   C. $990.   D. $1452.

76. Which of the following would not normally be paid by a tenant under a net lease of a commercial building?

   A. Ad valorem taxes on the property
   B. Hazard insurance on the building
   C. Custodial service
   D. Mortgage amortization

77. A property manager collects rents on a 10 unit building as follows: Two apartments rent for $250. per month each, six apartments rent for $200. per month each, and two apartments rent for $175. per month each. Utilities average $200. per month and taxes average $250. per month. Assuming 100% occupancy, what would be the annual management fee, based upon a charge of 10% of gross rental collections?

   A. $160.   B. $205   C. $2460.   D. $1920.

78. Which of the following should take place first at a settlement meeting on a real estate sale?

   I. The seller should sign the deed before the buyer signs the mortgage or trust deed
   II. The buyer should sign the mortgage note and mortgage before the seller signs the deed

   A. I only B. II only C. Both I and II   D. Neither I nor II

79. Which of the following would not normally be prorated at the settlement of a real estate sale?

    A. rents paid in advance of settlement
    B. ad valorem taxes on the property
    C. insurance premiums on policies being assumed
    D. special assessments such as for street paving

80. On a closing statement for a real estate sale, a mortgage being assumed by a buyer would be shown as a

    A. debit to buyer and credit to seller
    B. debit to seller and credit to buyer
    C. debit to buyer only
    D. credit to seller only

81. A complete history of all instruments affecting the title of a parcel of real estate is known as

    I. an abstract of title
    II. color of title

    A. I only B. II only C. Both I and II D. Neither I nor II

82. Prorate the unpaid annual taxes on the sale of a property valued at $45,000 and assessed at 50% of value, taxed at the rate of 35 mills on an annual basis, if settlement takes place on June 15th.

    A. $426.56 debit buyer, credit seller
    B. $426.56 credit buyer, debit seller
    C. $360.94 debit seller, credit buyer
    D. $360.94 debit buyer, credit seller

83. Smith purchased a home in a state where the transfer tax was 50¢ per $500. of purchase price, or part thereof, less all assumed indebtedness. The terms of the purchase were a down payment of $12,250. and the assumption of an existing loan of $25,750. What was the amount of the transfer tax?

    A. $12.50   B. $125.   C. $12.25   D. $122.50

84. What would be the amount paid at settlement by a seller who agreed to pay 2 discount points on a sale, the terms of which were: price, $45,000.; loan, 90% of purchase price.

    A. $900.   B. $91.00   C. $810.   D. $81.00

85. Which of the following terms refer to the moment in time when the seller transfers title to the buyer to complete a real estate sale?

    A. settlement meeting
    B. title closing meeting
    C. close of escrow
    D. all of the above

86. The approach to appraisal which is likely to produce the highest estimate of value is the

      I. market data approach
     II. income approach
    III. cost approach

A. I only B. II only C. III only D. All should be equal

87. The period over which a property will yield a return on the investment, over and above the economic or ground rent due to the land is the

      I. age life
     II. economic life

A. I only B. II only C. Both I and II D. Neither I nor II

88. The term "recapture rate" as used in appraising refers to the

      I. period of time necessary to recoup an investment
     II. means employed to estimate depreciation on a building

A. I only B. II only C. Both I and II D. Neither I nor II

89. Which of the following would not be considered by an appraiser in estimating the value of an apartment building?

     A. net income
     B. recent sale price of comparable properties
     C. replacement cost
     D. acquisition cost to present owner

90. In appraising an apartment building having a net income of $9100., you decide on a capitalization rate of 14%. Your estimate of value by this method would be

A. $127,400. B. $65,000. C. $153,000. D. None of the above

91. Depreciation on real property is ordinarily calculated on

      I. land and improvements
     II. improvements only

A. I only B. II only C. Both I and II D. Neither I nor II

92. Architectural features of a building may be restricted by

      I. covenants in a deed
     II. building codes

A. I only B. II only C. Both I and II D. Neither I nor II

93. When a property is utilized for a purpose not in harmony with local zoning laws, this is said to be

        I. a nonconforming use
       II. a zoning variance

A. I only B. II only C. Both I and II D. Neither I nor II

94. Zoning laws are usually enacted at the

      A. local level
      B. state level
      C. federal level
      D. all of the above

THE NEXT THREE QUESTIONS REFER TO THE PLAT WHICH FOLLOWS

95. In making the survey for this plat, the surveyor traveled in

      A. a counterclockwise direction
      B. a clockwise direction
      C. both clockwise and counterclockwise directions
      D. impossible to tell

96. The term P.R.M. as shown on this plat refers to a

       I. monument
      II. bench mark

A. I only B. II only C. Both I and II D. Neither I nor II

97. Identify the property described below:

"Beginning at Point A, 545.99' on course N89°48'27"W to the point of true beginning, thence 125' on course S00°11'33"W, thence 80' on course N89°48'27"W, thence 125' on course N00°11'33"E, thence 80' on course S89°48'27"E to the point of true beginning." This describes lot number:
A. 87 B. 88 C. 89 D. 90

98.   Taxes on real property are

      I. determined on an ad valorem basis
     II. assessed at the local level, as opposed to state
        or federal level

A. I only   B. II only   C. Both I and II   D. Neither I nor II

99.   A tax levied to pay for paving streets in a subdivision is
a(n)

    A. improvement tax
    B. ad valorem tax
    C. capital gain tax
    D. special assessment

100.   A property having a market value of $80,000. is assessed
at 65% of value for tax purposes. The annual taxes are
$1274. The tax rate is

    A. $2.45/$100
    B. 24½ mills
    C. $24.50/$1000
    D. All of the above

VI. LICENSE LAW

101.   State laws requiring licensure for real estate brokers and salesmen are enacted

     I.   to elevate standards of competency
    II. to protect the public

A. I only B. II only C. Both I and II D. Neither I nor II

102.   The term "real estate," as used in license laws, means

     I.   freehold interests only
    II. all interests in land or improvements

A. I only B. II only C. Both I and II D. Neither I nor II

103.   A person would be construed to be acting as a broker or salesman

     I.   if he attempted to perform an act of real estate brokerage, for another, and for compensation
    II. only if such attempt was successful

A. I only B. II only C. Both I and II D. Neither I nor II

104.   Members of the real estate commission are

     I.   appointed by the Governor
    II. elected in a general election

A. I only B. II only C. Both I and II D. Neither I nor II

105.   License fees, etc., collected by the commission are

     I.   paid into the state treasury
    II. retained by the commission as compensation to the commissioners

A. I only B. II only C. Both I and II D. Neither I nor II

106.   In order to be licensed as a broker or salesman, you must

     I.   have a good reputation
    II. be competent to safeguard the public interest

A. I only B. II only C. Both I and II D. Neither I nor II

107.   Real estate salesmen are required to

     I.   be employed by a real estate broker
    II. pass an examination for licensure

A. I only B. II only C. Both I and II D. Neither I nor II

108. Real estate brokers and salesmen may act as such

      I. upon filing an application for licensure
    II. by securing a learner's permit

A. I only B. II only C. Both I and II D. Neither I nor II

109. Real estate brokers must

      I. maintain an office in this state
    II. carry their licenses with them at all times when engaged in the brokerage business

A. I only B. II only C. Both I and II D. Neither I nor II

110. Real estate salesman licenses are maintained in the custody of

      I. the employing broker
    II. the real estate commission

A. I only B. II only C. Both I and II D. Neither I nor II

111. Should a broker change the location of his office

      I. he must notify the Commission within 10 days
    II. he must secure new licenses showing the new address

A. I only B. II only C. Both I and II D. Neither I nor II

112. A salesman may transfer from one broker to another

      I. only with the permission of the original broker
    II. by filing an application for transfer

A. I only B. II only C. Both I and II D. Neither I nor II

113. A salesman may work as such

      I. only as a representative of his employing broker
    II. for any duly licensed broker

A. I only B. II only C. Both I and II D. Neither I nor II

114. Your license may be revoked for

      I. substantial misrepresentation
    II. making false promises

A. I only B. II only C. Both I and II D. Neither I nor II

115. Funds belonging to others must be

      I. kept in an escrow account
    II. turned over to the commission for safekeeping

A. I only B. II only C. Both I and II D. Neither I nor II

116. Rules and regulations governing real estate licensees are promulgated by

        I.   the state legislature
        II. the real estate commission

    A. I only B. II only C. Both I and II D. Neither I nor II

117. You may lose your license for

        I.   dividing commissions with unlicensed persons
        II. failure to work full time as a licensee

    A. I only B. II only C. Both I and II D. Neither I nor II

118. Before your license may be revoked or suspended

        I.   you must be given a hearing before the
             commission
        II. the commission must prefer charges against you
             in court

    A. I only B. II only C. Both I and II D. Neither I nor II

119. Should your license be revoked by the Commission

        I.   there is no appeal from this decision
        II. you may never again be licensed as a broker or
             salesman in this state

    A. I only B. II only C. Both I and II D. Neither I nor II

120. A violation of the license law is a

        I.   felony
        II. misdemeanor

    A. I only B. II only C. Both I and II D. Neither I nor II

121. Fines for violation of the licensing act are imposed by

        I.   the real estate commission
        II. the courts

    A. I only B. II only C. Both I and II D. Neither I nor II

122. Which of the following would be exempt from the requirement for licensure as a broker or salesman?

        I.   an attorney-at-law,while acting as such
        II. the owner of the property

    A. I only B. II only C. Both I and II D. Neither I nor II

123. Should an unlicensed person attempt to file suit for a commission on a real estate transaction

   I. he must secure a temporary license
   II. the action would not be accepted by the court

A. I only B. II only C. Both I and II D. Neither I nor II

124. Real estate brokers must

   I. display a sign on their offices identifying themselves as licensed brokers
   II. maintain an office in this state

A. I only B. II only C. Both I and II D. Neither I nor II

125. Records of the real estate commission, other than license examination records, are

   I. public records
   II. private, available only to the commission

A. I only B. II only C. Both I and II D. Neither I nor II

126. Funds of others which are received by salesmen must be

   I. deposited in an escrow account by the salesman
   II. turned over to the broker for deposit in an escrow account

A. I only B. II only C. Both I and II D. Neither I nor II

127. Copies of all written instruments on real estate transactions prepared by a licensee must be

   I. distributed to all signators of the instrument
   II. maintained by the broker

A. I only B. II only C. Both I and II D. Neither I nor II

128. Salesmen may not advertise in their own names

   I. without the broker's permission
   II. without naming the employing broker in the advertisement

A. I only B. II only C. Both I and II D. Neither I nor II

129. Your license may be revoked for

   I. placing a sign on property offering it for sale without the owner's consent
   II. incompetency

A. I only B. II only C. Both I and II D. Neither I nor II

130. Which of the following may be licensed as a real estate salesman?

      I. a natural person
    II. a corporation

A. I only B. II only C. Both I and II D. Neither I nor II

Uniform Licensing Examination for Real Estate Broker

Name: (Print)

Place of Testing:

City:

State:

Center Code No.

Today's Date:

Signature:

Copy Examination Number Here:

	1	2	3	4	5	6	7	8	9	0
	1	2	3	4	5	6	7	8	9	0
	1	2	3	4	5	6	7	8	9	0
	1	2	3	4	5	6	7	8	9	0
	1	2	3	4	5	6	7	8	9	0
	1	2	3	4	5	6	7	8	9	0

Be sure each mark is *black* and *completely fills* the answer space

PART I

	A	B	C	D
1	[]	[]	[]	[]
2	[]	[]	[]	[]
3	[]	[]	[]	[]
4	[]	[]	[]	[]
5	[]	[]	[]	[]
6	[]	[]	[]	[]
7	[]	[]	[]	[]
8	[]	[]	[]	[]
9	[]	[]	[]	[]
10	[]	[]	[]	[]
11	[]	[]	[]	[]
12	[]	[]	[]	[]
13	[]	[]	[]	[]
14	[]	[]	[]	[]
15	[]	[]	[]	[]
16	[]	[]	[]	[]
17	[]	[]	[]	[]
18	[]	[]	[]	[]
19	[]	[]	[]	[]
20	[]	[]	[]	[]
21	[]	[]	[]	[]
22	[]	[]	[]	[]
23	[]	[]	[]	[]
24	[]	[]	[]	[]
25	[]	[]	[]	[]
26	[]	[]	[]	[]
27	[]	[]	[]	[]
28	[]	[]	[]	[]
29	[]	[]	[]	[]
30	[]	[]	[]	[]

PART II

	A	B	C	D
31	[]	[]	[]	[]
32	[]	[]	[]	[]
33	[]	[]	[]	[]
34	[]	[]	[]	[]
35	[]	[]	[]	[]
36	[]	[]	[]	[]
37	[]	[]	[]	[]
38	[]	[]	[]	[]
39	[]	[]	[]	[]
40	[]	[]	[]	[]
41	[]	[]	[]	[]
42	[]	[]	[]	[]
43	[]	[]	[]	[]
44	[]	[]	[]	[]
45	[]	[]	[]	[]
46	[]	[]	[]	[]
47	[]	[]	[]	[]
48	[]	[]	[]	[]
49	[]	[]	[]	[]
50	[]	[]	[]	[]

PART III

	A	B	C	D
51	[]	[]	[]	[]
52	[]	[]	[]	[]
53	[]	[]	[]	[]
54	[]	[]	[]	[]
55	[]	[]	[]	[]
56	[]	[]	[]	[]
57	[]	[]	[]	[]
58	[]	[]	[]	[]
59	[]	[]	[]	[]
60	[]	[]	[]	[]
61	[]	[]	[]	[]
62	[]	[]	[]	[]
63	[]	[]	[]	[]
64	[]	[]	[]	[]
65	[]	[]	[]	[]
66	[]	[]	[]	[]
67	[]	[]	[]	[]
68	[]	[]	[]	[]
69	[]	[]	[]	[]
70	[]	[]	[]	[]
71	[]	[]	[]	[]
72	[]	[]	[]	[]
73	[]	[]	[]	[]
74	[]	[]	[]	[]
75	[]	[]	[]	[]

	A	B	C	D
76	[]	[]	[]	[]
77	[]	[]	[]	[]
78	[]	[]	[]	[]
79	[]	[]	[]	[]
80	[]	[]	[]	[]
81	[]	[]	[]	[]
82	[]	[]	[]	[]
83	[]	[]	[]	[]
84	[]	[]	[]	[]
85	[]	[]	[]	[]
86	[]	[]	[]	[]
87	[]	[]	[]	[]
88	[]	[]	[]	[]
89	[]	[]	[]	[]
90	[]	[]	[]	[]
91	[]	[]	[]	[]
92	[]	[]	[]	[]
93	[]	[]	[]	[]
94	[]	[]	[]	[]
95	[]	[]	[]	[]
96	[]	[]	[]	[]
97	[]	[]	[]	[]
98	[]	[]	[]	[]
99	[]	[]	[]	[]
100	[]	[]	[]	[]

PART IV

	A	B	C	D
101	[]	[]	[]	[]
102	[]	[]	[]	[]
103	[]	[]	[]	[]
104	[]	[]	[]	[]
105	[]	[]	[]	[]
106	[]	[]	[]	[]
107	[]	[]	[]	[]
108	[]	[]	[]	[]
109	[]	[]	[]	[]
110	[]	[]	[]	[]
111	[]	[]	[]	[]
112	[]	[]	[]	[]
113	[]	[]	[]	[]
114	[]	[]	[]	[]
115	[]	[]	[]	[]
116	[]	[]	[]	[]
117	[]	[]	[]	[]
118	[]	[]	[]	[]
119	[]	[]	[]	[]
120	[]	[]	[]	[]
121	[]	[]	[]	[]
122	[]	[]	[]	[]
123	[]	[]	[]	[]
124	[]	[]	[]	[]
125	[]	[]	[]	[]
126	[]	[]	[]	[]
127	[]	[]	[]	[]
128	[]	[]	[]	[]
129	[]	[]	[]	[]
130	[]	[]	[]	[]

EXCLUSIVE AUTHORIZATION TO SELL

SALES PRICE: $45,500.   TYPE HOME Rambler   TOTAL BEDROOMS 2   TOTAL BATHS 1½

ADDRESS: 700 W. Oak Street   JURISDICTION OF: Staunton

AMT. OF LOAN TO BE ASSUMED $ 19,222.21   AS OF WHAT DATE: 6/1/--   TAXES & INS. INCLUDED: Y   YEARS TO GO 14   AMOUNT PAYABLE MONTHLY $ 184.50   7½ % LOAN   TYPE G.I.

MORTGAGE COMPANY Star Light Ins. Co.   2nd TRUST $

ESTIMATED EXPECTED RENT MONTHLY $ TYPE OF APPRAISAL REQUESTED: Appraised at $45,500.

OWNER'S NAME Nick L. Pincher & wife, Penny   PHONES: (HOME)   (BUSINESS)

TENANTS NAME   PHONES: (HOME)   (BUSINESS)

POSSESSION 30 days   DATE LISTED: 4/11/--   EXCLUSIVE FOR 90 days   DATE OF EXPIRATION 6/9/19--

LISTING BROKER ABC Realty   PHONE   KEY AVAILABLE AT

LISTING SALESMAN   HOME PHONE: HOW TO BE SHOWN:

(1) ENTRANCE FOYER ☐ CENTER HALL ☐	(18) AGE 12 yrs	AIR CONDITIONING ☐	(32) TYPE KITCHEN CABINETS
(2) LIVING ROOM SIZE 11 x 14 FIREPLACE ☐	(19) ROOFING Slag	TOOL HOUSE ☐	(33) TYPE COUNTER TOPS
(3) DINING ROOM SIZE 9 x 11	(20) GARAGE SIZE 1 car	PATIO ☐	(34) EAT-IN SIZE KITCHEN ☐
(4) BEDROOM TOTAL: 2 DOWN 2 UP	(21) SIDE DRIVE X	CIRCULAR DRIVE ☐	(35) BREAKFAST ROOM X Nook
(5) BATHS TOTAL: 1½ DOWN 1½ UP	(22) PORCH ☐ SIDE ☐ REAR ☐	SCREENED ☐	(36) BUILT-IN OVEN & RANGE ☐
(6) DEN SIZE 10 x 14 FIREPLACE X	(23) FENCED YARD	OUTDOOR GRILL ☐	(37) SEPARATE STOVE INCLUDED X Gas
(7) FAMILY ROOM SIZE FIREPLACE ☐	(24) STORM WINDOWS X	STORM DOORS X	(38) REFRIGERATOR INCLUDED ☐
(8) RECREATION ROOM SIZE FIREPLACE ☐	(25) CURBS & GUTTERS X	SIDEWALKS X	(39) DISHWASHER INCLUDED ☐
(9) BASEMENT SIZE None	(26) STORM SEWERS ☐	ALLEY X	(40) DISPOSAL INCLUDED ☐
NONE ☐ 1/4 ☐ 1/3 ☐ 1/2 ☐ 3/4 ☐ FULL ☐	(27) WATER SUPPLY well		(41) DOUBLE SINK ☐ SINGLE SINK ☐
(10) UTILITY ROOM SIZE 6 x 8	(28) SEWER ☐	SEPTIC X	STAINLESS STEEL ☐ PORCELAIN ☐
TYPE HOT WATER SYSTEM: SWHU	(29) TYPE GAS: NATURAL ☐	BOTTLED ☐	(42) WASHER INCLUDED X DRYER INCLUDED X
(11) TYPE HEAT Oil HWBB	(30) WHY SELLING		(43) PANTRY ☐ EXHAUST FAN ☐
(12) EST. FUEL COST $300/ yr			(44) LAND ASSESSMENT $ 4300.
(13) ATTIC ☐	(31) DIRECTIONS TO PROPERTY		(45) IMPROVEMENTS $ 19000.
PULL DOWN STAIRWAY ☐ REGULAR STAIRWAY ☐ TRAP DOOR X			(46) TOTAL ASSESSMENT $
(14) MAIDS ROOM ☐ TYPE BATH			(47) TAX RATE
LOCATION			(48) TOTAL ANNUAL TAXES $ 815.50
(15) NAME OF BUILDER			(49) LOT SIZE 80 x 136
(16) SQUARE FOOTAGE 2080 (52 x 40)			(50) LOT NO 1 BLOCK 4 SECTION
(17) EXTERIOR OF HOUSE Frame			Forest Hills Subd.

NAME OF SCHOOLS: ELEMENTARY: JR. HIGH:

HIGH   PAROCHIAL:

PUBLIC TRANSPORTATION:

NEAREST SHOPPING AREA:

REMARKS: Venetian blinds and carpets included. Attic insulated with rock wool.

Date: April 11, 19--

In consideration of the services of ABC Realty (herein called "Broker") to be rendered to the undersigned (herein called "Owner"), and of the promise of Broker to make reasonable efforts to obtain a Purchaser therefor, Owner hereby lists with Broker the real estate and all improvements thereon which are described above (all herein called "the property"), and Owner hereby grants to Broker the exclusive and irrevocable right to sell such property from 12:00 Noon on April 11, 19 -- until 12:00 Midnight on June 9, 19--, 19 (herein called "period of time"), for the price of Forty five Thousand Five Hundred Dollars ($ 45,500.) or for such other price and upon such other terms (including exchange) as Owner may subsequently authorize during the period of time.

It is understood by Owner that the above sum or any other price subsequently authorized by Owner shall include a cash fee of 6 per cent of such price or other price which shall be payable by Owner to Broker upon consummation by any Purchaser or Purchasers of a valid contract of sale of the property during the period of time and whether or not Broker was a procuring cause of any such contract of sale.

If the property is sold or exchanged by Owner, or by Broker or by any other person to any Purchaser to whom the property was shown by Broker or any representative of Broker within sixty (60) days after the expiration of the period of time mentioned above, Owner agrees to pay to Broker a cash fee which shall be the same percentage of the purchase price as the percentage mentioned above.

Broker is hereby authorized by Owner to place a "For Sale" sign on the property and to remove all signs of other brokers or salesmen during the period of time, and Owner hereby agrees to make the property available to Broker at all reasonable hours for the purpose of showing it to prospective Purchasers.

Owner agrees to convey the property to the Purchaser by warranty deed with the usual covenants of title and free and clear from all encumbrances, tenancies, liens (for taxes or otherwise), but subject to applicable restrictive covenants of record. Owner acknowledges receipt of a copy of this agreement.

WITNESS the following signature(s) and seal(s):

Date Signed: April 11, 19--

Listing Broker ABC Realty

Address   Telephone

Nick L. Pincher _____ (SEAL)
(Owner)

Penny Pincher _____ (SEAL)
(Owner)

BROKER EXAMINATION

Use the information from the listing and contract, plus the information given below, to complete the closing statement for the Pinchers to Dweller sale. Use existing loan balance, and do not include clerk's fees, credit report fees, etc. Title examination $117.25; title insurance, $37.50; preparation of deed, $25; preparation of the deed of trust, $20; survey, $45; annual taxes have not been paid for 1973; buyer to furnish new hazard insurance policy at cost of $90 for a 3-year policy. Loan discount, 1 percent, paid by seller; loan service fee, 1 percent; recording tax, $.20 per $100. Use a 30-day method of computation. Day of settlement accrues to the benefit and/or expense of the purchaser.

1. Your listing on the Pincher home will expire on

    I. July 11, 19__
    II. June 11, 19__
    A. I only B. II only C. Both I and II D. Neither I nor II

2. The monthly payment on the Pincher's existing loan includes

    I. principal, interest, taxes, and insurance.
    II. principal and interest only.
    A. I only B. II only C. Both I and II D. Neither I nor II

3. The den in the Pincher home is

    I. in the basement
    II. on the second floor
    A. I only B. II only C. Both I and II D. Neither I nor II

4. The Pincher home contains

    I. 2,080 square feet.
    II. 2 bedrooms
    A. I only B. II only C. Both I and II D. Neither I nor II

5. The tax rate on the Pincher home is

    A. $3.50/1000   e. 35 mills
    B. $3.50/100   d. All of the above

    A. I only B. II only C. Both I and II D. Neither I nor II

6. In the Pincher-Dweller contract, the cash down payment is to be

    I. $6825.
    II. $5325.
    A. I only B. II only C. Both I and II D. Neither I nor II

7. The loan to value ratio of the 1st D/T loan is

    I. 70%
    II. 80%

    A. I only B. II only C. Both I and II D. Neither I nor II

8.   Chattels included in the Pincher-Dweller sale include

            I. gas range, washer, dryer and venetian blinds
            II. gas range, washer, dryer and venetian blinds, and
                 carpet in bedrooms.
      A. I only   B. II only   C. Both I and II   D. Neither I nor II

9.   The second D/T loan in the Pincher-Dweller sale

            I. is a purchase money loan.
            II. is a balloon loan.
      A. I only   B. II only   C. Both I and II   D. Neither I nor II

10.   The contract calls for the earnest money deposit

            I. to be held by the seller until settlement
            II. settlement to be held on June 21, 19__
      A. I only   B. II only   C. Both I and II   D. Neither I nor II

11.   The purchase price is shown on the closing statement as a

            I. debit to purchaser and credit to seller.
            II. credit to purchaser and debit to seller.
      A. I only   B. II only   C. Both I and II   D. Neither I nor II

12.   The first D/T loan proceeds are shown as a

            I. debit to purchaser.
            II. credit to seller.
      A. I only   B. II only   C. Both I and II   D. Neither I nor II

13.   Hazard insurance is shown on the closing statement as

            I. a debit to purchaser and credit to seller.
            II. a debit to purchaser only.
      A. I only   B. II only   C. Both I and II   D. Neither I nor II

14.   The earnest money deposit paid by the Dwellers is

            I. $1500.
            II. shown as a credit to purchasers.
      A. I only   B. II only   C. Both I and II   D. Neither I nor II

15.   The balance on the Pincher's first D/T loan is

            I. $9,222.21
            II. a debit to the seller only.
      A. I only   B. II only   C. Both I and II   D. Neither I nor II

16.   The prorated amount of the annual taxes is

            I. $387. +
            II. $430. +
      A. I only   B. II only   C. Both I and II   D. Neither I nor II

17.   The prorated taxes are shown as a

            I. debit to purchaser and credit to seller.
            II. debit to seller and credit to purchaser.
      A. I only   B. II only   C. Both I and II   D. Neither I nor II

18. The amount of the agent's commission is
          I. $2730.
          II. shown as a debit to seller.
    A. I only   B. II only   C. Both I and II   D. Neither I nor II

19. Expenses for the preparation of the deed are borne by the
          I. seller.
          II. purchaser.
    A. I only   B. II only   C. Both I and II   D. Neither I nor II

20. The charge for preparation of the deed is
          I. $20.00
          II. $25.00
    A. I only   B. II only   C. Both I and II   D. Neither I nor II

21. Attorney's fee for title examination is a
          I. debit to purchaser
          II. credit to purchaser
    A. I only   B. II only   C. Both I and II   D. Neither I nor II

22. Title insurance is an expense to the
          I. seller.
          II. purchaser.
    A. I only   B. II only   C. Both I and II   D. Neither I nor II

23. Preparation of the first D/T is an expense borne by the
          I. mortgagee.
          II. seller.
    A. I only   B. II only   C. Both I and II   D. Neither I nor II

24. The amount of the loan service fee is
          I. $455.
          II. $364.
    A. I only   B. II only   C. Both I and II   D. Neither I nor II

25. The charge for loan service fee is an expense to the
          I. purchaser.
          II. seller.
    A. I only   B. II only   C. Both I and II   D. Neither I nor II

26. Loan discounts are in this instance
          I. $364.
          II. paid by the seller
    A. I only   B. II only   C. Both I and II   D. Neither I nor II

27. The expense of the survey is borne by the
          I. lender.
          II. purchaser.
    A. I only   B. II only   C. Both I and II   D. Neither I nor II

28. The second D/T to the seller is
          I. a debit to seller.
          II. a credit to purchaser.
    A. I only   B. II only   C. Both I and II   D. Neither I nor II

29. Which of the following is correct?

>   I. The first D/T is shown as a debit to the purchaser
>   and a credit to the seller.
>   II. The first D/T is shown as a credit to the purchas-
>   er and a debit to the seller.

A. I only B. II only C. Both I and II D. Neither I nor II

30. The amount due from purchaser to close is

>   I. a debit to purchaser.
>   II. a credit to purchaser.

A. I only B. II only C. Both I and II D. Neither I nor II

31. A land developer bought 15 acres of land at $1,500 per acre.
    On this land she built 12 houses at an average cost of
    $20,000 each. She also spent $25,000 on recreational improve-
    ment. If she wants to realize a 20% profit on her investment,
    what must each house sell for?

    A. $29,687.50   B. $28,500.00   C. $26,250.00   D. $27,343.00

32. An investor wants to purchase an 8-unit apartment building
    where each unit rents for $187 a month. How much should he
    pay for the building if he wants to earn 11% on his invest-
    ment?

    (a) $17,952   (b) $13,600   (c) $163,200   (d) $93,620

33. A builder buys land for $30,000, spends $50,000 for streets,
    $645,000 for 25 houses, and $45,000 for miscellaneous. He
    borrowed all the money at 12% per annum for five months. If
    he wants to make a 15% profit, how much must he sell each
    house for?

    (a) $37,121   (b) $35,741   (c) $35,421   (d) $37,191

34. A man owns 10 apartments and has an option of two rental
    plans: Option #1 at $100 a month including utilities; or
    Option #2 at $80 a month not including utilities. Utilities
    are $120 a month. The better choice is based upon the fact
    that:

>   (a) Option 1 pays $960 more than Option 2;
>   (b) Option 1 pays $960 less than Option 2;
>   (c) Option 1 pays $1200 more than Option 2;
>   (d) Option 1 pays $1200 less than Option 2.

35. A home is presently valued at $42,012. What was the original
    value of the home if it has been appreciating an average of
    .4% per annum and is 20 years old?

    (a) $23,300   (b) $38,900   (c) $45,700   (d) $41,800

36. A house was assessed at 65% of value for taxes. The tax rate was $3.50 per $100. Ten years later the same rates were used, but the taxes had increased by $409.50. How much had the market value of the house increased?

    (a) $117,000   (b) $180,000   (c) $11,700   (d) $18,000

37. A home was purchased 3 years ago for $35,000. It was listed for sale at a price that represented a 20% profit. If the seller accepted an offer that was $3,000 below list price, what would she receive after paying the 6% commission?

    (a) $39,480   (b) $36,660   (c) $36,480   (d) $36,900

38. The buildings on a 150' by 180' lot cover 25% of the lot. 15% of the front footage of the lot for the entire depth is sold to the State. How many square feet of land not covered with buildings is retained by the owner?

    (a) 27,000   (b) 16,200   (c) 10,800   (d) 13,500

39. A house was built eight years ago for $36,000 on a $10,000 lot. Four years later, half of the lot was sold for $11,000. If the house has appreciated 3/4% per year and the appreciation remained constant on the lot, what is the current value of the retained property?

    (a) $38,160   (b) $49,160   (c) $50,160   (d) $55,160

40. A real estate analyst states that the return on a 10-year investment is, on the average, equal to cost. Which is below average:

	COST	ANNUAL INCOME
(a)	$28,000	$ 3,000
(b)	$45,000	$ 4,200
(c)	$75,000	$ 8,000
(d)	$98,000	$10,000

41. A subdivider is selling eight lots that are 75' x 120'. Which will give her the highest selling price?

    | (a) | $1.50 per square foot; |
    | (b) | $13,600 per lot; |
    | (c) | $185 per front foot; |
    | (d) | $110,000 for the entire parcel |

42. A person borrows $ 4,500 at 7 1/2% interest to improve his store. If he pays back the loan at the end of eight months in one payment, how much did he pay?

    (a) $4,753   (b) $4,725   (c) $4,500   (d) $225

43. A street assessment was assessed on a parcel of land in the amount of $219.00. It was to be paid off in 10 equal installments. The owner has paid six payments. As of July 1 of this year the interest rate is 7% per annum on the declining balance. What would be the balance due January 1 of the following year, including principal and interest?

    (a) $87.60   (b) $93.72   (c) $90.67   (d) $113.33

44.

	House 1	House 2	House 3
Listed for	$88,000	$37,000	$67,750
Sold for	82,000	36,500	66,500

Mr. Wood, an investor, contracted with a broker, American Real Estate Associates, Inc. to sell his properties, shown as House 1, House 2 and House 3. All houses sold and the broker received his commission which was 8% of the first $90,000 plus 2% of everything over that amount based on total sales. How much more commission would the broker have received if a straight 6% commission rate had been charged?

    A. $2310
    B. $7750
    C. $2000
    D. None; the broker would get less money

45. You have the management contract on an aprtment house and are to receive 3 1/2% of the gross rentals as commission. You collect for one month as follows: $500 for each of 2 units; $400 for 1 unit; with $140 paid out in repairs. How much was the net amount paid to the owner that month?

    (a) $711   (b) $1,260   (c) $1,211   (d) $1,549

46. Mr. Ryan sold a home for $18,880 which was 18% over what he had paid for it four years ago. The property was taxed at 60% of Ryan's cost and at a tax rate of $.045 per dollar per year. Mr. Ryan's expense of ownership amounted to 3% of the assessed tax value each year. How much did mr. Ryan lose on the sale?

    (a) $1,523.20   (b) $408.00   (c) 768.00   (d) No loss

47. A property that was listed for $30,000 was sold for $26,000 with the purchaser agreeing to pay the sales commission of 6%. How much did the purchaser save by paying the broker's commission and the lower price instead of paying the seller the listed price?

    (a) $640   (b) $240   (c) $2,440   (d) $4,000

48. It cost a builder $8,000 to build a house last year. Since then building costs have risen 45% and then decreased 11 1/2% below this high point. How much would it cost him to build the same house today?

(a) $12,666   (b) $10,666   (c) $10,266   (d) $10,626

49. If the taxes on a $20,000 house assessed at $15,000 are $255 per year, how much would the taxes be on a house in the same area which is worth $30,000 and is assessed at $25,000?

(a) $425.   (b) $225.   (c) $5,000.   (d) $500.

50. On November 15, you bought a house. The taxes for the fiscal year July 1st to June 30th of $480 have not been paid. The fire insurance policy costing $90 for the calendar year has been paid. There is also a public liability policy for one year issued May 15th. That policy cost $30 and has also been paid. Does the seller owe the buyer or vice versa - and how much?

(a)   Seller owes the buyer $193.75;
(b)   Buyer owes the seller $193.75;
(c)   Seller owes the buyer $153.75;
(d)   Buyer owes the seller $153.75.

51. A residence located in an area where there are factories and plants, and where there is much smoke and dust is suffering from

       I. physical depreciation
     II. economic obsolescence.

A. I only B. II only C. Both I and II D. Neither I nor II

52. Which of the following is most likely to have a percentage lease in a commercial area?

A.   Kellogg Supermarket
B.   Ford Foundation
C.   Municipal Utility Company
D.   Government Agency

53. The value of a leasehold estate is equivalent to

       I. the rent the lessor receives
     II. the rent plus the land value

A. I only B. II only C. Both I and II D. Neither I nor II

54. The value of a leased fee is

       I. the amount of rent produced and the reversionary
         interest.

       II. the rent plus the improvements.
A. I only B. II only C. Both I and II D. Neither I nor II

55. The highest and best use of a property is determined by one

      I. that produces the highest net yield over the longest period of time.
     II. that allows for the tallest building.

A. I only B. II only C. Both I and II D. Neither I nor II

56. One of the following is not an approach used in appraising.

      I. Market data.
     II. Condemnation.

A. I only B. II only C. Both I and II D. Neither I nor II

57. A lease for years ends upon

      I. the death of either party.
     II. agreement of the parties.

A. I only B. II only C. Both I and II D. Neither I nor II

58. A mortgaged property

      I. cannot be sold without the consent of the mortgagee.
     II. can be conveyed by the grantor making a deed to the grantee.

A. I only B. II only C. Both I and II D. Neither I nor II

59. The written instrument that accompanies a mortgage is

      I. the deed.
     II. the note.

A. I only B. II only C. Both I and II D. Neither I nor II

60. A characteristic of a note as opposed to a mortgage is that

      I. it creates a personal liability
     II. it does not hypothecate the property

A. I only B. II only C. Both I and II D. Neither I nor II

61. The Fair Housing Act does not apply to

      I. a private organization not operated for commercial purposes.
     II. an individually owned private residence sold through a real estate company.

A. I only B. II only C. Both I and II D. Neither I nor II

62. Violations of the Fair Housing Act must be reported

        I. within 30 days.
       II. to the Attorney General.

A. I only B. II only C. Both I and II D. Neither I nor II

63. The Fair Housing Act prohibits

        I. blockbusting.
       II. discrimination in the use of a multiple listing
           service.

A. I only B. II only C. Both I and II D. Neither I nor II

64. A tenant's responsibilities extend to

        I. prevention of waste by third parties
       II. liability for injury to third parties.

A. I only B. II only C. Both I and II. D. Neither I nor II

65. It may be said that homegeneity in a neighborhood

A.   creates stability in values.
B.   increases prices.
C.   decreases value.
D.   has no effect on value.

66. A federal savings and loan association holds membership in

        I. F.S.L.I.C.
       II. Federal Home Loan Bank.

A. I only B. II only C. Both I and II D. Neither I nor II

67. A mortgage loan correspondent

        I. lends money of his clients and financial institu-
           tions.
       II. lends his own money.

A. I only B. II only C. Both I and II D. Neither I nor II

68. An abstract of title

        I. insures the title
       II. gives a history of the title, including the encum-
           brances against the property.

A. I only B. II only C. Both I and II D. Neither I nor II

69. A person in open, notorious, exclusive, and continuous possession of property for a stated period of time may claim ownership by

       I. adverse possession.
      II. quitclaim deed.

A. I only B. II only C. Both I and II D. Neither I nor II

70. Equity in a property is

       I. the value over and above the mortgage.
      II. the cash down payment made at time of acquisition

A. I only B. II only C. Both I and II D. Neither I nor II

71. A fiduciary relationship exists

       I. between the broker and the client.
      II. between the broker and the client's attorney.

A. I only B. II only C. Both I and II D. Neither I nor II

72. A tenant in common may sell

       I. with the premission and approval of the other tenants in common.
      II. at any time, without permission or approval.

A. I only B. II only C. Both I and II D. Neither I nor II

73. When an owner-seller finances the sale, it is known as

       I. secondary financing
      II. deferred purchase money mortgage

A. I only B. II only C. Both I and II D. Neither I nor II

74. When a person secures a right to buy a property at a definite price and pays an amount of money for this right, he is said to have

       I. an option.
      II. a contract for deed.

A. I only B. II only C. Both I and II D. Neither I nor II

75. One of the below is not a limitation on ownership of property

A.   Police power
B.   Escheat
C.   Taxation
D.   Title Search

76. When an applicant applies for V. A. financing

        I. the V. A. uses its own appraisers.
       II. the V. A. will accept an appraisal of another.

A. I only B. II only C. Both I and II D. Neither I nor II

77. F. H. A.

        I. plans housing.
       II. builds housing

A. I only B. II only C. Both I and II D. Neither I nor II

78. When a purchaser is required to sign a statement that he occupies or intends to occupy the house, he is securing

        I. a V.A. guaranteed loan.
       II. an F.H.A. insured loan.

A. I only B. II only C. Both I and II D. Neither I nor II

79. The before and after technique is used in

        I. condemnation.
       II. cost approach.

A. I only B. II only C. Both I and II D. Neither I nor II

80. The difference between the cost of replacement and current valuation is equal to

        I. accrued depreciation.
       II. assessed valuation.

81. Capitalization is based upon

        I. net earnings.
       II. gross income.

A. I only B. II only C. Both I and II D. Neither I nor II

82. V.A. closing costs

        I. must be paid in cash.
       II. may be paid by anyone.

A. I only B. II only C. Both I and II D. Neither I nor II

83. In a lease with an escalation clause

    I. the rent could increase 100 percent.
    II. the lessee has an option to renew for another
        year.

A. I only B. II only C. Both I and II D. Neither I nor II

84. Under a net lease, a tenant is least likely to pay

    A. Taxes.
    B. Utilities.
    C. Depreciation
    D. Mortgage Amortization.

85. When there is a meeting of minds, it may be said that there is

    I. a completed contract.
    II. an offer and acceptance.

A. I only B. II only C. Both I and II D. Neither I nor II

86. Which of the following listings would be least likely to have
    a specified commission?

    A. Net listing.
    B. Open listing.
    C. Exclusive listing.
    D. Multiple listing.

87. Where a mortgage is held by a corporation, partnership, or
    association, the holder is called the

    A. mortgagee.
    B. vendor.
    C. vendee
    D. mortgagor.

88. Nonconforming use is a use

    I. in violation of a zoning ordinance.
    II. for which a speicific exception to zoning ordin-
        ance has been obtained.

A. I only B. II only C. Both I and II D. Neither I nor II

89. Surety of good title is best evidenced by

    A. certificate of title.
    B. title insurance.
    C. quitclaim deed.
    D. color of title.

90. A lease

>   I. could be subordinated to a mortgage.
> II. could not be subordinated to a mortgage.

A. I only   B. II only   C. Both I and II   D. Neither I nor II

91. A fiduciary relationship could exist between a principal and all the following, except

>   A. Executor.
>   B. Administrator.
>   C. Trustee.
>   D. Appraiser.

92. Duly means

>   A. according to custom.
>   B. in a true direction.
>   C. as duty demands
>   D. in an appropriate and timely manner.

93. An appurtenance is

>   A. an attachment to a property.
>   B. a right of way.
>   C. a right or improvement belonging to and passing with a principal property.
>   D. an impertinent, rude remark.

94. To convey most nearly means

>   A. buy.
>   B. warrant.
>   C. obligate.
>   D. transfer.

95. A commitment is an

>   A. agreement.
>   B. decree.
>   C. privilege.
>   D. encumbrance.

96. The Habendum Clause is found in

>   A. a will.
>   B. a mortgage.
>   C. a deed.
>   D. an exclusive listing.

97. A mortgagee is

     A. a buyer.
     B. a lender.
     C. a borrower.
     D. a seller.

98. A lease is ended if

     A. the tenant dies.
     B. the landlord dies.
     C. the property is sold during the lease period.
     D. none of the above.

99. Lenders may protect their loan for real estate by use of

     I. a mortgage
    II. a deed of trust.

A. I only   B. II only   C. Both I and II   D. Neither I nor II

100. Survivorship cannot exist among

     I. joint tenants.
    II. tenants in common.

A. I only   B. II only   C. Both I and II   D. Neither I nor II

101. State laws requiring licensure for real estate brokers and salesmen are enacted

     I. to elevate standards of competency.
    II. to protect the public.

A. I only   B. II only   C. Both I and II   D. Neither I nor II

102. The term "real estate", as used in license laws, means

     I. freehold interests only.
    II. all interests in land or improvements.

A. I only   B. II only   C. Both I and II   D. Neither I nor II

103. A person would be construed to be acting as a broker or salesman

     I. if he attempted to perform an act of real estate
       brokerage, for another, and for compensation.
    II. only if such an attempt was successful.

A. I only   B. only   C. Both I and II   D. Neither I nor II

104. Members of the real estate commission are

> I. appointed by the Governor.
> II. elected in a general election.

A. I only B. II only C. Both I and II D. Neither I nor II

105. License fees, etc., collected by the commission are

> I. paid into the state treasury.
> II. retained by the commission as compensation to the commissioners.

A. I only B. II only C. Both I and II D. Neither I nor II

106. In order to be licensed as a broker or salesman, you must

> I. have a good reputation.
> II. be competent to safeguard the public interest.

A. I only B. II only C. Both I and II D. Neither I nor II

107. Real estate salesmen are required to

> I. be employed by a real estate broker
> II. pass an examination for licensure.

A. I only B. II only C. Both I and II D. Neither I nor II

108. Real estate brokers and salesmen may act as such

> I. upon filing an application for licensure.
> II. by securing a learner's permit

A. I only B. II only C. Both I and II D. Neither I nor II

109. Real estate brokers must

> I. maintain an office in this state.
> II. carry their licenses with them at all times when engaged in the brokerage business.

A. I only B. II only C. Both I and II D. Neither I nor II

110. Real estate salesman licenses are maintained in the custody of

> I. the employing broker
> II. the real estate commission

A. I only B. II only C. Both I and II D. Neither I nor II

111. Should a broker change the location of his office

       I. he must notify the Commission within 10 days.
      II. he must secure new licenses showing the new
          address.

A. I only B. II only C. Both I and II D. Neither I nor II

112. A salesman may transfer from one broker to another

       I. only with the permission of the original broker.
      II. by filing an application for transfer.

A. I only B. II only C. Both I and II D. Neither I nor II

113. A salesman may work as such

       I. only as a representative of his employing broker.
      II. for any duly licensed broker.

A. I only B. II only C. Both I and II D. Neither I nor II

114. Your license may be revoked for

       I. substantial misrepresentation.
      II. making false promises

A. I only B. II only C. Both I and II D. Neither I nor II

115. Funds belonging to others must be

       I. kept in an escrow account.
      II. turned over the commission for safekeeping.

A. I only B. II only C. Both I and II D. Neither I nor II

116. Rules and regulations governing real estate licensees are
promulgated by

       I. the state legislature.
      II. the real estate commission.

A. I only B. II only C. Both I and II D. Neither I nor II

117. You may lose your license for

       I. dividing commissions with unlicensed persons.
      II. failure to work full time as a licensee.

A. I only B. II only C. Both I and II D. Neither I nor II

118.   Before your license may be revoked or suspended

       I. you must be given a hearing before the Commission.
      II. the Commission must prefer charges against you in court.

A. I only B. II only C. Both I and II D. Neither I nor II

119.   Should your license be revoked by the Commission,

       I. there is no appeal from this decision.
      II. you may never again be licensed as a broker or salesman in this state.

A. I only B. II only C. Both I and II D. Neither I nor II

120.   A violation of the license law is a

       I. felony.
      II. misdemeanor.

A. I only B. II only C. Both I and II D. Neither I nor II

121.   Fines for violation of the licensing act are imposed by

       I. the real estate commission
      II. the courts.

A. I only B. II only C. Both I and II D. Neither I nor II

122.   Which of the following would be exempt from the requirement for licensure as a broker or salesman?

       I. an attorney-at-law, while acting as such.
      II. the owner of the property.

A. I only B. II only C. Both I and II D. Neither I nor II

123.   Should an unlicensed person attempt to file suit for a commission on a real estate transaction,

       I. he must secure a temporary license.
      II. the action would not be accepted by the court.

A. I only B. II only C. Both I and II D. Neither I nor II

124.   Real Estate brokers must

       I. display a sign on their offices identifying themselves as licensed brokers.
      II. maintain an office in this state.

A. I only B. II only C. Both I and II D. Neither I nor II

125. Records of the real estate commission, other than license examination records, are

> I. public records.
> II. private, available only to the Commission

A. I only B. II only C. Both I and II D. Neither I nor II

126. Funds of others which are received by salesmen must be

> I. deposited in an escrow account by the salesman.
> II. turned over to the broker for deposit in an escrow account.

A. I only B. II only C. Both I and II D. Neither I nor II

127. Copies of all written instruments on real estate transactions prepared by a licensee must be

> I. distributed to all signators of the instrument.
> II. maintained by the broker.

A. I only B. II only C. Both I and II D. Neither I nor II

128. Salesmen may not advertise in their own name

> I. without the broker's permission.
> II. without naming the employing broker in the advertisement.

A. I only B. II only C. Both I and II D. Neither I nor II

129. Your license may be revoked for

> I. placing a sign on property offering it for sale without the owner's consent.
> II. incompetency.

A. I only B. II only C. Both I and II D. Neither I nor II

130. Which of the following may be licensed as a real estate salesman?

> I. a natural person.
> II. a corporation

A. I only B. II only C. Both I and II D. Neither I nor II

ANSWER KEY
FOR
TESTS AND EXERCISES

TRUTH IN LENDING

1.	B	8.	B
2.	C	9.	X B
3.	D	10.	B
4.	D	11.	C
5.	C	12.	A
6.	X C	13.	X A (See note)
7.	C		

REAL ESTATE LICENSE LAW

1.	D	26.	C	51.	D
2.	B	27.	D	52.	X D
3.	D	28.	X D	53.	A
4.	B	29.	A	54.	B
5.	D	30.	A	55.	X B
6.	B	31.	B	56.	D
7.	C	32.	A	57.	D
8.	D	33.	C	58.	X D
9.	B	34.	C	59.	C
10.	X B	35.	X A	60.	D
11.	X C	36.	C	61.	C
12.	D	37.	X D	62.	C
13.	D	38.	D	63.	A
14.	C	39.	X D	64.	X D
15.	B	40.	X A	65.	X D
16.	D	41.	X B	66.	D
17.	C	42.	A	67.	B
18.	B	43.	D	68.	X A
19.	D	44.	C	69.	D
20.	X D	45.	C	70.	C
21.	B	46.	B	71.	B
22.	D	47.	C	72.	A
23.	C	48.	D	73.	D
24.	D	49.	B	74.	C
25.	X D	50.	D	75.	X D

IMPROVED PROPERTY SUMMARY CARD PROBLEMS

Problem No. 1		Problem No. 2	
1.	B	1.	A
2.	A	2.	B
3.	C	3.	B
4.	B	4.	C
5.	C	5.	A

CLOSING STATEMENT PROBLEMS

No. 1		No. 2		No. 3		No. 4	
1.	D	1.	B	1.	A	1.	B
2.	B	2.	B	2.	B	2.	C
3.	C	3.	A	3.	A	3.	B
4.	D	4.	C	4.	A	4.	A
5.	A	5.	A	5.	B	5.	A
6.	B	6.	B	6.	D	6.	B
7.	B	7.	B	7.	A	7.	B
8.	A	8.	B	8.	B	8.	B
9.	C	9.	A	9.	A	9.	A
10.	B	10.	D	10.	A	10.	D
11.	B	11.	B	11.	C	11.	C
12.	D	12.	A	12.	B	12.	A
13.	A	13.	A	13.	A	13.	B
14.	D	14.	B	14.	D	14.	B
15.	B	15.	A	15.	A	15.	D
16.	C	16.	B	16.	C	16.	D
17.	A	17.	D	17.	D	17.	D
18.	D	18.	B	18.	A	18.	C
19.	A	19.	A	19.	B	19.	A
20.	D	20.	C	20.	A	20.	B

NOTE: See Page 109. At bottom of page, paragraph: "NOTE." is wrong. First mortgages are subject to complete disclosure.

Errors or changes in text:
P. 56. V.A. guarantees $17,500.
P. 32. Re Dower. See Blue Book.
P. 30 Re Tenant at sufferance. Not a trespasser, because possession was obtained lawfully.

P. 86. See note on Q.7, Fair Housing.
MATH QUESTIONS: Page 250, Q. 71. In the diagram, indicate the distance horizontally as 56.5 ft.
Page 250, Q. 84, See solution diagram on page 308. The two 10' dimensions were omitted in the question.
Answer Q94, page 309. Change "loss" to "gain".

CONTRACTS	AGENCY & LISTINGS	REAL PROPERTY INTERESTS		APPRAISING
1. B	1. C	1. A	21. B	1. C
2. A	2. D	2. C	22. C	2. A
3. B	3. C	3. B	23. C	3. A
4. B	4. B	4. B	24. D	4. B
5. C	5. A	5. A (See note)	25. C	5. D
6. A B	6. A	6. B	26. C	6. B
7. B	7. B	7. A	27. A	7. A
8. D	8. D	8. C	28. C B	8. D
9. A	9. B	9. B	29. B	9. A
10. B	10. C	10. A	30. C A	10. C
11. A	11. D	11. A	31. C	11. D
12. D	12. B D	12. B	32. C	12. B
13. C	13. C	13. A	33. B	13. A
14. B	14. C	14. A	34. A D	14. B
15. B	15. A	15. B	35. A	15. D
16. B	16. C	16. A		16. A
17. C	17. C	17. D		17. C
18. C	18. D	18. D		18. A
19. A	19. B	19. B		19. A
20. C	20. B	20. A		20. B

FINANCING		TRANSFER OF TITLE		PLATS	FAIR HOUSING
1. B	21. A	1. B	21. B	1. D	1. A
2. C	22. B	2. A	22. A	2. B	2. C D
3. A	23. D	3. IV	23. B	3. D	3. C
4. A	24. C	4. B	24. A	4. A	4. C
5. D	25. B	5. B	25. B	5. C	5. C
6. C	26. C	6. A	26. D	6. B	6. C
7. B	27. A D	7. C	27. B	7. C	7. C See note.
8. A	28. A	8. C	28. C	8. B	8. C
9. B	29. B	9. A	29. B	9. A	9. C
10. B	30. A	10. D	30. B	10. B	10. B
11. A	31. A	11. A B		11. D	11. B
12. A	32. B	12. C		12. A	12. B
13. B	33. C	13. A			13. B
14. D	34. C	14. C			14. C
15. A		15. A			15. A
16. C		16. C			16. C
17. C		17. B			17. C See note.
18. B		18. B			18. D
19. A		19. A			19. A
20. A		20. A			20. C

NOTES: Fair Housing Q. 7: Answer II, as worded is wrong. Should read
"four or more". See also, Page 86, Par. 2a (3). Change "three or
more" to "four or more".

Fair Housing Q. 17: Answer I. Change "complainant" to "complaint".

CONTRACTS	AGENCY & LISTINGS	REAL PROPERTY INTERESTS		APPRAISING
1. B	1. C	1. A	21. B	1. C
2. A	2. D	2. C	22. C	2. A
3. B	3. C	3. B	23. C	3. A
4. B	4. B	4. B	24. D	4. B
5. C	5. A	5. A	25. C	5. D
6. A	6. A	6. B	26. C	6. B
7. B	7. B	7. A	27. A	7. A
8. D	8. D	8. C	28. C	8. D
9. A	9. B	9. B	29. B	9. A
10. B	10. C	10. A	30. C	10. C
11. A	11. D	11. A	31. C	11. D
12. D	12. B	12. B	32. C	12. B
13. C	13. C	13. A	33. B	13. A
14. B	14. C	14. A	34. A	14. B
15. B	15. A	15. B	35. A	15. D
16. B	16. C	16. A		16. A
17. C	17. C	17. D		17. C
18. C	18. D	18. D		18. A
19. A	19. B	19. B		19. A
20. C	20. B	20. A		20. B

FINANCING		TRANSFER OF TITLE		PLATS	FAIR HOUSING
1. B	21. A	1. B	21. B	1. D	1. A
2. C	22. B	2. A	22. A	2. B	2. C
3. A	23. D	3. IV	23. B	3. D	3. C
4. A	24. C	4. B	24. A	4. A	4. C
5. D	25. B	5. B	25. B	5. C	5. C
6. C	26. C	6. A	26. C	6. D	6. C
7. B	27. A	7. C	27. B	7. C	7. C
8. A	28. A	8. C	28. C	8. B	8. C
9. B	29. B	9. A	29. B	9. A	9. C
10. B	30. A	10. D	30. B	10. B	10. B
11. A	31. A	11. C		11. D	11. B
12. A	32. B	12. C		12. A	12. B
13. B	33. C	13. A			13. B
14. D	34. C	14. C			14. C
15. A		15. A			15. A
16. C		16. C			16. C
17. C		17. B			17. C
18. B		18. B			18. D
19. A		19. A			19. A
20. A		20. A			20. C

TRUTH IN LENDING

1.	B	8.	B
2.	C	9.	C
3.	D	10.	B
4.	D	11.	C
5.	C	12.	A
6.	A	13.	B
7.	C		

REAL ESTATE LICENSE LAW

1.	D	26.	C	51.	D
2.	B	27.	D	52.	A
3.	D	28.	B	53.	A
4.	B	29.	A	54.	B
5.	D	30.	A	55.	D
6.	B	31.	B	56.	D
7.	C	32.	A	57.	D
8.	D	33.	C	58.	B
9.	B	34.	C	59.	C
10.	C	35.	B	60.	D
11.	A	36.	C	61.	C
12.	D	37.	A	62.	C
13.	D	38.	D	63.	A
14.	C	39.	A	64.	A
15.	B	40.	C	65.	A
16.	D	41.	C	66.	D
17.	C	42.	A	67.	B
18.	B	43.	D	68.	C
19.	D	44.	C	69.	D
20.	A	45.	C	70.	C
21.	B	46.	B	71.	B
22.	D	47.	C	72.	A
23.	C	48.	D	73.	D
24.	D	49.	B	74.	C
25.	C	50.	D	75.	B

CLOSING STATEMENT PROBLEMS

No. 1		No. 2		No. 3		No. 4	
1.	D	1.	B	1.	A	1.	B
2.	B	2.	B	2.	B	2.	C
3.	C	3.	A	3.	A	3.	B
4.	D	4.	C	4.	A	4.	A
5.	A	5.	A	5.	B	5.	A
6.	B	6.	B	6.	D	6.	B
7.	B	7.	B	7.	A	7.	B
8.	A	8.	B	8.	B	8.	B
9.	C	9.	A	9.	A	9.	A
10.	B	10.	D	10.	A	10.	D
11.	B	11.	B	11.	C	11.	C
12.	D	12.	A	12.	B	12.	A
13.	A	13.	A	13.	A	13.	B
14.	D	14.	B	14.	D	14.	B
15.	B	15.	A	15.	A	15.	D
16.	C	16.	B	16.	C	16.	D
17.	A	17.	D	17.	D	17.	D
18.	D	18.	B	18.	A	18.	C
19.	A	19.	A	19.	B	19.	A
20.	D	20.	C	20.	A	20.	B

IMPROVED PROPERTY SUMMARY CARD PROBLEMS

Problem No. 1		Problem No. 2	
1.	B	1.	A
2.	A	2.	B
3.	C	3.	B
4.	B	4.	C
5.	C	5.	A

SOLUTION TO CLOSING STATEMENT

PROBLEM NO. 1

SETTLEMENT STATEMENT WORKSHEET

	BUYER'S STATEMENT		SELLER'S STATEMENT	
	DEBIT	CREDIT	DEBIT	CREDIT
Purchase price	$33,000.00	$	$	$33,000.00
Taxes, prorated	350.82			350.82
Title examination	163.25			
Insurance, prorated	49.49			49.49
Earnest money deposit		1,000.00		
Purchase, 2 window A/C's	200.00			200.00
Agent's Commission			1,980.00	
Title insurance	66.00			
New 1st D/T loan		26,400.00		
Pay-off 1st D/T loan			17,546.19	
Rent, 7-1-73 to 7-15-73		125.00	125.00	
2nd D/T to seller		3,300.00	3,300.00	
Recording tax, deed	66.00			
Recording tax, 1st D/T	52.80			
Recording tax, 2nd D/T	6.60			
Preparation of 2nd D/T	20.00			
Preparation of 1st D/T	20.00			
Due from buyer to close		3,169.96		
Due seller to close			10,649.12	
TOTALS	$33,994.96	$33.994.96	$33,600.31	$33,600.31

SOLUTION TO CLOSING STATEMENT

PROBLEM NO. 2

SETTLEMENT STATEMENT WORKSHEET

	BUYER'S STATEMENT		SELLER'S STATEMENT	
	DEBIT	CREDIT	DEBIT	CREDIT
Purchase price	$26,250.00	$	$	$26,250.00
Taxes, prorated		156.00	156.00	
Hazard insurance assumed, prorated	58.50			58.50
Title examination	125.00			
Agent's commission			1,575.00	
Preparation of deed			30.00	
Title insurance	52.50			
Preparation of 1st D/T	25.00			
Pay-off 1st D/T			8,440.00	
Pay-off 2nd D/T			900.00	
Earnest money deposit		500.00		
1st D/T loan proceeds		21,000.00		
Recording tax, deed	52.60			
Recording tax, 1st D/T	42.00			
Balance due seller to close			15,207.50	
Balance due from buyer to close		4,949.60		
TOTALS	$26,605.60	$26,605.60	$26,308.50	$26,308.50

SOLUTION TO CLOSING STATEMENT

PROBLEM NO. 3

SETTLEMENT STATEMENT WORKSHEET

	BUYER'S STATEMENT		SELLER'S STATEMENT	
	DEBIT	CREDIT	DEBIT	CREDIT
Purchase price	$32,000.00	$	$	$32,000.00
Insurance	99.00			
Title examination	160.00			
Preparation of deed			30.00	
Taxes, prorated		263.47	263.47	
Preparation of deeds of trust	25.00			
Title insurance	84.50			
1st D/T loan proceeds		24,000.00		
Agent's commission			1,920.00	
2nd D/T to seller		3,200.00	3,200.00	
Earnest money deposit		1,000.00		
Rent, 7-1-73 to 7-15-73	120.00			120.00
Pay-off 2nd D/T			2,028.00	
Pay-off 1st D/T			14,652.00	
Loan service fee - 1%	240.00			
Recording tax, deed	64.00			
Recording tax, 1st D/T	48.00			
Recording tax, 2nd D/T	6.40			
Due seller to close			10,026.53	
Due from buyer to close		4,383.43		
TOTALS	$32,846.90	$32,846.90	$32,120.00	$32,120.00

SOLUTION TO CLOSING STATEMENT

PROBLEM NO. 4

SETTLEMENT STATEMENT WORKSHEET

	BUYER'S STATEMENT		SELLER'S STATEMENT	
	DEBIT	CREDIT	DEBIT	CREDIT
Purchase price	$35,000.00	$	$	$35,000.00
Hazard insurance premium	145.00			
Earnest money deposit		1,000.00		
Taxes, prorated	393.00			393.00
Survey	55.00			
Pay-off sewer lien			250.00	
Loan discount	332.50		332.50	
Title examination	225.00			
Agent's commission			2,100.00	
Loan origination fee	332.50			
Preparation of deed			30.00	
1st D/T proceeds		33,250.00		
Title insurance	122.50			
Preparation of D/T	25.00			
Pay-off 1st D/T			20,771.34	
Mortgage insurance premium	166.25			
Recording tax, deed	70.00			
Recording tax, D/T	66.60			
Balance due from buyer to close		2,683.35		
Balance due seller to close			11,909,16	
TOTALS	$36,933.35	$36,933.35	$35,393.00	$35,393.00

ARITHMETIC

Problems on Percentages

1. (a) .375   (b) .45   (c) .03   (d) 1.05

2. (a) 47%   (b) 125%   (c) 7.5%   (d) 82.5%

3. (a) $\dfrac{12.5}{100} = \dfrac{1}{8}$ (b) $\dfrac{30}{100} = \dfrac{3}{10}$ (c) $\dfrac{75}{100} = \dfrac{3}{4}$ (d) $\dfrac{5}{100} = \dfrac{1}{20}$

4. (a) $\dfrac{1}{16} = 16\overline{)1.0000}\;\;.0625 = 6.25\%$ (b) $\dfrac{2}{5} = 5\overline{)2.00}\;\;.40 = 40\%$

   (c) $\dfrac{7}{10} = 10\overline{)7.00}\;\;.70 = 70\%$ (d) $\dfrac{3}{8} = 8\overline{)3.000}\;\;.375 = 37.5\%$

5. (a) $3\overline{)3.75}\;\;1.25$ (b) $4\overline{)1.8}\;\;.45$ (c) $8\overline{)10.2}\;\;1.275$ (d) $16\overline{)12.00}\;\;.75$

6. (a) $37.5\overline{)168.7.5}\;\;4.5$ (b) $222.75\overline{)182.00.}\;\;8.$

   (c) $6.75\overline{)84.37.5}\;\;12.5$ (d) $5.5\overline{)126.5.}\;\;23.$

7.
(a)	(b)	(c)	(d)
.4375	1.80	17.5	101.75
x 22.5	x 2.3	x .065	x .25
21875	540	875	50875
8750	360	1050	20350
8750	4.140	1.1375	25.4375
9.84375			

8.
(a)	(b)	(c)	(d)
28.225	16.37	18.5	7.65
+ 101.65	+ 22.8	+ 6.75	+ 9.35
129.875	39.17	25.25	17.00

9.
(a)	(b)	(c)	(d)
123.5	17.075	88.	76.20
- 48.75	- 12.5	- 22.6	- 43.
74.75	4.575	65.4	33.20

10. $\dfrac{\$26{,}790}{.94}$ (P) = \$28,500. = selling price (B)
     (R)

11. $\begin{aligned}\$10{,}000 &= \text{net cash to owner}\\ \underline{14{,}863} &= \text{1st D/T payoff}\\ \$24{,}863 &= \text{net price (P)}\end{aligned}$

   Rate = 1.00 (100%) - .06 = .94 (R)

   24,863 (P) = .94 (R) x B

   $\dfrac{24{,}863}{.94}$ = \$26,450 = selling price

12. $150/month interest x 12 months = $1,800/year interest

   $$\frac{\$1,800 \text{ interest (P)}}{.075 \text{ interest rate (R)}} = \$24,000 \text{ loan (B)} = .75 \text{ value}$$

   $$\frac{\$24,000 \text{ (P)}}{.75 \text{ (R)}} = \$32,000 = \text{price of house (B)}$$

13. $$\frac{.06 \text{ annual interest rate}}{12 \text{ months}} = .005 \text{ interest/month}$$

   $10,000 x .005 = $50 interest 1st month
   $80.00 payment - $50.00 interest = $30 principal 1st month

   $10,000 original loan amount $80.00 payment 2nd month
   -    30 principal payment 1st month   -49.85 interest
   $ 9,970 balance 2nd month $30.15 principal payment
   x .005 interest rate   2nd month
   $ 49.85 interest payment 2nd month

14. .20 listing commission
   +.35 sales commission
   .55 of total 6% commission to salesman

   .06 x .55 = .0330 = salesman's commission rate

   $$\frac{\$955.35}{.033} = \$28,950 = \text{selling price}$$

15. $45,900 = 100% (original price) + 8% (profit)

   $$\frac{\$45,900}{1.08} = \$42,500. = \text{original price}$$

16. $712.50 monthly rent x 12 months = $8,550/year rent

   $8,550 (P) = Rate x $95,000

   $$\frac{\$8,550}{95,000} = .09 = \text{annual rate of return}$$

17. $18,050 = (R) x $19,000 sale price

   $$\frac{\$18,050}{\$19,000} = .95 \text{ net to seller}$$

   1.00 = gross price = $19,000
   .95 = net to owner =   18,050
   .05 = agent's comm. = $ 950

18. $28,000 sale price x .06 commission = $1,680 total commission

   $1,680 x .15 listing commission = $252 listing commission

   $$\$1,680 - \$252 = \frac{1,428}{3} \text{ sales comm.} = \$476 \text{ sales commission}$$

19. $800 x .06 = $48.00/year interest

    $48 x .5 (1/2 year) = $ 24 = interest
                               + 800 = principal
                               $ 824 = total payment

20. $31,000 x 1.15 = $35,650 asking price

    $35,650 x .80 (1.00 - .20) = $28,520 sale price

    $31,000 - $28,520 = $2,480 loss

    $2,480   = .08 loss
    $31,000

21. $18.75 interest for 6 months x 2 = $37.50/year interest

    $37.50 interest/year = .075 or 7 1/2% interest
    $ 500

22. .075   annual interest = .00625/month interest
    12   months

    $10,000 x .00625 = $62.50 interest 1st month

    $90 payment - $62.50 interest = $27.50 principal 1st month

    $10,000 - $27.50 = $9,972.50 x .00625 = $62.33 interest

    $90 - $62.33 = $27.67 to principal 2nd month

23. $840/month x 12 months = $10,080 annual rent

    $10,080   = $72,000 = cost of property
    .14

24. Cost of property =   1.00 (100%)
    Plus profit   = + .25 (25%)
                         1.25
                       x .20   reduction
                         .25   reduction from asking price

    1.25 - .25 = 1.00   Result: You broke even.

25. 12,000   = 12 x $4.75 = $ 57 /year
    1,000   x 3 years
                                 $171

    $171 x .80 (20% savings) = $136.80 cost of policy

    Policy purchased: Year-1966   Month-9   Day-25
    Policy expires: 1968   21   25
    Policy assumed: 1968   11   10
    Remaining life: 0 year   10 months 15 days

    $136.80   = $3.80/month = policy cost
    36 months

    $3.80 x 10.5 months = $39.90 charge to buyer

26. $\dfrac{\$288}{12 \text{ months}}$ = $24/month tax   Oct. 15 to Dec. 31 = 2.5 months

$24. x 2.5 = $60

27. $\dfrac{14,000}{100}$ assessment = 140 x $2.60 rate = $364 tax

28. $\dfrac{\$503.25}{\$3.25}$ tax = 155 x 100 = $15,500 assessment
    rate

29. $\dfrac{\$19,400}{100}$ = 194 $\dfrac{\$533.50}{194}$ tax = $2.75/$100 = rate
                              assessment

Problems on Area and Volume

1. 508.2   Length $\dfrac{101,640}{43,560}$ /Acre   = 2.333 or 2 1/3 Acres
    x   200   Width
    ─────────
    101,640.0 Area

2. $ 57.50   price per front foot
    x   90   feet, frontage
    ─────────────
    $ 5,175.00   selling price

3. 18' x 20' = ceiling area   = 360 sq. ft.
    8' ceiling height x 20' = 160 sq. ft. x 2 walls   = 320 sq. ft.
    8' ceiling height x 18' = 144 sq. ft. x 2 walls   = 288 sq. ft.
                                                                ─────────────
    Total area walls and ceiling   = 968 sq. ft.
      Less: 5'(60") x 10' (120") = window area   = 50 sq. ft.
                                                                ─────────────
                                                                  918 sq. ft.
      Less: 3' x 7' = 21 sq. ft. x 2 doors   = 42 sq. ft.
    Total area to be painted   = 876 sq. ft.

4. To find square root of 6889:

        90 x 90 = 8100
        80 x 80 = 6400

    Answer is more than 80', less than 90'. Number ends in 9;
        3 x 3 = 9, so try 83

    83' x 83' = 6889 sq. ft.

    $\dfrac{\$4,565}{83'}$ price/front foot = $55/front foot
    frontage

5. $\dfrac{200'}{2}$ = 100' x 217.8' = 21,780 sq. ft.

    $\dfrac{21,780}{43,560}$ sq. ft. = .5 acre x $4,000 = $2,000 sale price
    sq. ft./acre

6.   120' x 6' = 720 sq. ft. in 1st area
     90' x 6' = 540 sq. ft. in 2nd area
      6' x 6' =   36 sq. ft. in 3rd area
              1,296 sq. ft.

$\dfrac{1{,}296 \text{ sq. ft.}}{9 \text{ sq. ft./sq. yd.}}$ =   144 sq. yds.   = total area

$\dfrac{144 \text{ sq. yds.}}{6 \text{ (36" divided by 6")}}$ =   24 cu. yds.

7.   22' (length) x 18' (width) x 10' (height) = 3,960 cu. ft.

     3,960 cu. ft. x .45/cu. ft. = $1,782

8.   120' x 6' = 720 sq. ft. in 1st area
     90' x 6' = 540 sq. ft. in 2nd area
              1,260 sq. ft.

     Less 6' x 6'   36 sq. ft. overlap
                   1,224 sq. ft.

$\dfrac{1{,}224 \text{ sq. ft.}}{9 \text{ sq. ft./sq. yd.}}$ =   136 sq. yds.

$\dfrac{136}{6 \text{ (36" divided by 6")}}$ sq. yds.   =   22.667 or 22 2/3 cu. yds.

9.   660' frontage divided by 2 = 330' (1/2 base)

     330' x 1,320 (1/4 mile = altitude) = 435,600 sq. ft.

$\dfrac{435{,}600 \text{ sq. ft.}}{43{,}560 \text{ sq. ft./Acre}}$ = 10 Acres

10. 33' x 45' x 10' = 14,850 cu. ft.

$\dfrac{14{,}850 \text{ cu. ft.}}{27 \text{ cu. ft./cu. yd.}}$ = 550 cu. yds.

     550 cu. yds. x $2.50 = $1,375

11. $\dfrac{22.5'}{2}$ = 11.25'   (1/2 base)

     11.25' x 8' x 30' = 2,700 cu. ft.

$\dfrac{2{,}700 \text{ cu. ft.}}{27 \text{ cu. ft./cu. yd.}}$ = 100 cu. yds.

Supplemental Arithmetic Problems

1. $1,700 x .05 = $85/yr. interest

     April 15 to January 15 = 9 months = .75 x $85 = $63.75

2. $15,000 x .06 = $900 total commission $900
    10 showings @ $10 each = $100 expense   −100
                                                       $800

3. $20,000 x 1.08 = $21,600 1st sale price
    Less. . . . . 19,440 2nd sales price
                         $ 2,160 Loss

    2,160   =   10%
    ──────
    21,600

4. $126 x 1/12 = $10.50/month tax $ 10.50
                                                x   3.5
    September 15 to December 30 = 3.5 months $ 36.75 Refund

5. 75 x $193.50 = $14,512.50

6. $85 x 1/2 = $42.50   lease commission

    $85 x .05 = $4.25/month x 17 months = $72.25 manage-
                                                      ment commission
    $42.50 + 72.25 = $114.75 total commission

7. $16,710.40 net cash + $679.60 expense = $17,390 net price

    $17,390 divided by .94 = $18,500 total price

8. 6 x 60 = 360
    6 x 90 = 540
    6 x   6 =   36
                 936 sq. ft.

    936 sq. ft.   = 104 sq. yds.
    ─────────────
    9 sq. ft./sq. yd

    36"   = 6 (1/6 yd.)
    ───
    6"

    104 sq. yds.   = 17.33 cu. yds.
    ───
    6

9. 60 x 120 = 7,200 sq. ft. = 3,600 sq. ft.
                   ─────
                     2

10. 726 x 200 = 145,200 sq. ft.   = 3.3 Acres
                    ──────────────────
                    43,560 sq. ft./Acre

11. Sq. root of 9216 = 96 = frontage of lot

    96 x $40 = $3,840 = cost of lot

    62' x 24' x 27' = 40,176 cu. ft. = $10,044 = cost of bldg.
                           ──────
                             4

    $10,044 + $3,840 = $13,884 total cost

12. $21,750 x .80 = $17,400 x 6.45/100 = $112.23 P & I
     $17,400 x .30 = $ 5,220 x 1/12   =   4.35 insurance
     $21,750 x .60 = $13,050 x .25 *   =   32.63 tax
                                               $149.21 total monthly
           *In the above computation,   payment
           .25 = 1/12 x $3.00 = 1 month's tax.

13. 180' x .45 = 81' x 6' = 486 sq. ft.

     $$\frac{486 \text{ sq. ft.}}{9} = \frac{54}{9} = 6 \text{ cu. yds.}$$
                     (36" divided by 4")

14. 486 x 80 = $388.80 labor
     $18 x   6 =   108.00 concrete
                    $496.80 total

15. $12,000 x .72 = $86.40 x 2.7 = $\frac{\$233.28}{36 \text{ months}}$ cost = $6.48/mo.

     September 20, 1966 to May 10, 1968 = 1 yr., 7 mos., 20 days =

     19 2/3 months x $6.48/month = $127.44 refund

16. 37.5% = 6/16 + 3/16 (corn) + 1/16 (dwelling) = 10/16

     10/16 = 5/8; 5/8 + 75 Acres = 8/8 - 5/8 = 3/8;

     hence 75 acres = 3/8 or 25 acres = 1/8;

     25 acres x 8 = 200 Acres

17. 45' x 45' = 2,025 sq. ft. x .25 = $506.25 cost of lot

     25' x 25' = 625 sq. ft. x 10' = 6,250 cu. ft.

     6,250 cu. ft. x .60 = $3,750 cost of building

     $506.25 + $3,750 = $4,256.25 cost

18. 100% - 20% = .80 x 45 = .36 + .20 = 56% of total
                                                       to salesman
     $\frac{\$756}{.56}$ = $1,350 = total commission

     $\frac{\$1,350}{.06}$ = $22,500 price

19. $282 x 1/30 = $9.40/day x 12 = $112.80

20. $750 x 12 = $\frac{\$9,000/yr.}{.12}$ = $75,000

21. $375/yr. x 1/12 = $31.25/ month

     January 1 to June 15 = 5.5 months x $31.25 = $171.88

22. 200' x 210' = 42,000 sq. ft. total area

    8 lots x 50' x 90' = 36,000 sq. ft. to lots

    42,000 - 36,000 = 6,000 sq. ft. to roads = 1/7th = 14.28%

23. Policy expires: 67 years 4 months 15 days
                      66 years 7 months 25 days
                                8 months 20 days   remaining

    $144.72 x 1/36 = $4.02/mo. x 8 2/3 mos. = $34.84 refund

24. 400' x 490.5' = $\frac{196,200}{43,560}$ sq. ft. = 4.5 Acres

25. August 15 to December 31 = 4.5 months

    $150/yr. x 1/12 = $12.50/mo. x 4.5 mos. = $56.25

26. 48' x 33' = 1,584 sq. ft. Main House
    10' x 20' = 200 sq. ft. Family Room
                1,784 sq. ft. x $12.50/sq. ft. = $22,300 cost

27. $20,000 x .80 = $16,000 x $3.50/mo. = $56.00/yr. dwelling
    $ 6,000 x .80 = $ 4,800 x $4.25/mo. = $20.40/yr. furnishings
                                          $76.40

    $76.40 x 1/2 yr. = $38.20 savings

28. $9.75 x 1/3 = $3.25/month

    August 15 to December 31 = 4.5 months

    $3.25 x 4.5 months = $14.63 refund

29. $5,000 x .05 = $250 x .10 = $25 listing commission

    $250 x .5 = $125 sales commission

    $125 sales commission - $25 listing commission = $100

30. $24,500 x .16/$100 = $39.20/yr. x 2.5 yrs. = $98 for three
                                                       years
    $98 x 1/36 = $2.72/month

31. 1 sq. mile = 640 acres

    .5 mile x .25 miles = .125 sq. miles x 640 Acres = 80 Acres

32. $1,800 divided by .06 = $30,000 price

33. $12,000 x .80 = $9,600 x $2.80 = $26.88/yr. dwelling
    $ 4,000 x .80 = $3,200 x $3.30 = $10.56/yr. furnishings
                                     $37.44/yr. total premium

    $37.44 x 1/2 year savings = $18.72 savings

34. $12,000 x .06 = $720/yr. x 1/12 = $60/mo. interest, 1st

month

September 20 to October 1 = 1/3 month

1/3 month x $60 = $20 interest

35. $200 = 5% appraised value

$200 divided by .05 = $4,000   = 2/3 value
If $4,000 = 2/3 value, then . . .   2,000   = 1/3 value
                                       $6,000   = Total

36. 1 acre = 160 sq. rods; area of triangle = 1/2 base x altitude

88 x 1/2 = 44 x 24 = 1,056 sq. rods

1,056 sq. rods divided by 160 (sq. rods/Acre) = 6.6 Acres in
field
6.6 acres x $175/acre = $1,155 price

37. $250.24 divided by $7,820 = $3.20/$100 rate

38. $330 x .06 = $19.80 divided by 2 = $9.90 interest for 6 mos.

$330 + $9.90 = $339.90 x 1/6 = $56.65/month

39. $22,500 divided by 100 x .20 = $45

40. $36,500 total cost = $20,000 @ .0075 = $150.00
                           $16,500 @ .005 =   82.50
                                             $232.50 total cost

41. (1) $95,000 = 105% (original price + 5%)
     (2) $95,000 =   95% (original price - 5%)

$95,000 divided by .95 = $100,000 cost first parcel
$95,000 divided by 1.05 = $90,476.19 cost second parcel

$100,000 - $95,000 = $5,000 loss first sale
$ 95,000 - $90,476.19 = $4,523.81 gain from second sale

$5,000 loss - $4,523.81 gain = $476.19 net loss on transaction

42. Builder should accept offer "A." Greater discount.

43. 1/4 = .25 not usable
     3/5 = .60 under cultivation
              .85 other than meadow

1.00 Total = 400 Acres
-.85   x.15
 .15   60 Acres in meadow

44. $5,600 net income = .08 or 8%
     $70,000

45. $1,375 = P; 5% = R; $\frac{P}{R} = B$

$\frac{\$1,375}{.05}$ = $27,500

46. $12,000 $12,000
 x .20 down payment − 2,400
$ 2,400 cash needed $ 9,600 loan

$9,600 x .085 = $\frac{816}{12}$ (annual interest) = $68/mo.
        12 mos.   x 7 mos.
              $476 interest

47. $30,080 + $1,920 = $32,000 sale price = $4.00/sq. ft.
  200' x 40' = 8,000 sq. ft.

48. 1.00 − .20 = .80

$\frac{\$8,000}{.80}$ purchase price = $10,000 market value & resale price

$10,000 − $8,000 = $\frac{\$2,000}{\$8,000}$ profit = .25 or 25% rate of profit

49. $\frac{\$69,000}{1.15}$ = Income   = $60,000 Original cost
    (1.00 orig. cost +   Parcel No. 1
    .15 gain)

$\frac{\$69,000}{.80}$ (1.00 − .20 loss) = 86,250 Original cost
                Parcel No. 2
            $146,250 Total original cost
           −138,000 Total resale price
           $ 8,250 Loss

50. $15,000 x .80 = $12,000 insured value
        x .72 /100 premium
       $ 86.40 total premium = $2.40/month
        36 months
3/1/67 to 7/1/68 = 16 months remaining

16 x $2.40 = $38.40 due from buyer

51. $\frac{\$720}{12}$ = $\frac{\$60}{30}$ /month = $2 day
      days

10 months x $60/month = $600
11 days x $2/day = 22
         $622 credit to buyer

52. $7,000 x .65 = $4,550 assessed value

$4,550 x .065 = $295.75 tax

53. 36' = 12 yds; 9' = 3 yds; 4" = 1/9 yd.

12 x 3 x 1/9 = 4 cu. yds. x $15 = $ 60.00 concrete cost
36' x 9' = 324 sq. ft. x $.20 =   69.80 labor cost
              $129.80 total cost

54. $14,200   net to seller
    +   50   advertising
    $14,250 = $15,000 sale price
      .95

55. $210 semiannual interest x 2 = $420 annual interest

    $420 = $5,250 loan x 2 = $10,500 appraised value
    .08

56. $15,500 x 1.10 = $17,050

57. 80 x 100 = 8,000 sq. ft. x .25 = $ 2,000 $ 2,400
    $5.00/front foot x 80 ft.   =   400   x 1.15
                                             $ 2,400 $ 2,760
                                                        +   500
                                                        $ 3,260

58. 70' x $60 = $4,200 sale price x .06 = $252 commission

59. $300 x 12 months = $3,600/yr. = $40,000 investment
                             .09

60. 2.5 x 6 = .15 total depreciation; 1.00 - .15 = .85

    $21,250 = $25,000 original value
      .85

61. $15,000 x .97 = $ 14,550
    $ 3,500 x .90 =   3,150
                       $ 17,700 insurable loan

62. 300' x 73' = 21,900 sq. ft. = .5$^+$ Acre
                     43,560

63. 15' = 5 yds.; 27' = 9 yds.; 5 x 9 x $11.50 = $517.50

64. 72' x 122' = 8,784 sq. ft.

    $5,006.88 = $.57 per sq. ft.
      8,784

65. $50 = $1,000
    .05

66. .06 x .5 = .03 = salesman's rate of commission

    $10,500 = $350,000
      .03

67. $625 = $125/month x 12 months = $1,500/yr. interest
     5

    1,500 = .075 interest rate
    20,000

68. $2,500 = $2,000/lot original cost
    1.25   x   5 lots
               $10,000 total original cost

69. 120 acres x 160 bu. x $1.40 = $\frac{\$26,880}{.055}$ = $\frac{\$488,727.27}{120}$ = $4,072.73/acre (answer)

70. $50,000 x .12 = $6,000 - (12 x $450) = $600 net

$175 x 12 = $2,100 rent received - $600 net = $1,500 savings (answer)

71. (40 x 40) + (10 x 56.5) = 1,600 + 565 = 2,165 sq. ft. (answer)

72. A = 5 x 10 =   50
B = 10 x 15 =   150
C = 5 x 10 =   50
D = 80 x 90 = 7,200
Total   7,450 sq. ft. x $17 = $126,650. (answer)

73. (1) 80 - 3 = 77 acres x 2 = 154 lots x 50 x 100 = 770,000 sq. ft. for houses

(2) 43,560 x 80 = 3,484,800 sq. ft.

(3) $\frac{770,000}{3,484,800}$ = .22 or 22% (answer)

74. (1) Cost = $28,000 + $500 = $28,500

(2) $28,500 x 1.15 = $32,775
(cost + profit)

(3) Less $15,000
from sale of lots

$17,775 (answer)

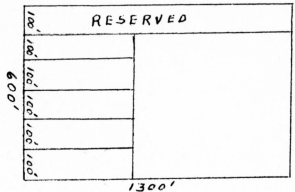

75. (1) (12 x $250) + (10 x $300) x .80 = $4,800/month rent rec'd.

(2) $4,800 x 12 mos. = $57,600 - $7,600 = $\frac{\$50,000}{.10}$ net = $500,000

76. (1) (400 x 400) - (1/2 x 50 x 100) = 157,500 sq. ft. x $1/sq. ft. = $157,500.

(2) ($100/day x 360 days) - $250 expense = $\frac{\$35,750}{.10}$ = $357,500

(3) $357,500 - $157,500 = $200,000 (answer)

77. Cost: Site $464,000
100 rooms @ $15,000   1,500,000
Over-ride 2% x $1,500,00   30,000
Pool (10x50x10x120%)   6,000
Total cost $2,000,000

Income: 100 rooms x 20 x 360 x .80 $ 576,000
Restaurant, 400 x 360   144,000
Total income $ 720,000
Less expenses (40%)   x   .60
$ 432,000

$\frac{\$432,000}{\$2,000,000}$ = .216 or 21.6% return (answer)

78.   ($1,500 x 12) - $6,000 = $\frac{$12,000}{.08625}$ = $139,130

79.   (1) $112,000 - $32,000 = $80,000 value of bldg.

       (2) 40 yrs - 14 yrs. = 26 yrs; ($80,000 x 26/40) = $52,000 depreciated
                                                              value of bldg.

       (3) $52,000 + $32,000 = $84,000 present value (answer)

80.   (1) 100 Ac. x $3,400 = $340,000 cost of land
       (2) 25 Ac. x $1,000 = $25,000 value of timber
       (3) 100 Ac. x .20 for streets = 20 Ac. for streets
       (4) 10 Ac. x 40' streets = $\frac{435,600 \text{ sq. ft.}}{40}$ = 10,890 lin. ft. to 40' st.

       (5) 10 Ac. for 30' streets = $\frac{435,600 \text{ sq. ft.}}{30}$ = 14,520 lin. ft. to 30' st.

       (6) 10,890 + 14,520 = 25,410 x $10 = $254,100 cost of streets
       (7) 100 Ac. x $3,400/Ac. =   340,000 cost of land
       (8) Total cost $594,100 (total cost)
       (9) $594,100 x 1.10 (profit) = $653,570 - 25,000 timber = $628,570
       (10) 80 Ac. x 2 lots/Ac. = 160 lots
       (11) $\frac{$628,570}{160 \text{ lots}}$ = $3,928+ per lot

81.

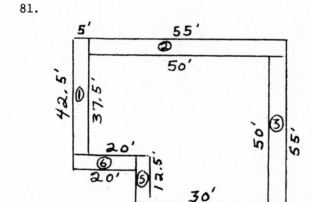

                                        42.5'   (1)
                                        55.0'   (2)
                                        55.0'   (3)
                                        35.0'   (4)
                                        12.5'   (5)
                                        20.0'   (6)
                                       ‾‾‾‾‾‾‾
                                        220.0'
                                         x 5
                                       ‾‾‾‾‾‾‾
                                      1,100.0' total sq. ft. (answer)

82.   (1) 1.00 (#1) + 1.25 (#2) = 2.25

       (2) $\frac{$22,500}{2.25}$ = $10,000 x 1.25 = $12,500 (answer)

83.   10,000 = 100
       100 x $25/front ft. = $ 2,500 land cost
       2,000 x 30 x .035x1.10 = $\frac{23,100}{}$ bldg. cost
                                 $25,600 total cost (answer)

84.

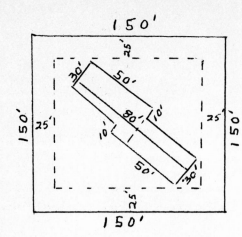

Size of usable lot = 100x100 = 10,000 sq. ft.

10,000 x .90 = 9,000 sq. ft.

House size (30x30)+(20x40)+(30x30) =
    900 + 800 + 900 = 2,600 sq.ft.

9,000 - 2,600 = 6,400 sq. ft. (answer)

85.　(1) 600 x 600 = $\frac{360,000 \text{ sq. ft.}}{2}$ = 180,000 each bldg. and lot

(2) 180,000 x $4/sq. ft. = $720,000 cost of bldg.

(3) $\frac{180,000}{9}$ x $3/sq. yd. = $60,000 cost of asphalt

(4) $\frac{2,400 \text{ ft.}}{3}$ x $2/lin. yd. = $1,600 cost of curb

(5) $720,000 + $60,000 + $1,600 + $67,800 = $849,400 total cost
(6) $849,400 x .10 = $84,940 x .70 = $59,458 (answer)

86.　House = $60,000 x .90 x $2/$1,000 = $108
Pers. Ppty. = $20,000 x .90 x $3/$1,000 = $\underline{54}$
                                                $162 total

$162 x 3 = $486 x 1/3 = $162 (answer)

87.　$20,000 x .08 = $1,600 x .25 = $400

88.　(1) 43,560 sq. ft. x 1/4 = $\frac{10,890}{100}$ = 108.9 ft. front

(2) 10,890 x $1 = $10,890 cost x 1.50 = $16,335 = cost + profit
(3) $16,335 + $3,400 + $65 = $\frac{\$19,800}{.90}$ = $22,000 final sale price

(4) $22,000 = $202/front foot (answer)

89.　125 x 35 x 25 x $.38 = $41,562.50
125 x 35 x $9 = $\underline{-39,375.00}$
                         $ 2,187.50 savings (answer)

90.　(1) $175 x 12) - ($395 + $75 + $150) =
        $2,100 - $620 = $1,480 net/yr.
(2) $\frac{\$1,480}{\$14,800}$ = .10 or 10% (answer)

91. $4,400 x 12 = $ 52,800.
$7,364.22 + $1,723.31 + $5,237.28 + $3,674.19 = $\underline{17,999.}$
                                            $ 34,801. net return

92.   Jones's Value   Smith's Value

        $21,500.00 $23,750.00

      - 8,080.04 Equity ($4,873.02 + $3,207.02)   -4,873.02

      $13,419.96 . . . . . . Encumbrance $18,876.98

93.

                                    Listed price = $35,000

     (1) $30,000 + $2,600 + $327=   32,927 cost

                                 $ 2073= .063 or 6.3% (answer)

                                 $32,927

94.   (1) $16,200 - $15,250 = $950 difference in cost

       (2) $10,200 x 1.03 = $10,506 x 1.03 = $10,821.18 - $10,200 = $621.18 int.

       (3) $950 - $621.18 = $328.82 loss

95.   4 x $95 x 12 x .35 = $1,596 = .042 = 4.2%

                          $38,000

SALESMAN EXAM ANSWERS

1. B	31. D	61. C	91. B	121. B
2. A	32. D	62. A	92. C	122. C
3. D	33. C	63. D	93. A	123. B
4. C	34. D	64. C	94. A	124. C
5. D	35. D	65. B	95. B	125. A
6. A	36. A	66. B	96. B	126. B
7. B	37. A	67. C	97. B	127. C
8. B	38. D	68. A	98. C	128. C
9. A	39. D	69. A	99. D	129. C
10. B	40. C	70. D	100. D	130. A
11. A	41. B	71. C	101. C	
12. D	42. C	72. D	102. B	
13. C	43. A	73. C	103. A	
14. B	44. C	74. C	104. A	
15. D	45. C	75. D	105. A	
16. A	46. C	76. D	106. C	
17. C	47. B	77. C	107. C	
18. A	48. D	78. A	108. D	
19. C	49. C	79. D	109. A	
20. A	50. C	80. B	110. A	
21. C	51. B	81. A	111. C	
22. B	52. A	82. C	112. B	
23. B	53. D	83. A	113. A	
24. A	54. B	84. C	114. C	
25. C	55. C	85. D	115. A	
26. C	56. C	86. C	116. B	
27. A	57. A	87. B	117. A	
28. B	58. C	88. A	118. A	
29. B	59. B	89. D	119. D	
30. B	60. D	90. B	120. B	

BROKER EXAM ANSWERS

1. D	31. B	61. A	91. D	121. B
2. A	32. C	62. D	92. D	122. C
3. D	33. D	63. C	93. C	123. B
4. B	34. A	64. C	94. D	124. C
5. D	35. B	65. A	95. A	125. A
6. A	36. C	66. C	96. C	126. B
7. B	37. B	67. A	97. B	127. C
8. C	38. B	68. B	98. D	128. C
9. C	39. D	69. A	99. C	129. C
10. B	40. B	70. A	100. B	130. A
11. A	41. C	71. A	101. C	
12. D	42. B	72. B	102. B	
13. B	43. C	73. B	103. A	
14. C	44. C	74. A	104. A	
15. B	45. C	75. D	105. A	
16. A	46. D	76. A	106. C	
17. B	47. C	77. D	107. C	
18. C	48. C	78. A	108. D	
19. A	49. A	79. A	109. A	
20. B	50. C	80. A	110. A	
21. A	51. B	81. A	111. B	
22. B	52. A	82. A	112. B	
23. D	53. D	83. A	113. A	
24. B	54. A	84. D	114. C	
25. A	55. A	85. B	115. A	
26. C	56. B	86. A	116. B	
27. D	57. B	87. A	117. A	
28. C	58. B	88. C	118. A	
29. D	59. B	89. B	119. D	
30. B	60. C	90. A	120. B	

NOTES

NOTES

NOTES

NOTES